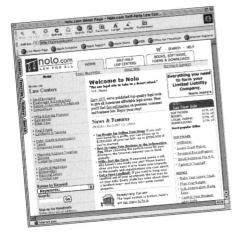

1st edition

How to Run a
Thriving
Business

Strategies for Success and Satisfaction

by Ralph Warner

FIRST EDITION	OCTOBER 2004
Editor	RICH STIM
Book Design	TERRI HEARSH
Proofreading	SUSAN CARLSON GREENE
Index	THÉRÈSE SHERE
Printing	DELTA PRINTING SOLUTIONS, INC.

Warner, Ralph E.
   How to Run a Thriving Business: Strategie for Sucess and Satisfaction/ by Ralph
   Warner.
      p.   cm.
   Includes index.
   ISBN 1-4133-0104-5 (alk. paper)
    1. Small business--Management. 2. Success in business. I. Title: Thrive and prosper. II.
Title.

HD62.7 .W374 2004
658'.022-dc22   2004055213

Quantity sales: For information on bulk purchases or corporate premium sales, please
contact the Special Sales Department. For academic sales or textbook adoptions, ask for
Academic Sales. Call 800-955-4775 or write to Nolo, 950 Parker Street, Berkeley, CA 94710.

Acknowledgments

Believe it or not, this book took me four years to write, during which time I was frequently diverted to other Nolo tasks. I'm not sure I ever would have found the willpower to finish had it not been for the encouragement of my production assistant Susan Cornell. I am also indebted to Susan for many good ideas.

My friend Rich Stim was an inspired editor, who made many substantive and creative suggestions. The result is a much-improved book.

Nolo's inimitable researchers, Stan Jacobsen and Ella Hirst, contributed much valuable material to this book, allowing me to at least occasionally back my opinions with fact.

Huge thanks to Terri Hearsh, who designed this book. Terri's sharp eye spotted several errors and omissions, allowing me to fix them with no need to be embarrassed by conscientious readers.

Finally, just as this book was going to press, George Miller introduced me to the wit and wisdom of Richard "Kinky" Friedman, of The Texas Jewboys. My life will never be the same.

Acknowledgments

Table of Contents

Index

Introduction

"Skate to where the puck is going to be, not where it has been."

–Wayne Gretzky

Running a profitable, life-enhancing small business can't be as tough as, say, climbing Mt. Everest without oxygen—after all, we all know many average souls who have done it. At the same time, we know the great majority of small business start-ups are kaput before they reach their fifth birthday. So if making a comfortable living as the owner of a business you are honestly proud of is a realistic goal, how come so few people accomplish it? And more important, what do you need to know to happily and profitably trek to the top of your personal small business mountain?

For more than 30 years, I've led Nolo, a small publisher of self-help law and business books that began in the corner of a bedroom and now employs almost 100 people and publishes hundreds of books, plus software and a website full of free legal information. Along the way, I've concluded that the so-called secrets to small business success are not really hidden at all. Most of the key things small business owners need to get right are out in the open, where anyone who's paying attention can spot, understand, and embrace them. As long as you are savvy enough to develop a customer-focused enterprise you truly care about, which at the same time is designed from the start to produce a substantial profit, you'll succeed. And if, in addition, your business finds a way to engage the hearts and minds of its customers and employees in an effort to make even a small slice of the world a little bit better, it will thrive.

Sound easy? Not so fast. Building a prosperous business you, your customers, your employees, and even your competitors respect will take a lot of effort and, usually, at least several or more years. But it's something I can help you learn how to do.

Many of the lessons I have learned at Nolo and discuss here are directly at odds with the advice you'll most often read in the business press. In fact, I believe that to truly thrive and prosper, you often must turn conventional business advice on its head. For example, I believe the entrepreneur who regularly puts in 60 or 70 hours per week is more likely to fail than the one who gets the job done in a normal workweek. This puts me at odds with much of the business press, which routinely features entrepreneurs who proudly brag that their success is the result of working their fingers to the bone. Too bad that none of these profiles point out an owner who more sensibly designs her business so she can work a 40-hour week, by learning to substitute smarts for hours and to delegate key tasks, both key skills highly predictive of success. In addition, because the person who works a shorter week will have enough time and energy to cope with life's many other important concerns, she is far more likely to avoid owner burnout and stick with her business over the long term, itself a huge, but seldom remarked on, predictor of entrepreneurial success.

At first glance, a couple of my prescriptions for success, such as "Drive a Modest Car" or "Pay Your Bills Early," may seem almost trivial. Certainly you won't find them featured in most business school courses. Nevertheless, I hope to convince you that embracing these habits will be far more significant to your long-term success than would be acquiring many flashy business skills, such as teaching yourself how to install a new computer network or even mastering a double-entry bookkeeping system. That's because I'm convinced that if you alienate your employees by flaunting your success, or engender distrust and anger throughout your business's creditor network by habitually paying bills late, you will recover little by keeping a great set of books on a state-of-the-art computer, a task you would anyway probably be wise to delegate.

Some of my other advice, such as "Understand How You Make a Profit," may at first appear so obvious as to hardly bear discussion. Not so. Too many new entrepreneurs, full of enthusiasm and vision, fail precisely because they never understand what it will take to make their business truly profitable. All too often, their moneymaking plan consists of little more than opening a shop, restaurant, consulting firm, or other small business and hoping that at the end of the month they'll sell enough so that the bottom line will be printed in black ink. Sorry, while an entrepreneur's own belief that all will go well is undoubtedly an asset, optimism is not a business plan. Long before you open your doors for the first time, you must be able to explain in a paragraph or two exactly how and when your small enterprise will make substantial money.

Let me also point out what this book is *not* designed to accomplish. Specifically, it does not cover the many important day-to-day skills that go into running any small business, including, among many others, accounting, information management, legal organization, and inventory tracking. Books such as *Small-Time Operator*, by Bernard Kamoroff (Bell Springs), *The Small Business Start-Up Kit*, by Peri Pakroo (Nolo), and *Legal Guide for Starting and Running a Small Business,* by Fred S. Steingold (Nolo) are among the many essential small business titles that will help you get up to speed in these areas. But again, as important as it is to master practical business skills, it's my strong belief that mastering the keys to success I discuss here will have far more impact on your business's core effectiveness.

I've drawn my sometimes counterintuitive theories about how to succeed in small business both from my years at Nolo and by studying the successes and failures of other entrepreneurs. Out of both personal curiosity and a determination to run Nolo business better, I've paid close attention to how others approach critical entrepreneurial problems. I've watched as a small minority of brilliant businessowners have learned to pick a business with a competitive edge, imbue it with a sense of purpose, keep it innovative and fresh over many years, and target and inspire employees to be loyal and productive. In fact, understanding what makes excellent small businesses hum has become a bit of a hobby. Whenever I encounter a seemingly successful enterprise I'm unfamiliar with, whether it involves helping contractors reduce workers' compensation premiums, plucking ducks for hunters, patenting new plant varieties, or running the busiest hair salon in town, I immediately want to puzzle out what makes it tick financially. And I don't mean the myriad day-to-day details that keep the "busy" in all businesses, but the core entrepreneurial facts that position the particular enterprise to produce a good profit year after year. Often, I'm disappointed. Given their core costs for things like rent and salaries, and their anticipated sales volume and unit profit margins many will never earn enough to justify their owners' time investment and personal commitment.

But not infrequently I encounter businesspeople who clearly understand how to design an efficient and profitable operation. Recently, for example, I met Philip, an urban animal trapper I called when raccoons tried to turn my lawn into a mud pit. Looking at Philip's business, I immediately saw he had discovered a much-in-demand, albeit unusual, service, which he could provide to a large local audience for a good price. And best of all, his overhead was rock bottom—he needed little more than a trunk full of humane livetraps, an answering machine in the corner of his living room, a bag of cat food, and knowledge of the ways his prey behaved. Because Philip had worked for years as a city animal control officer, he knew how to catch raccoons and other suburban pests such as skunks and possums. Perhaps even more important, he was thoroughly familiar with the affluent neighborhoods subject to raccoon depredations where customers would pay well and usually upfront for his service. Voilà, I thought admiringly, Philip is in great shape to further develop a business that will succeed over the long term. Sure, like all small business owners, Philip would be wise to take other steps discussed in this book, such as diversifying his business by developing innovative new services (deer-proofing yards, perhaps). And he'll need to figure out ways to encourage his high-profit customers to recommend his business to others and, assuming it continues to grow, he'll have to hire and keep good employees. But he has a solid foundation to build on.

But it isn't only exotic businesses, such as animal trapping, I discuss here. Often the best opportunities are to be found in high-demand service businesses, such as home repair, plumbing and heating, tutoring kids, home health services, financial planning, consulting, and other well-populated fields. Precisely because these are areas of high customer demand, they routinely attract large numbers of providers, many of whom will soldier along for years without ever achieving real success. But a substantial minority who understand how to build and market a better business will achieve an impressive and lasting prosperity.

Although good old fortune can play a short-term role in separating the highly successful entrepreneur from her more pedestrian peers, my own Nolo experience convinces me I really can teach you how to make your enterprise stand above the common herd.

I discuss all these keys to success in this little book. I hope you enjoy it, and that it inspires you to look at your own business with a new eye. ■

1

Build a Meaningful Business

On June 16, 1997, I walked out of my office on Nolo's second floor editorial area to see a group of editors gathered around Steve Elias, Nolo's associate publisher. Steve was holding a single sheet of paper. My curiosity piqued, I joined the others and was just in time to hear him read:

"The Unauthorized Practice of Law Committee [of the State of Texas] has received information that you may have engaged in activities which constitute the unauthorized practice of law ... you are requested to provide the undersigned investigation with a written response to the foregoing description of your activities within ten days."

Although the rest of the letter was full of similar muddy legalese, one thing was clear— the legal establishment of the State of Texas had begun legal proceedings against Nolo, which if successful could lead to our books and software being banned from sale in America's second most populous state—an action that would almost surely lead to lawyers of other states also attempting to suppress our publications.

How a Tiny Business Took on the Texas Legal Establishment

Given the freedom of press protection of the U.S. Constitution's First Amendment, how could Texas even contemplate banning self-help legal books and software? Unfortunately, the organization behind the Supreme Court's letter, the Texas Unauthorized Practice of Law Committee (UPLC), had a ready answer. Their legal strategy was to categorize Nolo and—we later learned—several other self-help law publishers, as unlicensed charlatans bent on providing Texas consumers with bogus legal information. Thus categorized, our books and software fell under the provisions of Section 81.102, of the Texas Government Code, a Depression-era law that prohibited the practice of law by unlicensed individuals. Since even the U.S. Supreme Court had found that a state's ability to protect its citizens by adopting professional licensing laws could trump free speech claims, Nolo was clearly in for the fight of its life.

My first thought was to pull all of our employees together and as calmly as possible explain the serious threat we suddenly faced—before rumors of impending legal disaster in Texas could race through Nolo's headquarters. But before I could step towards the intercom, Steve said "I see this as a great opportunity to spread the word about how Americans really do have the right to access their laws without lawyer intervention. Nolo has been given a golden opportunity to play offense."

As I looked at the Nolo editors gathered around Steve, and saw they were smiling and nodding, I relaxed. Nolo staffers, fully grounded in our "Law for All" mission, were not panicked by the Texas attack. Although there would be a need to promptly explain the dangers we faced to all Noloids, clearly a crisis meeting wasn't required.

Fortunately, when all of Nolo's 80 employees understood what the Texas legal establishment was trying to do, most were similarly optimistic.

And it wasn't simply an effort to put their heads in the sand. Like virtually everyone who has been long associated with America's legal system, Noloids knew that being "right" isn't necessarily enough. A well-heeled opponent like the State of Texas can wear down any small business with a long legal battle and millions of dollars in legal bills with the result that even a favorable judgment may only be a Pyrrhic victory.

But Noloids also knew from prior run-ins with lawyer trade groups that fighting back was the best way to spread the word about our little company and its core mission to make America's legal system more accessible, affordable, and democratic. Indeed, way back in 1971 then tiny Nolo achieved its first marketing success after the president of a prestigious California bar group warned that using Charles "Ed" Sherman's *Do Your Own Divorce in California* was akin to ingesting poisoned Tylenol.

Our initial conclusion that the Texas legal establishment was serious about banning our publications was confirmed in the spring of 1998 when we were instructed to appear at a closed-door hearing before the Texas UPLC in Dallas. This was to be our official chance to respond to charges that selling our books and software amounted to the unauthorized practice of law.

But before I tell you how our battle with the Texas legal establishment played out, let me go back a few years to briefly explain how Nolo's deeply embedded culture of standing up for the legal consumer developed. In 1971, Charles "Ed" Sherman and I founded Nolo after spending several years as legal aid lawyers in the Bay Area. Working for a federally funded, community-based legal assistance program in the late 1960s, we were tasked with providing legal help to thousands of low-income people, most of whom had never previously met a lawyer. As you might guess, helping the legally disenfranchised was an exhilarating experience for a couple of middle class guys still in their mid-twenties. But unfortunately our years as legal aid lawyers were marred by one huge unhappy reality;

every day we turned away scores of people with serious legal problems because their modest, working-class incomes rendered them ineligible for free legal help.

To truncate a much longer story, after several years of referring thousands of these working poor citizens to local lawyers we knew they couldn't possibly afford, we sensed an entrepreneurial opportunity. Starting with Ed's breakthrough *How to Do Your Own Divorce in California*, we founded Nolo to provide self-help legal alternatives to the millions of average Americans priced out of our legal system by the profession's high fees.

Over the almost 27 years from Nolo's founding to our brush with Texas, Nolo deliberately hired and trained people who shared this populist vision. Toni Ihara, Steve Elias, Mary Randolph, Linda Hanger, and many, many more Noloids joined our company drawn by our core commitment to building a profit-making enterprise that was at the same time committed to making our legal system more accessible and democratic.

Among the many ways we built this idea of legal reform into our corporate business, a few stand out. Most important, symbolically, we added the phrase "Law for All" to the word Nolo as our official business identifier. Of more substantive significance, we encouraged our legal editors to testify at public and legislative hearings advocating a more democratic legal system, and for many years devoted roughly a third of our free newspaper, *The Nolo News*, to legal reform issues such as rewriting laws with plain English, tasking the courts with providing simple forms and instructions to the self-represented, and making courtrooms welcoming rather than intimidating for nonlawyers.

When our print publication was replaced by Nolo.com as the main way to communicate with our fast-growing constituency we included a prominent "Democracy Corner" section to continue our evangelism in favor of leveling the legal playing field for the self-represented. Finally, and probably most important to convincing our employees and knowledgeable customers that Nolo practiced what it preached, we used some of the profits generated by our bestselling titles to subsidize the niche publication self-help law books. Referring to these in house as "soul of Nolo" books, we did this much in the spirit of a pharmaceutical lab that spends time and money to find the cure to an obscure disease. Even though we knew any potential profit would be somewhere between tiny and nonexistent we also knew that the information was both badly needed and available nowhere else. To take just two examples, way back in the mid-1980's we published a title for grandparents who suddenly found themselves parenting their grandkids and were in need of a low-cost legal guardianship. And even earlier, we published another to help financially pressed stepparents who wanted to adopt their new spouses' children.

In short, when the Texas legal establishment challenged Nolo's continued ability to sell our publications in that state, we were psychologically and culturally ready to embrace the struggle. No question we were also sobered by the prospect of the high costs of fighting an organization with huge financial resources. And we were ever mindful that if we took a wrong legal step and lost our fight, the growing but still immature national self-help law movement would likely be set back by at least a decade. But despite all this we also couldn't help feeling excited. And why not—without intending to, the Texas UPLC had handed Nolo a huge media canvas on which we hoped to paint a persuasive picture of how America's legal profession regularly conspired to place their own profit and privileges ahead of the right of all Americans to affordable legal access.

Enough history. Let's get back to the fight. As you might expect Nolo's immediate response to the UPLC summons was not to roll over and beg for mercy (as several other self-help law publishers did). Instead Nolo challenged the committee! Among other things, we promptly asked:

- Had any Texas citizens had been harmed by Nolo's products?

- Which of our hundreds of publications were being investigated? (We even sent the committee a catalogue and a pencil to ease their task of identifying the worst culprits.)

- What were the names of the people on the UPL committee (theretofore kept secret)?

- What procedures would be followed—for example, could Nolo question witnesses?

When the UPL refused to address any of our requests, we immediately went public with the details of the proceedings, something that was all but unprecedented in the hush-hush world of unauthorized practice of law investigations.

Then, with the invaluable help of Austin civil liberties litigator Peter Kennedy, Nolo filed a lawsuit in the Supreme Court of Texas, challenging the secretive, inquisition-like investigatory procedures being followed by the UPLC and asking that the Supreme Court of Texas order the UPLC to disclose the requested information. The subsequent oral argument before the Texas high court was covered by dozens of news organizations.

Although the ensuing legal battle took two years and featured many more legal and technical twists and turns than are of interest here, four key factors—all stemming from Nolo's commitment to building a meaningful business based on the idea of law for all—were crucial to our eventual victory. (See www.nolo.com/texas/index.cfm for the full story.)

Unity of Purpose

First, as already mentioned, virtually everyone at Nolo was unified by our business's long-standing commitment to create a more democratic legal system. Also, our convictions had already been repeatedly tested over the years when state bar association officials attacked and criticized both the broad concept of self-representation and Nolo's growing arsenal of books and software (often claiming that a person who represents herself has a fool for a client). We had considerable experience in fighting back. For example, when several prominent attorneys, including the late Melvin Belli, claimed that filling out a simple check-the-boxes, fill-in-the-blanks legal form was akin to doing your own brain surgery, we responded by asking, "Does it really take three years of law school to confuse a hair cut with a major operation?"

Nolo also gained conviction by observing how trailblazers in other new fields acquired strength from the unfair attacks of established economic interests. For example, we studied how pioneers in the organic food business had turned the strident derision of the chemical and pesticide industries into a marketing bonanza. Similarly, it was easy to see that one of the biggest assets of auto safety experts, affordable funeral advocates, and low-carb food pioneers was the over-the-top attacks of the vested interests threatened by their new ideas.

Credibility

A second, huge Nolo asset was that many people in the media already knew and trusted us. When we sent out press releases explaining how the Texas legal establishment was trying to use an obscure law to ban our books, many reporters paid attention because we had long been a leader of the affordable legal access movement. Instead of having to convince them from scratch that our publications offered people of average means a reasonable alternative to $250-an-hour lawyers, we were able to quickly get them to focus on the details of how the Texas UPLC was primarily interested in protecting lawyers' economic turf. As a result, over 1,000 Texas and national media outlets covered our battle, including *The Wall*

Street Journal, CNN, ABC News, The Chicago Tribune, and *The L.A. Times*. A major *New York Times* piece was even reprinted in the *International Herald Tribune,* which meant the story of how Texas lawyers threatened to gun down our small company went worldwide. And every time the Texas vs. Nolo story seemed to be getting stale, a member of the Texas UPLC could be counted on to revive it by saying something inflammatory. For example, panel chairman Mark Ticer told *Time* magazine that "Ninety-nine percent of the people we deal with [individuals and companies like Nolo charged with unauthorized practice of law] should be in jail." As Steve Elias said to me, "With an enemy like this, you almost don't need friends!"

Public Support

The third important element of Nolo's success was provided by many direct supporters. When we filed our lawsuit against the UPLC, Nolo was joined by both the Texas Library Association (representing the great majority of Texas librarians), and the prestigious American Association of Law Librarians. To say the least, the principled support of Nolo by these two highly respected librarian's groups added greatly to Nolo's assertion that our dispute really did raise fundamental issues of free speech, free press, and access to justice.

Loads of individual Americans, many of them influential, also supported Nolo. Their help took two broad forms. The first involved many hundreds and possibly thousands of people who, after hearing or reading about our story, contacted either the Texas UPLC, the Supreme Court of Texas, or the Texas Legislature on our behalf. Letters, faxes, and emails poured in to these organizations from consumers and businesspeople who had used our books as well as academics, librarians, and even some lawyers and judges who supported our right to publish them. In one example, Thomas D. Russell, Professor of Law and History at University of Texas Law School wrote, "The current attempt to shut down Nolo Press within Texas is a reprehensible and pitiable attempt by weak-minded lawyers who fear that they lose power and wealth when independent-minded Texans buy Nolo Press books and peer beneath the priestly robes of Texas lawyers." (See www.nolo.com/texas/Professor.html for the full text of Professor Russell's letter.)

Customer Support

The fourth key element in our struggle was a group of individual Texans, each of whom had successfully used our books or software (and in the process saved many thousands of dollars in legal fees). We needed individuals to join our lawsuit filed in Austin, Texas, so we sent invitations to 32 customers in that area. Remarkably, 28 said yes. Because such a large group of plaintiffs was simply too hard to manage on our limited budget, we eventually chose six. We included people who had used our materials to start businesses, make wills, and file for divorce. In sworn legal declarations, all these people responded to the UPLC's core charge that Nolo's publications somehow *practiced* law, by stating that they had no trouble telling the difference between a Texas lawyer and a Nolo book.

The evening before we filed our court papers, all of the plaintiffs gathered at our Austin law firm where Peter Kennedy reviewed the significant legal issues at stake. The atmosphere was earnest and electric. I stood and looked into the faces of the librarians and public-spirited Texans who had volunteered to join our lawsuit with no expectation of personal gain. Their sincere, unselfish gesture to protect access to the law struck me as an intensely patriotic stance and I was reminded of the many thousands of similar protest gatherings which had been held throughout American history from the town meetings that preceded the American

Revolution, and the pre-Civil War period's abolitionist movement through struggles of the 1950s for civil rights. Shaking my head to clear it of the ghosts of patriots past, I thanked everyone for his or her principled support and asked each to say a few words about why they had volunteered without any compensation to join a highly controversial lawsuit against the Texas legal establishment. Almost to a person, the answer was that each believed that our little company—and even more important the self-help law message we enunciated—was a force for the good in the world. And if the lawyers of Texas thought they could drive us out of the state without a fight, they better think again.

The Finale

And now for the end of our drama. Instead of an Alamo-like showdown, it ended in a series of legal whimpers. In the summer of 1999, in the face of our lawsuit (and the legal maneuverings of several other self-help law publishers), the Texas legislature adopted House Bill 1507 which altered the state's UPL statute to state that the practice of law does not include "written materials, books, printed forms, Internet sites or similar media, as long as the items clearly indicate that they are not prepared by a person licensed to practice law in this state". Of course this had been our position from the start and our books and software had long carried a similar disclaimer.

But quibbles aside, the new law was great news. Not only was our two-year fight finally over, but it had ended on our terms. And although it had cost Nolo a small fortune, our books and software sales—driven in large part by all the favorable publicity we received—actually increased enough over the next few years to make us financially whole. And, in a bit of poetic justice, Texans, it turned out, became some of our best customers, purchasing more Nolo books and software than the citizens of any state, except our home state of California.

How to Make Your Business Meaningful

Enough about Nolo? Let's turn now to how you can make your business stronger by imbuing it with a positive purpose. For some businesses—solar engineering, recycled lumber, or ethical investing—altruism is built into the company's purpose. The challenge for these businesses is typically to deepen and broaden the sense of commitment by making sure employees, contractors, and even suppliers fully understand and buy into it.

If, as is more likely, your business doesn't come with a built-in sense of mission—for example you're a lawyer, you run a restaurant, or you do landscaping—it will be your job to create one. Fortunately, with a little creativity it isn't hard to align even the most prosaic of enterprises with a positive goal. Here are a few examples:

- A coffee shop serves "fair trade" coffees while educating its customers that by so doing, it both serves a better cup of java and helps provide a living wage to desperately poor Central American coffee farmers.

- A publisher of a financial newsletter provides a website to educate non-English speakers about sound personal money management practices.

- An eyeglass shop develops a program with local homeless shelters to provide desperately needed glasses to the poorest among us.

- A computer service and repair outfit develops a low-cost recycling program for old computers.

This list could easily run off the bottom of the page. For those who want to learn more about how to transform an everyday business into a meaningful one, I recommend *True to Our Roots, Fermenting a Business Revolution*, Paul Dolan (Bloomberg Press). Dolan, President of Fetzer

Vineyards of Mendocino, California discusses how in the early 1990s Fetzer committed itself to beginning a highly controversial program of making wine from organically grown grapes.

Fast forward fifteen years and Fetzer's sustainable viticulture approach is now widely recognized, respected, and emulated. It turns out that growing grapes without heavy doses of chemical fertilizers is not only better for the land, better for the water, and better for the vineyard workers; it's also better for the taste of the wine. As has proved true in so many other businesses, Fetzer's commitment to serve the greater good also turned out to be very beneficial for its bottom line. It's cheaper to grow grapes organically, employees are healthier and happier, and new customers are attracted both to sustainable viticulture and better tasting wine.

If you are still wondering how you might best develop a sense of purpose for your enterprise and whether doing so would be worth the trouble, take a long walk and think about four concepts:

- sustainability
- education
- service, and
- excellence.

I suggest these four because experience has shown that countless businesses have successfully embraced one or more to deepen their sense of purpose. Let's take a moment to consider each.

Sustainability

In the words of Ernest Callenbach, author of *Ecology: A Pocket Guide* (University of California Press, 1998), from a human point of view, a sustainable society is one that satisfies its needs without diminishing the prospects of future generations. In our petroleum-centric, throwaway economy, any business that advances the idea of resource sustainability—whether via solar or wind power, organic agriculture, "green" construction techniques, resource recycling, or in dozens of other ways—is almost automatically a force for the good. This is especially true if, like Fetzer Vineyards, your business is able to successfully change from an old-style resources-be-damned paradigm to one that treats physical resources and human beings as nonexpendable.

Of course, in our highly wasteful world, winemaking is just one of thousands of business endeavors that can be transformed by the concept of sustainability. For example, the owner of a small local gardening service who shows customers how to grow beautiful plants with half the water and no chemical fertilizer makes a significant commitment to the betterment of all of our lives. And so does a printer who features recycled papers and nonchemical inks. Even an accountant who helps customers substantially reduce the amount of paper needed to prepare their tax returns makes a meaningful contribution.

Superior Service

A second way to imbue your business with a sense of purpose is to dedicate it to providing truly superior customer service. Since many small businesses at best provide spotty help to consumers, designing your operation so that it is accessible, responsive, cheerful, and competent will almost immediately set it apart. And for good reason, since by putting your patrons needs first, you have created a remarkable thing—a business that is at the same time helpful and unselfish. Just as all of the world's religions and many of its other not-for-profit enterprises honestly attract people by emphasizing these virtues, so, too, can your small business.

Example 1:

When prospective customers call Phil, a home repair contractor, the phone is picked up by an answering machine. Phil tries to return calls each evening but doesn't always succeed—especially when he has had a long, frustrating day. When Phil finally does talk to callers it's often to tell them he's too busy to fit their job in. The result of Phil's poor call return policy is that he ends up not working for three out of every four people who call. That's really too bad since Phil frequently experiences periods when no one calls and he doesn't work.

Example 2:

Now suppose that Phil realizes his business model is broken and decides to fix it by making customer service his first priority. To this end, Phil contacts five quality competitors and invites them to join in setting up a customer referral and support network. When a potential customer calls Phil or one of the other contractors during a busy time, she'll be referred to another member of the group who can more promptly fit the job in. And oh yes, because five contractors now work together they can now afford a part-time scheduler who will return every call within two hours.

It's easy to see how this approach allows Phil and the other home repair contractors to provide better service. And, of course, it follows that the satisfied customers are likely to recommend the contractors group to others, thereby creating new business. (See Chapter 8, Market Your Business Creatively, to better understand the principle of word-of-mouth marketing.)

Pleasing customers is one way of providing superior service. A second is to provide assistance to your community. By giving something back to your municipality (or to an electronic community, if yours is a Web-based business), your enterprise establishes an honest connection to real people that chain stores and out-of-town franchises can never achieve.

For example, Phil and his group of contractors can further elevate their service beyond promptly returning calls and responding to emergencies by committing to work with a local jobs center to help train a low-income minority apprentice—a young person who would otherwise find it hard to to learn contracting skills. By jointly mentoring an aspiring contractor in an on-the-job program, the six entrepreneurs could make a real difference in a young person's life. And assuming that they found appropriate ways to tell their customers about their program, chances are many would cheer them on.

Education

But as important as the concepts of sustainability and service are to building a meaningful business, a strong commitment to education normally offers the best way for most small businesses to instill a sense of honest purpose in their operations. Without being too corny about it, we tend to regard those who teach to be worthy of our respect—and that goes for everything from teaching golf and cooking to woodworking and novel writing. Providing instruction taps into the almost universal human respect for knowledge and the ability to do things better.

Add to this respect for learning the fact that most Americans are inveterate self-helpers, anxious for information that will allow them to improve their own lives. It's easy to see why consumers are drawn to businesses that teach them useful skills. And lest you doubt this, think for a moment about the literally thousands of popular magazines, self-help books, and even TV and radio shows that prosper by instructing people how to better accomplish an almost infinite list of tasks, from fixing their cars or learning French, to making over their own bodies, finding a mate, or raising an obedient spaniel.

In short, virtually every business, including yours, has a chance to deepen its sense of mission and purpose by educating customers.

Example:

Walter's Barbershop is a relatively new addition to the Main Street scene in a small mid-western city. Like all barbershops, Walter's cuts hair. But in an effort to set his business apart from at least its less fastidious competitors, Walter commits himself to maintaining a super-clean, uncluttered environment. In addition, he adopts a flexible staffing pattern backed by an easy-to-access reservation system so as to both reduce waiting time and accommodate as many customers as possible during busy periods.

So far so good, but several other barbershops in town have also thrown off their sleepy old ways. In short, although Walter's commitment to cleanliness and service is a definite marketing plus, it doesn't convincingly distinguish his business. To do that Walter decides to educate men about healthy hair care and effective remedies to reverse baldness. He does this by creating a little niche in his waiting area, complete with attractive information sheets explaining the pros and cons of different types of shampoos, conditioners, and dandruff treatments along with copies of reliable consumer testing reports and other comparative hair product data.

In addition, Walter provides up-to-date information about the advantages and disadvantages of all legitimate anti-baldness treatments and techniques along with material debunking the many hair growth scams. Finally, Walter provides a comprehensive list of reputable local doctors who treat hair loss, hair weave specialists, wigmakers, and other area businesses that help cancer patients and others cope with sudden baldness.

As mentioned, virtually every type of business can improve its relationship with their customers by providing access to life-enhancing information. But to really succeed by adopting an education-first approach, you'll need to capture the imaginations of all your business's key stakeholders, including its employees, contractors, suppliers, employees, and even any investors. With everyone on board, a good customer education program can create a sense of deep-seated pride that can greatly improve every aspect of your operation.

Example:

Joe's Hardware occupied the corner of Main and Maple in downtown Riverview ever since Joe I opened it in 1946 after returning from service as a sergeant in Patton's 3rd Army during World War II. But in 2004, with more competition soon to come from a big box store planned for a commercial area ten miles away, Joe III clearly saw that the old store's relatively small physical size plus its lack of free parking doomed it to a marginal future. So Joe III decided to make a big move to a strip mall a half mile away, taking over the space vacated by a large chain drugstore. Not only was the new building's footprint double the size of the old one's, but it was surrounded by half an acre of free parking and came with an efficient loading dock, something the old store lacked. Nevertheless, Joe III worried that by abandoning his family's charming and much-loved downtown shop in favor of a more efficient, but far less sexy retail environment he risked losing many longtime customers.

To keep the loyalty of Joe's long-term customer base and hopefully to win back former customers who had gone elsewhere after becoming frustrated by the old store's lack of selection, Joe III decided to fundamentally change the way his business operated, by designing the new store around a strong educational component. This took two main forms. First, Joe's Hardware leased a small empty space next door to its new location and turned it into a classroom where it could hold free classes for do-it-yourselfers. Focused on practical subjects like pouring concrete, building decks, and replacing worn-out plumbing fixtures, Joe's self-help sessions would be taught by local contractors, manufacturers' reps, decorators, architects, and a couple of authors of self-help building guides, all of whom would accept modest fees in exchange for the highly desirable opportunity to market their own services, products, and publications.

Joe's Hardware's second teaching initiative was to hire a group of retired home repair and building contractors as senior clerks, each willing to work 10 to 15 hours per week for a reasonable wage. Eventually, Joe's stable of in-store experts included plumbers, electricians, carpenters, tile layers, and general contractors, each available to answer do-it-yourself questions and help patrons select merchandise. And to make it easy for customers to easily connect with the right expert, Joe's published a monthly schedule of their work times on its Internet site and in flyers.

Joe suspected that the occasional customer came to him for free advice and then tried to save a few dollars by buying from the big box store, but he quickly saw that this wasn't a significant economic threat. That's because in the first year after the move, both Joe's Hardware's gross revenue and net profit almost doubled as newly empowered customers purchased more and told their friends that almost any do-it-yourself home improvement job would go better with the help of the knowledgeable folks down at Joe's.

Don't take money from investors who don't understand your mission.

Sadly, the many good reasons why a business benefits by investing in concepts like sustainability, education, and service are lost on many investors whose goal is to pump up short-term profit, often by selling the business. So before you take money from anyone, be sure they also buy into the idea that building a meaningful business is the best way to build value in the long run.

Excellence

Depending on the type of business you operate, excellence can be defined in many ways: highly accurate, relentlessly innovative, most accessible, or cleanest, for example. Arguably, a commitment to excellence should be a part of every enterprise, and that it isn't, by itself, a discrete way to do business. But I don't buy it. In my experience, because many, if not most, small businesses are run in a mediocre fashion, a true dedication to providing customers with the highest quality goods and services is a significant way to imbue it with purpose.

Or to put it more bluntly, the excellent business is almost always regarded by its customers as transcending its market niche. In my field of self-help law publishing for example, Nolo stands out not only because of our commitment to affordable legal access, but because our materials are clearly so much better and more helpful than those of our competitors. So much better, that over and over our customers tell us that they simply can't believe we can publish professional quality materials in a low-cost paperback format. And, of course, this isn't an accident—Nolo consistently and consciously invests more time, energy, money, and commitment in its products than do others in the field.

You may ask whether is it really cost effective to spend the extra time, money, and effort to run a truly excellent enterprise when many if not most customers will be satisfied with "pretty good"? Or put another way, will your employees, customers, and the rest of the people in your network really value your business more highly because you consciously work to achieve the highest possible standard? The answer is a resounding yes—especially in fields where there are lots of competitors.

Your commitment to excellence will also furnish everyone connected with your business with a sense of pride. Or put another way, in the world of small business where dirty windows, cluttered sales areas, and disinterested service is so often the norm, your commitment to consistently do better will quite properly be seen as something special. And it won't only be your customers who will respond positively. Employees, independent contractors, and others in your network will not only be proud of being associated with your excellent operation, but willing to contribute their enthusiastic support.

To see how a commitment to excellence can even transform a large industry, consider how relatively quickly and definitively Honda and Toyota achieved worldwide respect during the last quarter of the 20th century, based on their determination to make the most reliable, repair-free cars. The fact that in our new century these two excellently run companies have also embraced the concept of sustainability by introducing higher-mileage, less-polluting electric-gas hybrid vehicles has only deepened the esteem in which their many loyal customers hold them. And of course Honda's and Toyota's commitment to excellence means that people who work for these companies are not only proud of what they do but understand that it's up to them to be sure that the highest standards continue to be met.

Similarly, at Nolo, everyone in the building is proud of the fact that our people-oriented, plain-English legal materials are the most accurate and up to date, bar none. Thus when a customer writes or emails us a success story, whoever receives it typically forwards it to everyone. But instead of telling you more about how Nolo communicates its quality advantage to its customers and longtime media fans, let's focus on how a more typical small business might apply the concept of excellence to improve a key aspect of its operations.

Example:

Cindy and her brother Abraham inherited the Ace Garage when their dad, Woody, died. Ace had been repairing cars in Lake Port for over fifty years. But like so many car repair shops, it looked its age. In the last decade of his life, Woody simply hadn't had the energy or inclination to make significant improvements.

Cindy and Abraham immediately agreed that big changes were needed if the garage was to provide a comfortable income over the next several decades. They focused first on cleaning up what they had to admit was a typically filthy garage. With the help of a team of professional cleaners and painters, Cindy, Abraham, and their employees cleaned and painted almost everything, from the service bays and office to the driveway and the roof. Even the gumball machine got a coat of new red paint. And it wasn't just the building that was scrubbed and shined—enough new overalls were ordered so that every Ace employee would have a clean pair each morning. Not surprisingly, when the refurbished, new Ace reopened in mid-January, Cindy and Abraham received lots of praise, including even a picture of the garage and its striking new sign in the local paper. Best of all, business immediately increased almost 15%, with the result that they could project that the clean-up cost would be amortized in less than a year.

But Cindy and Abraham weren't done. They next set out to create a keep-it-clean culture at Ace. Instead of yelling at longtime employees when they reverted to their sloppy old ways, Cindy and Abraham demonstrated their personal commitment to cleanliness by adopting a Sunday clean-up strategy. If a mechanic fouled the floor or walls of his area during the week, or the oil an old clunker leaked on the driveway was still there Saturday evening, Cindy or Abraham would personally come in on Sunday to scrub and, if necessary repaint the offending area. As you might guess, it only took a couple of weeks of this gentle shaming before the garage was kept so clean Cindy and Abraham were free to find better ways to spend their day off.

Cindy and Abraham's next effort to distinguish their business was to install a small carwash unit in the back parking lot. Now, every car repaired by Ace was given a complimentary wash—and for a small optional fee an inside cleaning. Not surprisingly, customers who brought in cars both broken and dirty were delighted to pick them up both repaired and scrubbed—so pleased, in fact, that they frequently told their friends and relatives about Ace's superior service.

But running a clean repair garage wasn't Cindy and Abraham's only effort to improve Ace. Realizing that a few incompetently done repairs can alienate customers and drive up customer service costs, Ace began a campaign to improve its repair work. Mechanics were asked to refresh their skills through classes and seminars paid for by Ace that were designed to help them take maximum advantage of the new diagnostic machines Cindy and Abraham purchased with the help of a small bank loan. When one employee balked at learning "all the damn fool new technology" Cindy helped him find a job at a more traditional garage down the street. Although nothing was said about the reasons for the change, other Ace employees redoubled their efforts to maximize their skills.

To celebrate the end of their successful first year, Cindy and Abraham had a low-key staff holiday party at which they handed out red baseball caps with the number 55 (the age of the garage) on the front and the small words "ACE-Accuracy, Cleanliness & Excellence" embroidered just above the back adjustment strap. When many of their employees regularly wore their caps to work, the energetic duo knew they really had converted Ace into a garage with a mission.

■

2

Choose a Business You Care About

"To love what you do and feel that it matters—how could anything be more fun?"

—Katharine Graham

Especially if you haven't yet greeted your first customer, it may seem premature to focus on the importance of staying committed to your business over the long term. Best to think again. Most small businesses take three to five years to become solidly profitable, and at least several more to justify all the work and investment that went into their creation. But once profitable, a business can continue to make the cash register sing for many years, if not decades. In short, to enjoy the financial success you're hoping for, you need to be ready to run a marathon, not a sprint. And that means you'll want to pick a business you fundamentally care about, not just one you think will make big profits.

Picking the right business is a lot like picking the right spouse. "Till death do us part" is a long time—impossibly long if you and your spouse aren't a good fit. Running a small enterprise is much the same; you'll have many days when nothing goes right, and you'll inevitably wonder whether life doesn't have something better to offer. As with marriage, you'll hang in there only if the glue that brought you together in the first place has lots of stick.

A few people are lucky enough to create a business that springs directly from their hearts. They are what they do in the best sense of that phrase. But most of us aren't quite so fortunate—the best we can do is to start a business in a field we are interested in, but not in love with. We are content to fill teeth, sell golf clubs, or counsel dieters from 9 to 5 so we can raise a great family, spend time with our friends, and maybe even sing opera, scale mountains, or write poetry in our free time.

No problem, as long as you really do care about your business's core functions and find ways to invest them with meaning. That way, when the going gets tough, or even when you've been successful for several years and begin to feel boredom's first inevitable tugs, you'll be well-positioned to persevere. To carry on happily and profitably over many years, you will also need to periodically change and refresh many aspects of your business, something that will be much easier to accomplish if you respect and care about what you do.

Plan for the Long Haul

Given that, by most estimates, only about 20% of small businesses last even five years, it's easy to see that staying power, and not just a good idea or hard work, is key to success. Of course, small businesses fail for dozens of reasons. Financial mismanagement, poor customer relations, bad personnel decisions, fights between co-owners, and selling undistinguished products and services top the list. Especially in combination, these failings are quick business killers. But oddly, one of the commonest reasons small businesses close—especially after experiencing an initial burst of success—is often overlooked. "Entrepreneurial boredom" is the best description of this stealthy killer of seemingly healthy small businesses. Typically, it strikes just when a business begins to successfully emerge from its start-up phase, but is still fragile.

To prosper, most small businesses depend on the energy and entrepreneurial savvy of their owners, and if either begins to flag, it creates an immediate problem. A bored or depressed owner is likely to stop doing the many little things that made the business initially seem so special to its customers. A restaurant owner is no longer willing to stay late to greet the last customer; the proprietor of an imported fabric store refuses to travel frequently in search of new designs; or the owner of a haircutting boutique neglects freshening the window display. As these businesses begin to become as boring as their owners are bored, customers quickly sense the loss of entrepreneurial energy and look for more robust alternatives.

Typically, a business begins to lose momentum when the owner stops focusing on how to continuously improve every aspect of its operation, and instead adopts an "if it's not broken, don't fix it" attitude. This lackadaisical approach may work fine for several months or, if the business has a large following or a particularly well-defined competitive niche, maybe even a few years. But businesses that stand pat for an extended period— or until others copy or improve on their products or services—inevitably lose customers. And once a downward spiral begins, it is often too late to reenergize an operation enough to reclaim its position in the marketplace. Whether you give massages, provide home health care, install fences, or any one of thousands of other tasks, the smart and aggressive competitors who have passed you by are likely to be working hard to extend their new lead.

Although entrepreneurial boredom can damage businesses of any size—it took decades of producing mostly undistinguished cars to severely blemish once mighty General Motors—there are two reasons it is particularly lethal to small ones. First, little businesses rarely have the financial reserves to weather an extended downturn. Second, when old customers begin to disappear, few small enterprises can afford to spend enough on advertising or other marketing efforts to quickly attract new ones. They must rely instead on the slow process of gaining new business based on the positive word of mouth of satisfied customers, who are by definition beginning to be in short supply (or in a worst case, are no longer satisfied and are beginning to actively criticize the business). Or put another way, even if a somnolent business finally wakes up and introduces fresh and exciting products or services, it may run out of money before it can convince enough customers to give it another chance. Which, of course, goes far towards explaining why, when a downtrodden business is sold, the new owners' first steps are usually to put up an "Under New Management" sign and to attempt to change as many of the physical attributes of the business as possible. Thus a new owner will often try to signal a business reawakening by painting the building, holding a sale, and implementing a number of new marketing initiatives.

The Exception: Serial Entrepreneurs

Every generalization has its exceptions. So it is with the proposition that small business success depends on the caring involvement, if not passionate commitment, of its owner. Very infrequently, exceptional men and women start a series of successful businesses during long and profitable careers without seeming to give a hoot about their substance. Instead of following the normal formula of carefully building and nurturing a business over many years, they seem born with the knack of starting up and getting out of enterprises at just the right time. For instance, one man I know sequentially, and very successfully, started a small chain of men's clothing stores, a grapefruit orchard, a golf resort, a commercial real estate business, and a bank.

Most of the people who start or buy a number of disparate businesses in their lives share several traits. They love the dollars-and-cents side of entrepreneurship. The business of business fascinates them. They are also good at spotting potentially profitable niches before they become trendy. Probably most important, they are willing (even eager) to sell well before a business peaks in value.

Interestingly, most of the successful serial entrepreneurs I know love to play cards for money and are very good at it. But none of them gambles carelessly. Instead, they almost always know the mathematical odds for and against every bet, memorize cards as they are played, and pay lots of attention to the strengths and weaknesses of their fellow players. In short, they are attracted to the idea of taking chances, but disciplined enough to do everything possible to maximize their likelihood of success.

I have firsthand experience with just how important it is to choose a business you're genuinely interested in. Close to 35 years ago, I quit practicing law—something I found almost terminally boring—and helped start Nolo Press, a publisher of self-help law books and software. In doing so, I was fortunate to become involved in the following five endeavors I found (and still find) fascinating:

- mastering the expert systems that inform a number of consumer law areas that were largely unfamiliar to me, including estate planning, family law, and landlord/tenant law
- teaching nonlawyers how to solve legal and practical problems
- writing and editing
- participating in the business of book and software publishing, including, of course, starting and growing Nolo, and
- writing and speaking about the reforms necessary to make America's legal system more accessible, affordable, and democratic.

Had my attraction to any of these activities been less strong, I'm sure Nolo would never have survived its early unprofitable years, when one of its main assets was my unwillingness to quit. Even if it had lasted long enough to achieve profitability, chances are excellent that like so many other business founders, I would have gotten fed up with coping with the stream of day-to-day problems that are part of any enterprise, and sold it years ago. But because I still find it fun and rewarding to work on books and software that demystify complicated-seeming legal information, Nolo has had a chance to grow and mature into a large and profitable company.

Here are a few additional down-to-earth examples of why it's important to pick a field you are authentically attracted to:

- If you plan to go into the catering business, it will be far easier to scrub the kitchen three years from now if you truly care about food.

- If you plan to study chiropractic medicine, your practice is likely to do well only if you are fully committed to relieving your patients' pain. Just learning how the body works and how to competently manipulate it is unlikely to be enough to keep your interest over many years.

- If you plan to open a garage to repair German cars not because you like to get your hands dirty, but because the nearest BMW dealer is 50 miles away, chances are you'll make a hash of it. To take just one example, what will you do if your chief mechanic is sick? Far better to begin this type enterprise only if car repair is something you have a real affinity for. That way you'll be able to step in and help fix the cars when you need to.

- If you plan to open a dance studio to teach kids ballet, you should care deeply both about children and ballet. If dance is your passion, and teaching kids is just a way to pay your bills, chances are the snot-nosed little devils will drive you nuts long before you establish a solidly profitable business.

- If you plan to open a business to help people manage their retirement savings, it will help greatly if you have real compassion for older people, as well as skill picking investments. Otherwise, you probably won't survive all the inevitable stories of chronic illness, irresponsible children, and precocious grandchildren.

To emphasize how important picking the right business is, let's briefly look at an example of how owner boredom, combined with more than a dash of entrepreneurial hubris, combined to kill a successful clothing store I'll call Snapdragon. When Snapdragon opened in a popular business section of a good-sized university city, its exciting window displays of cutting-edge women's fashions proved irresistible to loads of customers. Passersby whose only thought was to grab a double latté at a neighboring coffee shop found themselves instead getting a far more expensive lift by buying a new outfit. Indeed, Snapdragon prospered so mightily that before it had been in business 18 months, a second location sprouted on the other side of town. And when that store also seemed poised to bloom, a third flowered in a shopping center ten miles to the north.

Imagine my surprise (shock would be a better word) when after another 18 months I walked by Snapdragon's original shop to find a going-out-of-business sale in progress. "Unbelievable" was the word that filled my head. I was so curious as to what had suddenly gone wrong, I called Kathy, a friend who had worked briefly as a part-time bookkeeper for Snapdragon's owner, Millie. I expressed my disbelief and asked Kathy to fill me in on Snapdragon's history.

"Millie's success resulted from her great eye for style," Kathy told me. "She saw that there was a niche for clothes that were in between the usual frumpy college-town look and the more upscale clothes you would find at a Saks or Nordstrom's. I heard several customers call this look 'bohemian chic,' but I'd just say Millie understood how to display bright colors, soft fabrics, and comfortable styles in an exciting way."

"But it must have taken more than that to create such a successful business," I said.

"A huge part of it was Millie's knack at designing a highly attractive shop," Kathy said. "In the first year, at least, she just seemed born to create a jazzy retail atmosphere. We had truly innovative window displays that she changed twice a month, hand-painted flowers on the dressing room walls, and even fashion shows before major holidays. Not only were the stores painted in inviting colors, Millie nailed every design detail so perfectly that women all over town were buzzing about Snapdragon. But it was clearly designing the shop, not selling clothes, that really turned Millie on. I mean, she usually wore shorts and a t-shirt."

"Whether Millie came to work in shorts or an evening dress, I still don't get why such a popular store closed in less than four years," I remarked.

"Making a lot of money fast actually made Millie dumber," Kathy replied. "Instead of putting aside a reserve for the inevitable bad period, she made a down payment on a nice house, bought a BMW, and went on a couple of expensive buying trips that were really just thinly disguised vacations. This ticked off a couple of good employees, who quit because they didn't receive expected raises. But the problems really developed when Millie began to lose interest in what really made the business work: clothing that was attractive and exciting to her particular customers. For example, she decided it was too hard to travel to trade shows every few months to find exactly the right fashions, and started buying the styles sales reps pushed on her. When lots of them turned out to be a little too Rodeo Drive for her audience, she tried to get back to her old formula. But by then, a couple other shops had opened nearby that combined decent style with lower prices, and Snapdragon never regained enough of its customers to return to its early level of profitability."

"Do you mean Snapdragon wasn't losing money when it closed?" I asked.

"Not really," Kathy answered. "After making a bundle for a couple of years and opening the other stores—which, incidentally, were never as profitable as the original and sapped Millie's energy since she never learned to delegate well—Snapdragon barely broke even in its third year. That next fall, Millie worked extremely hard and worried a lot, but she still made only a small profit. That's when she decided she'd had enough."

"So Millie closed a profitable business that until recently had done well?"

"Precisely. I think she never cared that much about selling clothes in the first place. When she decided to pull out, she tried to sell the business, but when the offers weren't that great, she saw she could make a lot more by having an extended going-out-of-business sale. She filled up all three stores to the brim before she announced a closing date. And she was right—the fact that Snapdragon would soon be gone forever caused all of her old customers to crawl out of the woodwork, with their checkbooks. She moved a year's inventory in three months and then she extended the closing date 60 days and made even more."

"What is Millie doing now?"

"Studying design, with the idea of opening a consulting business to help small businesses improve their visual presentations. And you know, I think if she sticks to it, she'll do really well. Millie was always happiest when she was in the front window area creating a wonderful display. Turning her design flair into a career should be a great choice."

How to Stay Interested in Your Business

Even in a business you care about, there is the obvious danger that boredom will eventually creep in. If you increasingly find reasons to be elsewhere—taking lots of vacations, attending trade shows, starting a side business, or spending lots of time on nonprofit boards or a government commission—it's time to reexamine your commitment. Even if you still put in a reasonable number of hours on the job, do you still have the intensity and creativity that put the business on the map? If, instead of coming up with—and more importantly, implementing—the steady stream of ideas needed to keep the business fresh, you're more worried about why you're shanking your seven iron or buying the perfect sailboat, your business is unlikely to continue to prosper.

The most insidious thing about entrepreneurial boredom is that typically, it springs from the very thing that makes a business successful in the first place: the intelligent repetition of many small tasks over many months and years. No question, it can be tough to continue to make excellent wine, soup, or soap day after day after day, or to teach ten great aerobics classes 49 weeks a year. If you doubt how different it can be to set a high standard and live up to it over the long term, think for a moment about the laundry/dry cleaning businesses in your area. Chances are good that only one or two excellent establishments have built up and kept a large and loyal following over an extended period while other shops have opened, done a seemingly decent business for a while, and then closed. It's likely that the winning establishments built their apparently unassailable market position because their owners stayed committed to providing excellent customer service for years, if not decades, while at least some of the businesses that folded did so because their owners just couldn't look at another dirty collar.

As someone who has run a business for close to 35 years despite being born with a low boredom threshold, I consider myself something of an expert on strategies to stay interested and even invigorated by one's business. Here are several that have worked for me.

Make Time to Do What You Enjoy Most

Hopefully, you were drawn to start your business because you were attracted to some core part of it. If you work as an authors' agent, you probably enjoy books. If you make cabinets, chances are you like the process of woodworking. Similarly, most successful golf teachers not only love the game, but enjoy helping others master it. And many people who sell real estate get a genuine thrill from matching someone to the perfect home.

But whether you simply like your field or have been lucky enough to turn a beloved hobby into a successful enterprise, actually running your business will inevitably involve many workaday aspects. Among literally dozens of other tasks, typically you'll need to crunch lots of paperwork, pay bills, mediate food fights between employees or contractors, placate customers, and probably coax the landlord to get broken equipment fixed or restripe the parking lot. In my experience, it's often while trying and failing to squeeze a week's worth of this type of work into a morning that business-killing boredom begins to corrode your interest in your company.

Instead of happily spending your hours on your business's fundamental work—the activity you found so attractive in the first place—you'll often find yourself too busy to get to it. If you're a furniture maker, instead of contentedly working in the shop with hammer and chisel, you're all too likely to find yourself in the office spending frustrating hours straightening out quality and collection problems with a big customer. If you're a golf pro, instead of being out on the practice tee—or better yet the links—you'll only be human if you resent the many hours you spend running the busy pro shop. And if you are an antiquarian bookseller who lives for literature and fine examples of the bookmaker's art, you'll likely hate long hours spent trying to decipher the intricacies of bookkeeping software.

Sound familiar? If so, call a halt and do something about it. Several times over the years, I've had to just say "hell, no" to additional administrative work while facing the need to rid myself of piles of busywork. And I didn't necessarily do this because I was overworked, but in order to have time to do the writing, editing, and other legal self-help activities I most enjoy. The good news is that if you follow my example, you'll not only stay in touch with what originally attracted you to your business, but also have the opportunity to empower your employees, contractors, and others you work with to competently handle many routine tasks. Because almost by definition many small business owners come with Control Freak stamped on their psyches, learning to delegate well can be as tough as it is essential. (See Chapter 11, Don't Work Overlong Hours.) But even in the unlikely event that you really are twice as smart and three times as hardworking as the people who will replace you, it's essential that you make time for the work you care about. If you don't, the chances that you won't stay interested in your business over the long term go way up. And if this happens, the odds your business will produce the continuing stream of healthy profits you hope for over the long term will drop just as fast.

Example:

Ed quit his job at one of the large Silicon Valley chip outfits and started his own website design consultancy, operating from a small office in a converted backyard garden shed. In the beginning, Ed did it all—fixing the balky printer, hunting for business, creating the custom websites that were the business's core product, and collecting the money. But as his business quickly prospered, Ed moved into an office building and recruited a couple of designer pals to help create the sites while he concentrated on bringing in more and more lucrative contracts. But the better Ed succeeded financially, the more dissatisfied he became with the hassles of running the business, at one point even considering closing and going back to the Silicon Valley treadmill.

That's when Beth, a business consultant and friend, suggested a different approach. She recommended that instead of hiring designers, Ed should hire an experienced marketer so that he could spend at least 50% of his time on the design side of the business. He took the advice, and the result was that even though WayCoolWebPlace's earnings declined slightly the next year, Ed had a smile on his face—always a good trade-off. And in the following year, as positive word about WayCoolWebPlace spread quickly over the Internet and the new marketing director gained traction, Ed's suddenly not-so-little business became highly profitable even as many other Web-related businesses began to have trouble.

Don't hire employees if you can't learn to delegate.

Some people really are born with an "I need to do it myself" gene. Even when they understand the need to delegate, they just can't. If this describes you, I strongly recommend that you operate a one-person business. True, by definition this will mean staying tiny, but it will also mean you have the opportunity to create a business that perfectly fits your personality. And if you choose and execute well, you'll still be able to make a very good living. Best of all, you'll never have to hold a meeting or get mad at others who just can't seem to see or do things exactly the way you want them to.

Develop New Business Approaches

If you're easily bored by routine, you have a choice: move from one business to another every few years in search of variety or use this trait as a catalyst for innovation in your existing enterprise. Unleashing your creativity is undoubtedly the most powerful cure for boredom and, sensibly harnessed, it can work wonders to make a good business better. Whether you're in a service, retail, manufacturing, or construction business, your customers will respond positively if your business regularly introduces new products and services. Even improving the way your business looks and sounds will almost always be positively remarked on by your customers.

One approach I find helpful when I get a bad case of the ho-hums is to pretend I am starting Nolo from scratch. Here are some questions I ask:

- What would a new Nolo look like?

- How would it communicate with its customers?

- Who would we hire, and how would we organize them?

- What current products would we no longer produce, and what would we replace them with?

- How would Nolo's old and new products be priced and marketed?

If your business is successful, you'll probably decide that you are already doing many things right, meaning that your mythical new enterprise would look similar to your existing one. But I have a hunch that if you are savvy enough to have created a superior business, you'll have no trouble finding dozens of significant ways to change and improve it. If so, what's stopping you from implementing at least some of your best ideas? High cost may be one answer. If so, you need to focus on the most powerful ones that can also be implemented at modest cost. And if a truly compelling new initiative will require a significant investment, be ready to raise the needed funds. If your business is solidly profitable, you can't afford not to make it better and, hopefully, in the process become re-excited about its prospects. If profitability is flagging and you have nevertheless decided to persevere, there is usually even more reason to consider implementing significant changes.

You can't do everything at once.

Some businesspeople have more ideas than they have time, people, and money to implement them. If this describes you, you'll need to choose well. Make sure the new products, services, and business methods you introduce really will enhance your enterprise's core competencies and, by extension, its profits. And before committing a major investment to any particular initiative, find a way to test it at lower cost.

Successful small business owners—especially those who become jaded operating the same old business—sometimes try to take a successful enterprise in a totally new and unexpected direction. For example, a successful landscape gardener I knew fell in love with making jewelry and hoped to transform his life by selling earrings to his gardening clients. Unfortunately, his customers found his enthusiasm for jewelry off-putting and not only resisted buying trinkets, but turned elsewhere to get their lawns cut. Similarly, a restaurant owner who tried to turn part of her establishment into an art gallery ended up with two failed businesses. As these little stories illustrate, there is a huge difference between innovating within a successful enterprise and embarking on a total departure from the tried-and-true. Very few of us, it turns out, are smart and disciplined enough to invent a second successful business while still running the first.

Invest Your Business With a Sense of Purpose

In Chapter 1, Build a Meaningful Business, I discuss in detail several reasons why it is important to align your business with an altruistic purpose, such as improving the environment, or teaching customers valuable new skills, to mention just a couple. It not only makes sense to do this because it is likely to make your business more profitable, but also because it will make it more interesting. And although I can point to no study proving it, I'm convinced that entrepreneurs are far more likely to stave off boredom and stay involved in their business over the long term if they believe in what they do.

Fire Yourself/Hire Yourself

When I get completely fed up with my day-to-day work responsibilities, I take a few weeks off. Often this is all I need to feel reenergized about Nolo. But three or four times over my career, even an extended vacation hasn't reawakened my entrepreneurial zeal. Instead, I've returned from a holiday feeling almost as enervated as when I left.

The first time this happened, the cause of my angst was not hard to figure out. In the early 1990s, with close to 50 employees and growing, Nolo had become too big and complicated for me to run on a daily basis while still setting aside enough time to focus on the essential task of developing new self-help law products. Gradually, as Nolo grew, the parts of the business that bored me had all but crowded out the parts that drew me to the office early on Monday morning with fire in my belly.

After more than a little soul-searching (my doctor would probably have said I was suffering from mild depression), I sat down and made a list of all the business tasks of which I was supposed to be in ultimate charge. This turned out to be a very long list, including creating new book and software titles, updating old ones, producing and printing them on time, creating a marketing plan for every product, operating a warehouse, supervising Nolo's retail store, seeing that Nolo had sensible personnel policies, creating a budget, supervising our accounting system, and helping produce the *Nolo News*, our quarterly newspaper, to mention just a few.

Deciding that the only thing I was both best at and enjoyed the most was Nolo's editorial function—developing Nolo's new self-help law content—I decided to fire myself from running all the rest. I knew I had made the right personal decision when for the first time in quite a while I found myself in a great mood. But I also knew my newfound euphoria wouldn't last long unless I could find the right person to competently lead all the essential business tasks I would no longer be responsible for. Fortunately, I knew just the person for the job: Linda Hanger, an experienced publishing executive and friend who had worked for Nolo many years before. And providentially, Linda, who was fed up with her increasingly miserable daily commute to her job, where she ran several divisions of a computer book publisher, agreed to become Nolo's president, a position she held from 1993 until 2004, when she resigned to head up Evan-Moor Educational Publishers.

But as you might guess, I still faced the huge challenge of getting out of Linda's way and letting her run the company I had cofounded and run for more than 20 years. To get this process off to a good start, Linda and I drew up a two-page document called "It's a Deal." In it, we listed the major functions of a publishing company, including writing and editing, layout and design, financial management, marketing, publicity, printing, warehousing, and shipping. We then made it clear that I remained the boss only of Nolo's book and software publishing activities. Linda would be in charge of all the rest. In addition, each of us reserved the right to express our opinions to each other (kibitz) about the decisions the other had made.

From the beginning, our division of labor worked. No question, facing up to the need to surrender long-held power was as wrenching as it was exhilarating. But the important point was that I survived it (with loads of help from Linda) because I clearly understood that only by voluntarily giving up power would I have enough time to do the self-help law work I loved. In short, firing myself from the parts of my job that had begun to depress me allowed me to rededicate myself to the work that had originally drawn me to help start Nolo. This lesson was so empowering I have applied it twice more when I experienced similar bouts of boredom. In 1998, I fired myself as Nolo's book and software publisher and hired myself to supervise Nolo's fast-growing Internet operations—then a relatively new and exciting area of our business that simply wasn't getting enough attention. Later, with Nolo's Web strategy largely in place, I turned the job over to people who better understood how to develop our Webby-winning website and hired myself as executive publisher, to integrate Nolo's traditional and new media efforts.

Each time that I gave myself permission to shuck off work that bored me and focus on tasks I looked forward to, I felt almost reborn. And best of all, I accomplished these personal transformations without selling the business, retiring, or becoming an absentee owner. Even more important, I allowed Nolo's estimable employees, many of whom have spent over 20 years with the company, a chance to continue to develop Nolo as a profitable enterprise. Whether your boredom threshold is high or low, one thing is sure: The longer you run a business, the more likely it is that you, too, will need to learn how to fire and rehire yourself.

Example:

Jed and Paul, brothers in their 40s, took over active management of their dad's vending machine business, Evergreen Vending, a decade ago. With about 500 machines in operation, mostly located at worksites with 50 to 150 employees, the brothers made a decent living in part because they both worked hard keeping the machines in good repair and full of soda and candy. Although the business was doing well, increasingly Jed wasn't. Many days he got up in the morning tired and grumpy, and told his wife that just making it through the day seemed like wading through acres of wet cement.

After ruling out physical illness, Jed's doctor explained that he was suffering from depression, a condition that could probably be improved by exercise, diet, and medication, but was undoubtedly also rooted in Jed's psyche (his soul, if you will). The doctor suggested that Jed knock off work for a week, take a look at how his life was going, and consider making some changes. Following this advice, Jed realized that he had come to hate the repetitive, boring nature of his job and that doing something about it was imperative. Either he had to sell his share of the business and find a new career (no easy task at age 46 with a limited education) or find a way to feel better about his part of the work.

Fortunately, Dave, Jed and Paul's dad still worked a couple of days a week to help out, made a good suggestion. Reasoning that 20% of the machines almost surely generated the majority of the profit, Dave proposed that instead of maintaining and filling the machines, Jed spend a couple of months crunching numbers to see whether he could come up with a plan to make the business more profitable. In the meantime, Dave and other family members would pitch in and cover Jed's routes.

To oversimplify more than a little, Jed quickly concluded that Dave's hunch was right—a minority of the machines made most of the profits. In part, this reflected the fact that vending machines located at design firms, architects' offices, and Internet-related businesses, where many employees worked nontraditional hours, produced far higher sales than those at warehouses, machine shops, and other 9-to-5 operations. And interestingly, Jed also established that a number of the more profitable businesses were located fairly close together in one part of Evergreen's territory, meaning that they could be serviced with a minimum of driving.

Finally, after talking to the people in charge of facilities at half a dozen of these companies, Jed reported that a number of them were hungry for additional machines stocking less traditional, but higher-margin, products, such as custom-brewed coffee drinks, low-carb snacks, and burritos and other frozen food that could be quickly heated in a microwave. As a result of Jed's work, and with Paul and Dave's enthusiastic agreement, Evergreen Vending dropped 100 of its least productive or most distant machines and replaced them with 150 machines at or near their most profitable locations. The result was a substantial increase in profits. Jed could now spend three days a week as marketing director so as to further improve financial results while hiring a new employee to cover his routes.

■

3

Understand How You Make a Profit

"Business is a good game—lots of competition and a minimum of rules. You keep score with money."
—Nolan Bushwell

You should be able to state in just a few sentences how your business makes—or plans to make—a substantial profit. The fact that so many entrepreneurs can't do this goes far to explain why so few small companies are truly profitable.

Never Be Vague About Money

Because Nolo has succeeded over the years, a number of friends, acquaintances, and even the best buddy of my second cousin have asked me to spend a few minutes discussing their business plans. When we sit down to talk, most of these folks are so excited about their entrepreneurial dreams they happily chatter on for hours. In one instance, I hardly got to say a word, but still received profuse thanks and a nice little present when the three-hour meeting was finally over. I guess by just listening I had confirmed the excited new businessperson's high opinion of her business prospects.

When I do finally get a chance to actually comment on a business idea, I typically ask for a short explanation of how the businessperson plans to make money, something that is usually missing from the original presentation. Often, the person acts surprised, as if I have not been listening. I remember one plaintively saying, "I've just told you the whole thing—don't you get it?"

I tried to explain that although she had told me a lot about her business vision—and maybe buried in there somewhere had been some information about how she hoped to make a profit—I hadn't quite understood the dollars and cents of her plan. I asked her to grab a napkin or the back of an envelope and quickly outline her key income and expense numbers.

The hopeful entrepreneur took a deep breath and again started in on the encyclopedic version of her plans, including even how she would spend the big bucks she planned to make. This time I interrupted to explain that describing entrepreneurial hopes is different than succinctly explaining how you'll make a profit. But what I really wanted to say was, "Get a job." That's because I strongly suspected that like most hopeful entrepreneurs who can't clearly explain how his or her business will earn a solid profit, this hopeful woman would fail to achieve the success she so eagerly sought.

One typical example of the pitfalls of this numbers-be-damned approach involved a very bright woman who saw a business opportunity in capitalizing on the popularity of a new type of stretching exercise. To exploit it, she decided to establish a national training and support center that would provide publications, products, and seminars to teachers and committed students. Excited about the possibilities and aware that similar groups had done well in fields as diverse as yoga, Jazzercise, and tai chi, she quickly established what amounted to a for-profit trade association for this new activity. Her first steps included trademarking a clever name, obtaining an 800 number, and sending out a press release describing her organization. When a prominent news magazine picked up on the press release and mentioned her new venture in a "news you can use" item, she received over 2,000 phone calls on her 800 line in less than two weeks. Too bad, she had nothing to sell—no newsletters, classes, instructional videos, or seminars. Even worse, instead of immediately focusing on the steps necessary to produce these income-producing items, she ran up a huge phone bill over the next six weeks excitedly talking about her vision to everyone who called, from exercise devotees to potential investors to just plain flakes. In fact, about the only thing she did right was to close down her money-losing operation a few months later after someone else grabbed her hoped-for market by quickly publishing what turned out to be a highly successful series of books, guides, and videos on the subject.

Another man I talked to at length wanted to create a series of 40-page booklets he named Antique Finders. Each booklet would be designed to help consumers in a particular geographical area locate the best antique shops. This enthusiastic, smart fellow had already spent hundreds of hours locating the best antiques retailers in several cities and writing clever descriptions of each. He had even paid a graphic designer to create mock-ups of his first three guides. But unfortunately, he had spent no time considering the first question I asked: "How are you going to sell enough of your pamphlets to make a profit, given that bookstores don't sell pamphlets and America has no pamphlet stores?"

His response was to again explain to me that because millions of Americans collect antiques, and there are even successful TV shows on the subject, surely there would be a huge demand for Antique Finders. When I again pointed out that while everything he said was true, it did not answer my question about how he was going to make a profit, he became annoyed. "Of course, I've thought about the sales side of the business. If it turns out that you are right and bookstores won't sell my pamphlets, I'm sure the antique stores themselves will."

I replied that I thought this was highly unlikely, since any antique store that carried his booklets would be promoting other stores that their customers might not otherwise know about. He literally scratched his head and said, "I didn't think of that."

Even though I strongly recommended that he spend no more time on this venture until he could come up with a convincing profit plan, his enthusiasm propelled him forward. One divorce and two years of entre-preneurial misery later, he had sold fewer than 1,000 pamphlets at a loss of almost $100,000. Although, mercifully, he eventually put his inventory of 25,000 pamphlets in storage and got a job, he still occasionally calls to tell me about some new idea he's had to turn his Antique Finders into a hot business.

Getting a Quick Plan on Paper

Opening the doors of a shop and hoping you sell enough Fiddlyhumps to make a decent living is almost always an effective prescription for failure. For starters, you need to know your costs: how much you'll spend purchasing the little critters, keeping them alive and happy, compensating your sales staff, paying the rent, and covering what is likely to be a surprisingly long list of other costs. Only then you can begin to figure out exactly how many Fiddlyhumps you'll need to sell each month, for how many dollars, to cover those expenses and have an adequate profit besides. Of course, being able to describe the details of how you'll make money won't guarantee success. You'll still have to create a marketing plan that really will result in your selling enough Fiddlyhumps at a high enough price. But understanding your numbers will give you a chance to succeed.

Unfortunately, it's extremely easy to skip over this dollars-and-cents step, a lesson I learned the hard way more than 25 years ago. One Fourth of July, then-tiny Nolo was invited to participate in a flea market sponsored by the Berkeley Coop, a consumer-owned grocery store. Nolo set up a booth that sold damaged and slightly out-of-date books for a dollar or two each, and almost literally raked in money.

That evening, with my pockets bulging with bills, I stopped by a friend's house for dinner and described my new vision to substantially increase Nolo profits by regularly selling Nolo's overstock at similar flea markets. Fortunately, one of the other guests, who had considerable retail experience, started to laugh. When I got over feeling hurt and asked why, he replied, "I bet when you add up all your costs, you worked a ten-hour day for practically nothing."

To prove him wrong, I got out pen and paper and we went to work. In addition to $20 to rent the space, $10 for supplies to make signs, and a $15 promotional fee to be included in the flea market's ads and flyers, the largest cost was paying the two Nolo employees who helped me run the booth and transport the books to and from the Nolo warehouse. Although both Noloids were happy to trade working on July 4th for time off on another day, this was nevertheless a considerable cost. And then there were a few hours of additional employee time to pack up the books the day before the flea market and unpack the ones that hadn't sold the day after. Add a couple dollars for gas, $10 to treat workers to lunch and it turned out we had netted about $80. If, instead of working a 12-hour day for no pay, I had also paid myself even $7 per hour, we would have lost money.

So much for my dreams of making a profit selling bargain-priced distressed books one by one. But as you can see, it wasn't until I carefully worked the numbers that I understood that this clearly wasn't a business Nolo wanted to be in. And fortunately, Nolo did eventually find a way to get a few bucks out of our big pile of distressed merchandise. We began selling much of it to what are called "remainder" outfits, companies that buy publishers' overstock for a few cents on the dollar and resell them to bookstores who resell them on bargain tables. Although following this approach we got far less per individual book, the fact that we sold in bulk with minimal overhead costs meant we not only made a profit, but also that I got to sleep in on the Fourth of July.

Okay, by now I hope you're convinced of the wisdom of grabbing paper and pen (or your computer) and on one page, describing how you make money now or, if your business is in the start-up phase, how you plan to earn it in the near future. Again, don't try to explain how your entire business will work as you would to a stranger. Just briefly set out exactly where your profits will come from.

Let me predict that doing this will turn out to be a little tougher than you first anticipated. To help you, the next sections contain some examples of brief profit statements written by businesspeople who have thought through how to accomplish this. Don't worry if you don't fully grasp every detail of these statements—again, these are back-of-the-envelope profit forecasts, not formal business plans designed to explain to a stranger how a business will operate.

The Wisdom of Writing a Formal Business Plan

If you borrow money from a bank or other professional lender or sell equity in your enterprise to a sophisticated investor, you'll almost surely be required to write a business plan, not just the quick profit forecast I discuss in this chapter. But even if you (or friends and family members) self-finance your start-up phase, I highly recommend that you prepare a formal plan describing every aspect of your business in detail and demonstrating how it will become profitable.

Your plan should contain at least two key number-crunching components. First, you'll need a profit and loss forecast, which helps tell you how much money you realistically need to get started, exactly what you'll spend it on and how you'll recover it, plus a nice profit.

Second, you'll need a cash flow forecast. This tool tells you when money will flow into and out of your business and alerts you should you be in danger of running out. Since even a theoretically profitable business can literally go broke if too much cash is tied up in accounts receivable, it's easy to see why it's crucial to manage cash as well as profits.

One good resource is the book *How to Write a Business Plan*, by Mike McKeever (Nolo). If you would rather let your computer do the walking, I recommend *Business Plan PRO* (Palo Alto Software).

Making Money in Service Businesses

The dollars and cents of service businesses tend to be easy to explain. When the main thing you're selling is time, it's relatively easy to understand what you need to do to make money, something that is usually much tougher if you run a retail or small manufacturing business. For example, to earn a good income, a lawyer needs only to sell a reasonable number of hours each year while keeping control of overhead expenditures. Similarly, if an attorney does poorly, it's usually easy to spot the problem—not enough clients paying for her hours—and to fix it by improving marketing efforts designed to bring in more work.

Similarly, other service providers, whether they are consultants, plumbers, music teachers, exterminators, or massage therapists, should quickly be able to state how many hours of time they must sell at any given hourly rate to operate a financially successful enterprise. In some fields such as plucking ducks for hunters, or making emergency house calls to unplug sinks or toilets, it's common to charge by the unit, or job, not the hour. Fortunately, the math is no harder. For example, if a successful duck plucker cleans and wraps 10,000 ducks per season at $4 each (before moving on to cleaning salmon for a similar fee), it won't be hard to subtract his costs of doing business to arrive at a profit figure. And even if you expand your business by renting more space or buying additional equipment, the math needed to figure out how the business will make a profit usually won't get much more complicated. As a general rule, whether you charge by the hour or by the job, as long as your service business can mark up its employees' labor three to five times, all will be well.

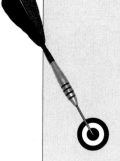

Selling services is generally better than selling stuff.

Chapter 16, Sell Services, Not Goods, details several fundamental reasons why it's usually better to operate a service business instead of a retail operation. The most important of these is that you can generally set and defend decent profit margins, because unless yours is one of the few service businesses that faces overseas competition, your business will compete against other local enterprises that must compensate workers similarly. By contrast, if you're a retailer or manufacturer, you will probably be competing against giant technology-driven companies that use their marketing clout to purchase goods produced by third-world workers at unbelievably low prices. Finally, precisely because you'll likely compete with other small fry, chances are your service business can be started with a relatively small investment.

Here are two decent profits statements for service businesses. As you'll see, each of these entrepreneurs has a good handle on the dollars-and-cents side of their operations.

Able, a House Painter

I'm a house painter with a two-man crew. To pay them, cover other expenses, such as the cost of my truck and equipment, pay my wife $15,000 to be a very part-time bookkeeper and scheduler, and net $90,000 or more to support my family, I need to gross about $215,000 per year. I accomplish this by charging customers $50 per hour for myself and each of my two workers; I pay my less-skilled employee $14 per hour and my highly experienced one $20 per hour.

Because I spend a good deal of time doing things that don't produce income, such as bidding jobs, maintaining equipment, keeping my crew supplied, and taking a vacation, I only bill about 800 hours of my own time each year. So, to meet my goal I need to charge at least 3,500 hours for my crew, which makes 4,300 hours all told. When the weather and the economy are both good, I can often do better, meaning I can earn the $90,000 I need to live on and put some money aside as well.

Able's Business—Doing the Numbers

Revenue

Crew	(3,500 hrs × $ 50)	$ 175,000	
Able	(800 hrs × $ 50)	40,000	
Total Revenue			$ 215,000

Expenses

Equipment		$ 20,000	
Office		10,000	
Marketing		5,000	
Wages & benefits (crew, bookkeeper)		90,000	
Total Expenses			125,000

Able's Personal Net $ 90,000

Employees cost more than you think

The only truly efficient business is a one-person operation. If you hire even a few people, otherwise productive time and energy must be diverted to communication, coordination and other management tasks, none of which makes the cash register ring. Recognizing this, it's important that each new employee you hire make a substantial contribution to your bottom line. If they do, great—your management efforts will more than pay for themselves. But if each employee you hire doesn't make your business substantially more profitable, you would probably do better to stop wasting your own productive hours on what is by definition a low-profit activity. Better to run a smaller business and concentrate on getting the maximum possible return for your own time.

Wilbur, an Attorney for Small Businesses

I try to work a 35-hour week, not counting hours I spend keeping up on my field through reading and attending legal education classes. With five weeks off each year, this means I have 1,645 hours to sell. I share an office with two other lawyers; my portion of office rent, salaries for our own full-time secretary and paralegal, and other expenses are about $100,000. In addition, I spend about $25,000 entertaining clients, taking classes, and subscribing to professional publications. Obviously, I have to cover this $125,000 nut before I pocket anything. My goal is to bill at least 80% of my 1,645 working hours (or 1,316 hours) at $225 per hour, bringing in just under $300,000. This leaves me with a net of about $170,000 after covering expenses. But because I also have a couple of retainer contracts (clients with continuing legal needs who pay up front for my time whether or not they use all of it) that net me substantially more than $225 per hour, I do a little better.

Wilbur's Business—Doing the Numbers

Revenue

Billable hours	$ 296,100	
Retainers	30,000	
Total		$ 326,100

Expenses

Office rent and secretarial services	$ 100,000	
Entertaining	15,000	
Publications, professional dues, classes	5,000	
Business travel	5,000	
Total		$ 125,000
Wilbur's Personal Net		$ 201,100

Making Money in a Manufacturing or Retail Business

Businesses that must carry inventory, like a store, or buy new materials or components, such as a manufacturer or publisher, face a tougher task than do service businesses in understanding how to make money. It follows that your back-of-the-envelope profit statement will necessarily be more complicated. And if something goes wrong with one part of your business, as would be the case if sales of a couple of new products are disappointing, you'll have a tougher job reducing expenditures than would a service provider. Nevertheless, it should still be possible to demonstrate that you understand what it takes to make a good living by producing a reasonably straightforward, albeit slightly longer, profit statement.

Here's the story of one business owner who does have a good handle on just what she needs to do to make a reasonable profit.

Felice, a Book Publisher

I publish regional guidebooks to restaurants, bed and breakfasts, excursions with kids, and the like. My goal is to gross $1 million a year and net a 9% profit, or $90,000. To do this, I need to develop and maintain a list of 20 core titles that sell 5,000 or more copies annually at an average cover price of at least $20.

If I meet that sales goal, I end up with $1 million after wholesalers and retailers take their 50% cut. My total cost to manufacture each book is about $2, or $200,000 per year, all told. I pay my authors a royalty of 10% of my net receipts (10% of $1 million, or $100,000). This leaves $700,000. I pay $40,000 annually to buy and lease equipment. Rent and utilities cost $30,000. Book storage and shipping cost $50,000. I pay my core staff of two editors, two marketers, one graphic designer, one secretary/receptionist, and a two-day-per-week bookkeeper, almost $350,000 per year, counting benefits. I freelance most other tasks I don't do myself, for a total expenditure of $140,000 annually. Additional miscellaneous expenses total $10,000. The $80,000 that's left is what I take out of the business each year.

Felice's Publishing Business – Doing the Numbers

Revenue

Gross sales at retail	$2,000,000	
Net receipts		$1,000,000

Cost of Goods

Manufacturing ($2 per book)	200,000	
Author royalties (10% of net)	100,000	
Total cost of goods		$ (300,000)

Expenses

Rent and utilities	$ 30,000	
Equipment (lease and purchase)	40,000	
Book storage and shipping	50,000	
Salaries and benefits for 6$^1/_2$ employees	350,000	
Payments to freelancers	140,000	
Miscellaneous	10,000	
Total expenses		($ 620,000)
Profit		$ 80,000

Unfortunately, most new shop owners, small manufacturers, and restaurant owners—with the exception, of course, of those who have a head for numbers and deep experience in the field—are not sure what it will take to make their enterprises profitable. This helps explain why so many seemingly popular small retailers come and go. Their owners, it turns out, never quite understood how much they needed to mark up their goods at a given sales volume and inventory level to cover their costs (rent, salaries, the cost of carrying inventory, marketing expenditures) and make a decent profit.

Goodwill doesn't count.

Often when naïve businesspeople pencil out the dollars and cents of a business, profit turns out to be thin or even non-existent, as was the case in my flea market example. Instead of just facing the truth that without adjustment the business won't work, it is common to argue that although start-up costs are high, exposing the business to lots of customers will eventually pay off (as if somehow a profit would eventually materialize from all the people Nolo introduced to its books at the flea market). Sorry, but business doesn't work that way. Each business endeavor should make economic sense on its own. And if it doesn't now, there is little chance things will be different in the future.

Of all business expenses, the substantial cost of keeping an inventory of merchandise is usually the least well understood and accounted for. For instance, if you typically carry $200,000 in inventory, your profits must be large enough to cover the cost of tying up this investment as well as all the other expenditures necessary to keep the doors open. If you use a bank line of credit to cover some or all of your inventory investment, the cost to carry inventory might be $10,000 to $20,000 per year, depending on how fast things sell.

Example:

Tamara dreamed of opening a shop specializing in handmade Southwestern furniture. She located a large, bright space near the affluent residential area that she expected to produce the bulk of her customers. Everything seemed great until she looked closely at the numbers and found that the cost of maintaining a large floor of furniture in a reasonably pricey location would gobble all her anticipated profits and then some. Disappointed, she pulled back and rethought her business plan.

The next year, she was back with a new one. This time, she would work with just a few high-end furniture makers. She would ask each to supply her with floor samples of their tables, chests, chairs and other items, allowing customers to place orders, for which they would pay in advance. Tamara would then transmit the orders to the workshops where the furniture was built. Free of the need to tie up money in inventory, Tamara next searched for and eventually found a much smaller, cheaper showroom in a light industrial area that was not too far from the upscale residential area from which she expected to draw most of her customers. Now, with far lower overhead costs, Tamara was able to come up with a back-of-the-envelope plan that showed her making a tidy profit.

Add a service component to a retail business.

A low-profit retail enterprise can often do far better if it also operates a higher-margin services operation. For example, a bookstore specializing in building and design books could also make referrals to contractors and builders, for which it would receive commissions. In this business model, the low-margin retail business is primarily designed to provide a steady stream of customers to the much higher-profit services business.

4

Start on a Shoestring

"Nothing great was ever achieved without enthusiasm."
—Ralph Waldo Emerson

You'll never succeed unless your business is adequately capitalized. You've probably heard or read this many times—but frequent repetition does nothing to improve bad advice. On the contrary, one of the biggest mistakes a novice business owner can make is to have too much money too soon.

Why Small Is Better

People who start their small business on the cheap, often in a garage, den, or some other scavenged space, and create their first goods or services with more sweat than cash, have the luxury of making their inevitable rookie mistakes on a small scale. And precisely because their early screw-ups don't bury them in debt, they are usually able to learn and recover from them. In short, assuming you really do have an idea for a better mouse-trap and the knowledge and passion needed to create a superior business to sell it, you'll almost surely do better if you have to count your pennies during your start-up stage. Hewlett-Packard, Apple Computer, and Nolo are just three examples of the many thousands of successful enterprises that called a garage or attic their first headquarters.

Starting a small business on the cheap also helps you more quickly determine whether or not your entrepreneurial idea really does have the potential to succeed. Absent money in the bank or your dad's checkbook, you must quickly face the truth. Can you sell enough whatchamacallits for enough pennies to pay your business expenses and put enough dollars in your pocket to buy groceries and pay the mortgage? If you can't, it's better to find out early and move on to something else.

By contrast, novices who begin a new business by rounding up investment capital or borrowing a wad of cash are likely to spend a substantial portion of it foolishly. Commonly, they pay for a nice office, state-of-the-art equipment, or a new vehicle instead of focusing their dollars on what really makes their business tick. By the time experience teaches them that a thick rug and leather couch don't help make a profit, it may be almost impossible to dig themselves out of their financial hole.

For a vivid example of this riches-to-rags scenario, consider how and why the dot-com balloon that soared so high at the end of the last century popped so quickly at the beginning of this one. Certainly, one big reason was that investors showered far too much money on inexperienced man-agers—people who had optimistic PowerPoint presentations, slick offices, and fat salaries but no authentic knowledge of how to run a profitable enterprise. But the flood of money also meant that even people with potentially sound businesses took them from idea to full-scale, heavily financed execution with no opportunity to learn how to become profitable. The fact that thousands promptly fell to earth despite starting with millions in the bank should come as no big surprise.

When the dot-com pioneers ran out of venture capital and flamed out, established enterprises in many fields, including toys, pharmaceuticals, cosmetics, and clothing, picked up the pieces of crashed companies for pennies on the dollar and began the patient process of business building. Executives of these seasoned enterprises knew the basic facts of business life, and many have succeeded.

But buying once-high flyers at federal bankruptcy court hasn't proved the only way to succeed in the world of e-commerce. Thousands of niche sites started on the cheap by ordinary folks investing and pinching their own pennies, have also done well. Whether it's selling jewelry made in Estonia, first editions of the work of 19th-century English novelists, or vintage baseball cards, plenty of small Web-based operators have been willing to learn the Internet ropes before, not *after* investing large sums.

Surely there are exceptions to the "frugal is better" start-up argument. After all, it's impossible to start an upscale restaurant on a shoestring, right? Don't be so sure. True, thousands of expensively equipped and decorated restaurants open every year. But it's also true that after an initial period of new-kid-on-the-block popularity wears off, most struggle and fail. Recognizing that location, marketing savvy, pricing and the state of the economy are among the many factors that determine which restaurants will be among the winners, undoubtedly the biggest reason why so many glitzy eateries struggle is that customers just don't find their food good enough to return over and over.

When a fancy, new restaurant begins to struggle, it's not hard to predict what will happen next. Faced with a half-empty dining room night after night, the worried restaurateur is likely to look for a quick fix: tinkering with the menu, attempting to copy the business practices of successful competitors, lowering prices, or offering "early bird" specials. If all this fails, the chef may be fired—or quit anyway because of all the new restrictions on his "artistic freedom." Given enough time, a persistent owner may begin to get the formula right. But by the time customers really are pleased with the food, service, and prices, it is often too late to save the business. Payments on the bank loan needed to cover all the expensive equipment and decor are likely to be far overdue, investors reluctant to put up more money, and even the owner's marriage may be headed for trouble.

Now let's look at an alternate scenario of opening a new restaurant—one, incidentally, that is based on a real story. It begins with Eileen, a young woman determined to start a small restaurant even though she has saved less than $10,000 and doesn't run with a deep-pocketed crowd. Although she knows a lot about food and loves to cook, Eileen realizes that before she reaches for her slim checkbook, her first task is to learn far more about the business. She starts by getting a job as a hostess at a successful restaurant she admires. Each evening after work she makes copious notes about what works and what doesn't. After four months, Eileen transfers to the food preparation side of the business and again spends every free minute studying and recording how the kitchen operates.

Eileen also finds and reads everything she can about operating a small restaurant at a profit. Before long she knows how much she'll need to mark up food and wine, and what percentage of her gross should go for rent, salaries, and to amortize the cost of equipment. And crucially, she understands that to succeed with a dinner house she'll absolutely need a license to serve beer and wine.

When Eileen believes she has learned enough of the basics, she sets up a meeting with an experienced commercial real estate broker to ask about the possibilities of getting into business on the cheap by taking over the lease of a failed restaurant. The broker confirms Eileen's hunch that a landlord with a building full of equipment but no tenant may be willing to take a chance on a new operator, even one with more energy than experience.

Whenever a small local restaurant or cafe goes out of business, Eileen checks out the situation, each time learning a bit more about what it takes to do a deal. Once or twice she seems close to leasing a desirable spot, but each time is beaten out by someone else with more money or experience. Finally, when the owner of the tatty old Red Brick Café has a stroke and the business simply closes because no one wants to take it on, Eileen gets her chance. Although the kitchen equipment is prehistoric, the dining area threadbare and the location marginal, two things are absolutely right: the rent and the easily transferable beer and wine license. By paying the retiring owner $8,000 for his equipment (half in cash and half with a promissory note to be paid over two years) and assuming the last year of his lease, Eileen is finally ready to begin.

Her first step is to give herself a few weeks to spruce up the place. Instead of calling an architect and planning to do lots of expensive remodeling, Eileen and a small army of her closest friends repaint the interior themselves. When she runs into what looks like a budget-busting problem—the old pink tablecloths are disgusting and the tables too scarred to go without—she improvises by filling in the dents and nicks with plastic wood and then painting the tables bright contrasting colors. Eileen then orders stylish but low-cost paper placemats just like the one she saved years ago from a cool little café outside Florence. Finally, she buys small inexpensive vases and dresses up each table with a fresh flower from her garden.

To reflect her strategy of serving just two or three gourmet entrées each evening at a very competitive price, Eileen renames the old place The Humble Gourmet. She reasons that if her food is good enough, price-sensitive customers who appreciate a quality meal will gladly forgo a big selection in exchange for an affordable bill. To this end she targets young adults without children and older empty-nesters who are either saving for retirement or have already retired, reasoning that both groups like to eat out a lot if they can do so at a reasonable cost. And to help people worried that on any given night they might not like anything on her small menu, Eileen decides to post her selections two weeks in advance, both on a board outside the restaurant and on a bare-bones website.

Understanding that her approach might take a while to catch on, and painfully aware that she has next to no financial cushion, Eileen sets out almost maniacally to promote The Humble Gourmet. Adopting the old saying "marketing is a contact sport" as her motto, she starts by sending a short letter to everyone on the extended mailing list she and her friends have been creating for over a year. Briefly explaining her dream of serving delicious, stylish food at a reasonable price and asking each person for their support, she includes a coupon good for a free dessert. When her letter-writing campaign turns out to be surprisingly successful, Eileen asks customers to add people to her mailing list, which she keeps posted along with a convenient pen just inside the front door. Impressed by her spunk, a surprising number of people contribute names, and a few even plan dinner parties at the restaurant.

Each evening, as patrons leave her restaurant after what she hopes has been an enjoyable meal, Eileen personally thanks them. She also hands out a little packet containing a cleverly designed Humble Gourmet refrigerator magnet along with a brief flyer explaining her dream of providing excellent food at a reasonable price. Many people smile, nod, and later deposit the flyer unread in their circular file. But pleased to receive the clever little magnet, a good number take the time to read Eileen's material. And best of all, a substantial minority are willing to come back often bringing their friends. To thank this core group of supporters, Eileen periodically holds a free wine-and-hors d'oeuvre party with music supplied by her boyfriend's ensemble (free, of course).

Eileen also adopts an unorthodox media strategy. Instead of trying to convince jaded restaurant critics that her kitchen produces the most exotic meals in River City, her press materials emphasize her determination to each night serve a small but interesting selection of excellent food at a very fair price. She also points out that she works with a couple of tiny family wineries to serve house wines that are both interesting and affordable. Attracted both by her modesty and pluck, critics who stop by are impressed by The Humble Gourmet's fun atmosphere and, given their lowered expectations, find that meals are pretty darn good. Before long, The Humble Gourmet is receiving favorable media mention, including a feature in an influential local weekly newspaper entitled "The Little Restaurant That Could" and a column in a major daily titled "Ambitious Food at a Modest Price."

After ten months of hard work, Eileen realizes that she has a potential success on her hands. But she is also wise enough to understand that her shoestring operation is stretched dangerously thin. Fortunately, now, with positive cash flow as well as black ink on the bottom line, she can afford to make improvements. She starts by talking to Tom, her landlord, about making essential changes to the kitchen. Tom, who has long since joined Eileen's core group of believers and is hopeful she'll remain as a long-term tenant, agrees to replace the wretched old stove and refrigerator with state-of-the-art models he is able to pick up cheap when a nearby restaurant fails. Even more important, Eileen dedicates some of her positive cash flow to hiring Mary, a talented cook with the experience to help her improve the variety and quality of the meals. And noticing that customers who get splinters are less likely to come back, she spends a few more dollars replacing the old tables with tasteful new ones. Now the cool placemats and fresh flowers really do look good.

But before she goes very far with her improvement plan, Eileen turns her attention to the lease, realizing that it's silly to further upgrade the restaurant until she and Tom have worked out a long-term deal. Understanding Eileen's needs almost as well as she does, Tom offers to remodel and expand the dining room if Eileen will agree to a five-year lease at a somewhat higher rent. At first Eileen hesitates, unsure that she is experienced enough to run a larger restaurant. And she also wonders if her customers will be turned off by a more upscale facility or drift away while the restaurant is closed for the six weeks it will take to get the work done.

Sensibly deciding to deal with these very different worries separately, Eileen first decides to confront her concern that she doesn't have enough experience to operate a bigger house. To this end she approaches Mary, her cook, and Rolf, her de facto business manager, and asks if they would be willing to become minority partners in exchange for making a long-term commitment to help her expand. When both answer yes, and the ink on their partnership agreement is dry, she asks them to join her in closely examining Tom's remodeling and expansion proposals. After much back and forth, they all agree on a plan that will increase seating capacity by 35% while changing the pleasantly down-to-earth character of the restaurant as little as possible. And after Eileen and her new partners sign the five-year lease, they work with Tom to execute the remodeling in the middle of the next summer, when many regular customers will be on vacation. The result is that in September of its third year, The Humble Gourmet reopens as one of the simplest, but nicest, restaurants in town, and Eileen and her junior partners join the ranks of successful local businesspeople. Eileen celebrates the event by retiring her 15-year-old Honda Civic in favor of a shiny new Saturn wagon.

How can you apply the lessons of Eileen's shoestring business success to your endeavor? Start by examining how she succeeded. First and most important, she focused most of her attention on the core value of her business: Gourmet food at a reasonable price. Second, short of cash, she made a virtue of frugality. And third, she determined who her customers were and adopted a marketing plan calculated not only to reach them, but to engage their enthusiasm so that they became The Humble Gourmet's active supporters. (See Chapter 7, Target Your Customers, for more on how to identify and reach customers intelligently.)

In every field there are many models for success (and even more ways to fail). No question, if you want to open a Spanish-style bistro with a tile floor, copper-topped bar, and an open kitchen, you'll have to invest more than Eileen did. But no matter how much you plan to spend, the key is to invest wisely—something that's very difficult to do unless you already know your field extremely well. If not, you'll almost surely be better off placing your money in a good-quality mutual fund and forgetting about being an entrepreneur.

Spending Money Wisely

Commonly, new businesspeople not only spend far too much for items they need, but also make expenditures that don't have the remotest possibility of benefiting the business. If I had $20 for every new entrepreneur I've seen lease a luxury car no customer will ever sit in, or expensively remodel an office only a few employees ever see, I could pave my patio with portraits of our seventh president.

The fastest way to make a dollar is to hang on to the one you already have; by definition, you get to keep the whole 100 cents. By contrast, earning a dollar by selling most types of goods or services is much tougher. After you first subtract your out-of-pocket costs of doing business, and then the value of your own time, you'll be lucky if you only need to gross $10 to pocket the same buck. So next time you are tempted to buy something you don't absolutely need, ask yourself how likely it is that your expenditure will quickly bring in ten times that amount in revenue. In most businesses, often the honest answer will be somewhere between a long time and never.

Here is a quick review of some kinds of expenses that commonly get out of hand, along with some commonsense suggestions for how to keep them in check. If you've already been in business for a while, you'll almost surely be able to add to the list.

Office Decor

Spending money to create an upmarket image may make some sense if you're selling expensive jewelry or running a posh hair salon. But in the great majority of small businesses, where you and perhaps a few employees are the only people who regularly use your office, it's a huge waste. It just doesn't make sense to drop a few thousand dollars so you can feel good sitting behind a cool new desk. Serviceable used office furniture, much of which has likely been repossessed from failed spendthrifts, is easily available for a fraction of the cost. And even if customers or clients will regularly visit your workspace, most will be more favorably impressed by a utilitarian atmosphere than one of opulence.

Electronic Gizmos

Many business owners could cut their electronic equipment expenditures in half and still be spending way too much. For reasons that have more to do with stroking one's ego than common sense, it's easy to toss away a lot of money on the latest model electronic organizer, digital camcorder, or other flashy gizmo your business never really needed in the first place. But even more money is wasted by purchasing "gold-plated" models of essential equipment such as computers, copiers, phone systems, and tools, when stripped-down but adequate models could be bought or leased for a fraction of the cost. If you really can't be happy without surrounding yourself with cool paraphernalia, at least buy it used. As with office furniture, great deals are commonly available at the going-out-of-business sales of less wise entrepreneurs.

It may be useful, in fact, to think of your cell phone as a proxy for your business spending habits. Recognizing that, especially if you're frequently on the move, this handy little tool will greatly increase your efficiency, it's also true that, if you hand one out to every employee, your bill is likely to go up a lot faster than your business's productivity. Or put another way, by purchasing basic phones and making them available only to people who really need them, and sensibly monitoring charges, businesspeople I know could cut their cell phone bill in half with no loss of income. And if they applied the same "half is more" discipline to most other business "coolest new model" expenditures, they would find it far easier to make a profit each month.

Advertising

Advertising is another place where inexperienced small business owners (and plenty of veterans as well) frequently waste significant dollars. As discussed in some detail in Chapter 8, Market Your Business Creatively, much, if not most, money paid for advertising could be far better spent in other ways. And this is doubly true when a business owner hasn't yet developed the experience to know which types of advertising are effective. Let's return for a moment to Eileen and The Humble Gourmet. Suppose instead of her letter-writing and word-of-mouth marketing campaign, Eileen had tried to promote her restaurant by ads in local newspapers or other media. Given the relatively high cost of buying even a few display ads, it's unlikely Eileen's advertising campaign could have come close to covering her expenses. No question, some types of ads, such as those in the Yellow Pages, can be cost-effective. But again, as further discussed in Chapter 8, generally, small business owners should advertise sparingly and only as part of a well-thought-out campaign carefully designed and tested to reach the most likely customers at an affordable cost.

Instead of splashing out lots of money advertising your business, plan to encourage satisfied customers to recommend your business to others. And remember, restaurant customers aren't the only people who make purchasing decisions based on positive word of mouth of knowledgeable friends. Whether you are a dentist, chiropractor, roofer, or painter, most of your new business will come by personal referral, not in response to ads. In Chapter 8, Market Your Business Creatively, I discuss a number of reliable ways a new business can get this referral process started.

Consultants and Professionals

Paying consultants and professionals, including lawyers and accountants, too much is another way many new businesspeople waste money. I've known a number of aspiring publishers whose first step has been to hire a consultant, often at upwards of $100 per hour, to help them get their business off the ground. Unfortunately, the information they purchased was rarely worth the cost. You can efficiently gather most of what you need to know to start a small business at a fraction of this amount in several ways: by apprenticing for an existing business, reading trade magazines, how-to books, and online business information, attending industry trade shows, and asking for free help and advice from people already in the business. This is not to say that it is never wise to hire an experienced coach to help with the start-up phase, only that if you plan to buy information at a hefty hourly rate, you should first glean as much as possible for free.

Example:

Jenny, an English teacher and lifetime amateur gardener, decides to retire early to write and publish a series of local gardening guides. By tightly focusing her horticultural advice on her extended metropolitan area's many microclimates, she believes she can create publications that will have a significant marketing edge over the one-size-fits-all national gardening books that dominate the market. Wondering how to print and distribute her planned titles, Jenny asks a friend to introduce her to Mavis, a successful local publisher of restaurant guide books. Mavis is kind enough to accept Jenny's lunch invitation, and the two women spend a pleasant hour bonding. When the coffee cups are cleared, Mavis smiles, reaches in her bag and gives Jenny a list of the printers, wholesalers, and retailers her company uses, remarking, "When I started, a very generous, established publisher did this for me, so now it's my turn to pass on the favor." She then explains that dealing successfully with established printers is mostly a question of being sure you are being offered a competitive price. Mavis goes on to explain how she has at least three printers bid on every title. Then explaining that it's much easier to write and manufacture a title than it is to sell it, she suggests that Jenny hire David McCloud, of the Tactical Bookmarketing Group, to help coax area wholesalers and retailers to stock Jenny's books.

Similarly, when it comes to the nuts and bolts of getting your business established as a legal and tax entity, there is no need to spend big bucks on professional help. Many sole proprietors should be able to pay less than $100 for all the licenses and permits they need to get started. If, instead, you decide to form a partnership, corporation, or limited liability company (LLC), you have available a plethora of top-quality self-help materials published by Nolo and others. Even if you choose not to do necessary legal work yourself, it makes sense to educate yourself on the basics before hiring a professional. That way, you won't be paying a lawyer upwards of $200 an hour to teach you routine legal information, but will be billed only for the tasks or advice you really need. For example, many lawyers charge upwards of $1,000 (often many dollars more) to form an LLC for your business, so you can enjoy freedom from personal liability for most business debts at the same time that you can report business taxes on your personal return. By contrast, you can safely and quickly accomplish this same legal task using *Nolo's LLC Maker* software for less than $60.

Further reading on small businesses.

Nolo also publishes an excellent series of small business books, including titles on starting a small business, 50-state incorporation, partnerships, forming an LLC, and many more. For more information, check out the free Small Business section of Nolo's online Legal Encyclopedia (www.nolo.com).

Employees

Rather than staffing a new business to meet your fondest hopes, it's far better to keep your money in the bank and start with a small staff, even if it means imposing on the goodwill of family and friends for a few months. This way, if business is slower to develop than you hope, no money will be wasted on unneeded wages. When and if you really need more employees, you'll be able to afford them. Even if once you open, business is surprisingly *robust*, and you need to hire additional help right away, keep control of your enthusiasm and staff up conservatively. Hiring temporary workers until you see how much permanent staff will really be needed can be one good approach.

Never try to impress new employees—or yourself—by throwing out overly generous salaries or benefits for managers and employees at the high end of your pay scale. During the start-up phase of your business, when every dollar is precious, it's essential to pay most workers fairly but modestly. (In Chapter 9, Hire and Keep Good People, I also explain why it does make sense to pay people at the very low end of your pay scale generously.)

Space

Dentists, lawyers, accountants, and consultants are among the small business owners who often convince themselves it's wise to invest lots of money in fancy digs. In fact, spending money on elegant offices is often counterproductive, because customers and clients understand exactly who is footing the bill. It's usually far better to spend half as much on modest but pleasant space, investing some of the dollars you save in providing free parking.

Upscale retail and other businesses that need to reach an affluent clientele also commonly overpay for a premium location. Many of these businesses would have a far better chance to succeed if they took the time to find a cheaper spot that nevertheless offered easy customer access. Then, instead of busting their budget on rent, they could use the same dollars to build a business so compelling that customers would seek it out. Should you doubt this is possible, think of the excellent small businesses you and many others patronize that are located in warehouse districts or other atypical locations. If they can find a way to pay a reasonable rent and still reach their customers, why can't you?

Many small businesses can be sensibly located just about anyplace, including a spare bedroom. This is certainly true of Internet businesses, some of which can operate from a large closet. So, especially if your business does not depend on walk-in traffic or personal contact with customers, don't pay for space you don't really need. ■

5

Get and Keep a Competitive Edge

"The secret of business is to know something that nobody else knows."

—Aristotle Onassis

reating and maintaining a clear edge over your competitors is crucial to small business success. Fortunately, there are lots of ways to positively distinguish your business in customers' minds. Too bad that just opening the doors and hoping lots of customers come aren't among them—if they were, many more businesses would succeed.

You would think that the value of building a business around a competitive edge would be obvious. Think again. It never seems to occur to most entrepreneurs to look for ways to outthink their competitors, which is a huge reason so many never become solidly profitable. All over America, independent coffee shops, not savvy enough to give people a good reason to prefer them, struggle for survival in the shadow of mediocre chain outlets. Similarly, the typical pet food outlet, chiropractor, sandwich shop, or freelance bookkeeping service enjoys little or no edge over the ever-present herd of similar businesses. True, because pets and people need to eat, and the IRS and sore feet are always with us, these look-alike businesses may nevertheless make a few dollars. But unless one of them designs itself around a clear and compelling edge, such as better knowledge, business methods, or a terrific location, it's unlikely to attract enough loyal customers to prosper over an extended period.

Even when an undistinguished small business does do well (perhaps because its location is great, its product or service is temporarily in short supply, or its prices are low), it is almost sure to attract competition. And unless the profitable business smartens up and finds a way to distinguish itself, these competitors will eventually find a way to siphon off customers. This, of course, is just what happened in the last few decades to many pioneering video stores, quick oil changers and photocopy shops. In each instance the new service was in demand, and businesses that entered these fields early often did very well. But because their business formulas were so easy to copy, deep-pocketed competitors quickly flooded in, and all but the cleverest small operators saw most of their profits vanish.

Convincing Customers That You're Special: An Overview

Building an edge into the very fabric of your business is crucially important to long-term success. Here's a short list of the best ways to do this (truly successful businesses typically find ways to combine several of these competitive advantages).

- **Unique knowledge.** Knowing more than your competitors is one of the best and most authentic ways to make your business stand apart. For example, Jen, a Korean-American, establishes a website aimed at providing up-to-date information about Korea's capitol city to Western business travelers and tourists. Relying on relatives and friends in Seoul to post up-to-the-minute information, Jen is able to keep the site fresh, exciting, and heavily trafficked. The happy result is that Korean hotels, restaurants, and other businesses that cater to Western visitors buy copious amounts of advertising space on her site.

- **A way of doing business that produces a clearly superior product.** Mountain Magic, a publisher of climbing guides whose editors are themselves cutting-edge climbers, produces far better mountaineering books than do traditional multisubject publishing companies, whose editors tend to be café-loving English majors.

- **An ability to produce or distribute products more efficiently than competitors.** Loads of small New Mexico galleries and shops sell jewelry, pottery, and other products handcrafted by a small roster of local artists and artisans. Looking to enter the business, Penny concludes that she can do better if she can broaden her market. Accordingly, she creates a catalog and website offering the wares of many skilled Native American silversmiths, potters, and weavers. This allows her to reach customers everywhere, without waiting for them to happen through Santa Fe or Taos, and justifies her decision to work with a larger group of creative people.

- **A deviant business model.** Loads of successful businesses are based on providing goods and services considered weird, deviant, or just plain strange by mainstream Americans. When entrepreneurs choose wisely, it's amazing how fast many of these oddball businesses do extremely well. If you doubt this, remember that businesses based on organic gardening, bodybuilding, and bicycle touring, which were commonly considered to be bizarre 40 years ago and are now as mainstream as many, are profitable. Businesses providing tattoos, body piercing, and sex toys offer more current examples of fields where the deviant became the norm seemingly overnight. As discussed in Chapter 1, Build a Meaningful Business, Nolo was founded, and in many ways still is, a deviant business, based on its message that people, not just lawyers, can competently cope with legal issues. The entrepreneurial point, of course, is that when a business is considered deviant, you are by definition embracing new ideas and pioneering a new field. And assuming you're right in picking an area which will soon attract others, the fact that you are near the head of the line should position you to reap substantial profits. To learn more about how and why deviant enterprises often succeed, grab a copy of *The Deviant's Advantage: How Fringe Ideas Create Mass Markets*, by Ryan Mathews and Watts Wacker (Crown).

- **A better location.** André dreams of opening a butcher shop like the ones he knew as a kid growing up in France. Realizing that it will be no easy task to compete with American supermarkets and warehouse clubs, André searches for an affordable location easily accessible to a large number of people who are willing to pay a little extra for superior meat. He finally finds it when a small storefront becomes available across the street from a popular specialty produce mart. Reasoning that many people who seek quality fruit and vegetables will also want to buy better meat, André moves in. When his hunch proves correct, a fish market, bakery, and coffee store follow, and the location is enhanced for all.

- **An innovative product that is hard or even impossible to imitate.** Walter makes unique toys, and protects each design by patenting it. He then markets his creations to toy companies that find it cheaper and easier to purchase the novel toys from Walter than to try to design around his patents.

- **Better customer access.** John, whose dry cleaning shop is located on a typical small city main street with inadequate parking, moves a few blocks to an out-of-business gas station, which allows him to rebuild his business around easy customer access. Not only can drivers now park free right in front of the shop, but John's well-staffed service counter means that a typical customer is in and out in less than three minutes.

- **Superior customer service.** Ivan, a mobile knife sharpener whose business is based on bringing a large, fully equipped van to businesses and other venues where people can conveniently get their knives sharpened, has a big competitive advantage over shop-based competitors.

- **Up-to-the-minute knowledge about a fast-developing field.** Jasmine, a young New England business attorney realizes that in her area lawyers are as common as March snow (and about as welcome). So, she specializes in cutting-edge biotechnology law concepts. Her specialized knowledge distinguishes her from 99% of the other business lawyers and, to biotech clients, makes her as welcome as spring's first crocus.

- **A distinctive business style.** Molly Wilson incorporates her three-person business, Wilson, Inc., which specializes in trying to find flaws in the websites of major corporations. Unlike her competitors, many of whom are barely housebroken hackers, Molly deliberately runs Wilson, Inc. in a buttoned-down way. This includes formal stationery, brochures, business cards, her own elegant website, and a state-of-the-art message-forwarding system, which allows her to quickly respond to phone calls when she is out of her office. All of her materials emphasize that her business is incorporated. As a result, large businesses looking to work with people who will "fit in" to a corporate environment and worried about the legal liability that can come with hiring unincorporated freelancers (the IRS may later treat them as employees, with resulting legal hassles and penalties) are far more comfortable hiring Molly than her more casual competitors.

- **Better marketing.** Jan and Adam market their business, Fresh Start Plumbing, primarily through the use of highly distinctive and beautifully maintained 1950s-style trucks painted a deep red with black fenders and gold lettering. Mounted on top of each truck's cab is a bronze plunger with a small white light built into the handle. Wherever Fresh Start's beautiful old trucks go, people notice and, as they do, many read the slogan on the side: "A good job starts with a good attitude."

- **Deeper experience.** The partners in a small architectural firm, BT Associates, tire of competing with dozens of other firms for residential and small commercial jobs. To learn about a hot new field, they volunteer to design, at no cost, an emergency response center for their county. When the center wins several design prizes, BT Associates is quickly able to parlay its experience into a leadership role in this specialized field. Almost immediately they begin to land a substantial percentage of the jobs they bid on. And even when a local firm can use its political connections to beat them out, it often contracts with BT Associates for behind-the-scenes design help.

What Makes Your Business Special?

What do you know, or what can you learn or do, that will give you a clear and valuable edge in your marketplace? And just as important, how easily could someone else copy it? If the answer is "easily," the fact that your business has an edge over its competitors won't be worth much in the long term unless, of course, you are able to continue to make the innovative changes needed to stay ahead. (See Chapter 6, Innovate Now and Forever.)

Example:

Julia owns The Top Slice Sandwich Shop in a busy downtown location in a small Midwestern city. On a summer vacation to Los Angeles, she spots a new food trend—a cross between a taco and a crepe, called a "craco." Believing that she has seen the future, and convinced the craco could be her ticket to prosperity, Julia rushes home and updates her menu. Yowser! Cracos fly out the door as fast as she can make them, and Julia has her most profitable quarter ever. Then reality hits. Julia's three main competitors, Bill's Coffee Shop, Noreen's Bakery, and Sandwich-A-Go-Go, fight back by introducing their own versions of the craco. Even more annoying, Bill and Noreen underprice Julia. With her competitive advantage gone as fast as it arrived, Julia's sales and profits fall back to their normal meager levels.

Fortunately, not all knowledge can be copied as easily as a sandwich recipe. Suppose, instead of staking her future on flogging a fad sandwich, Julia decides to turn her run-of-Main-Street sandwich shop into a high-quality soup, salad, and sandwich bar serving super-fresh baked goods and hearty soups made from fresh organic ingredients. To pull this off, Julia first needs to find growers and wholesalers who can supply her with organic produce daily. Once she creates this network, Julia must then install the equipment and master the cooking skills and management systems necessary to cost-effectively and consistently produce a changing array of top-quality food.

Assuming her new health-conscious, high-quality format attracts plenty of customers, Julia will now find it far easier to charge premium prices and defend her market niche. To compete effectively, her competitors will have to similarly reengineer their businesses, something that will take a lot more planning, effort, and investment than copying a trendy sandwich. And even if a competitor moves to open a similar operation, Julia should have ample time to further improve her business.

You may already know things that could make your business hard to beat. Take my friends Will and Cara, who for a number of years imported women's casual clothing from India under the name Radiant Imports. Using contemporary designs created in the U.S., this husband-and-wife team contracted to have Radiant's clothing line sewn in Madras, using Indian fabrics. Then, principally by taking orders at trade shows, Will and Cara sold their creations to retail clothing shops throughout the U.S. Although Radiant enjoyed a number of modestly profitable years, the fact that it had to compete with a swarm of similar importers meant that Will's and Cara's business was brutally price-competitive, making it difficult to really prosper. In addition, the fact that there were a number of similar suppliers made it tough for Radiant to collect from many underfunded boutiques; when Will and Cara stopped extending credit to a shop, it could simply order from others. What all this added up to was that despite Will and Cara's excellent designs, hard work, and exhausting travel schedule, Radiant simply couldn't sufficiently separate itself from its competitors. At the end of the day, they were just one more lookalike importer of contemporary Indian clothing.

Understanding that they needed to get out of the low-profit, high-volume end of the rag trade, Will and Cara decided to look for a more profitable and less volatile niche. After researching a number of possible new directions, they decided to make the most of their deep knowledge of how and where handloomed Indian fabrics were made. They started a business in high-end upholstery fabric—handmade, hand-dyed, high-priced cloth, bought in relatively small quantities by decorators and small custom upholstery shops serving an affluent clientele. Armed with fashionable Western designs, Will and Cara put together a network of skilled handweavers and dyers in several remote Indian villages they already knew well. Then, using familiar marketing techniques, such as displaying their wares at high-end trade shows and in upmarket upholstery fabric catalogs (as well as other creative strategies I've agreed not to mention), Will and Cara developed a network of upholstery shops and designers in the U.S. and Europe willing to pay well for a unique product. Over just a few years, Will and Cara, who called their new business Pushkar Designs, were able to translate their superior knowledge of how to create and market high-quality handmade upholstery fabric into a business that was simultaneously more creative, more stable, and more profitable than Radiant had ever been. Although several competitors tried to copy Pushkar's formula, few were willing to invest the time and care necessary to create and maintain a similar loyal network of highly skilled village-based handweavers. And crucially, the two that tried didn't last long, as they were never able to match Pushkar's proprietary system of quickly ramping up production of each season's most popular designs.

Building superior knowledge into your business is particularly important if you provide services that can be purchased from many others, such as house painting, financial planning, bill collecting, or children's dentistry.

Unless you can convince customers to highly value your services, you're in danger of having to compete only on price, something that is likely to consign you to the familiar small business treadmill of hard work for low profits. In the traditional professions, such as law, medicine, accounting, and engineering, licenses and degrees used to be proxies for knowledge—for example, patients were willing to pay well for the services of a doctor who graduated from a good medical school and had privileges at a prestigious hospital. Today, with a surplus of general practice providers in most professions, coupled with the price-depressing market clout of third-party payers such as insurance companies, it is far tougher to prosper. No matter what your profession or occupation—be it architecture, pediatrics, or teaching dog obedience—you'll normally find that the key to consistent profits is to go beyond the basic occupational activity and develop a specialty that customers will pay a premium for. Thus surgeons who specialize in difficult cardiac cases, lawyers with expertise in intellectual property, and architects who know how to design extra-secure "terrorist resistant" buildings are almost sure to do better in the years ahead than peers who don't specialize.

Example:

Tina paints houses. So do dozens of other local contractors. Because she realizes early on that she'll never prosper if she gets all of her jobs based on the lowest bid, Tina sets out to design a service people will pay a little extra for. Deciding that her skill with color is a competitive edge, Tina targets customers who want their houses to look distinctive. As part of getting her "color is cool" message across, Tina calls her business Color by Tina. More important, before she bids on a job, Tina insists on spending an hour talking color with each potential customer. This includes showing them a short video of other houses she has painted, looking at photos of houses with distinctive color schemes, and then creating a color mock-up showing what the customer's house would look like painted in various combinations. Tina waits to talk price until the customer has decided on the perfect color scheme. Typically, by this time the homeowner is enthusiastic about the project and impressed with Tina, meaning that she has a good chance to get the job without having to match the price of every lowball competitor.

In thinking about how to design an authentic knowledge edge into your business, it's important to realize that you are dealing with at least several moving targets. Not only do markets themselves constantly change and evolve, but a local or industry-specific edge that is extremely valuable one day can become almost worthless the next. Take the experience of Juan Sanchez, an immigrant from Mexico who arrived in the U.S. with little more than the clothes on his back. After a couple years of cutting lawns and cleaning houses, Juan decided to start a housecleaning service called Sparkle. Instead of pushing a broom himself, Juan organized small crews of workers whom he dispatched to customers' houses for a fast but thorough weekly cleaning. Juan not only hired and paid the cleaners, but made sure their Social Security and other benefit payments were made. In the 1990s, when the IRS began very publicly cracking down on prominent people who had neglected to make Social Security payments for their nannies and maids, Sparkle's assurance of legality proved to be a huge business edge. As a result, customers were willing to pay Sparkle a premium. And because Sparkle's service was as good as it was legally bulletproof, many remained loyal year after year, meaning that Sparkle's marketing costs were modest.

But as the new century began to unwind, several of the people who worked for Sparkle figured out how to emulate Juan's system. And when they did, it proved fairly easy for them to poach customers whose homes they, after all, already cleaned. Juan recruited more cleaners and customers, but found himself having to run faster just to stay even.

In short, Juan's edge, based on his ability to assure customers that Sparkle's workers were fully legal, was fast eroding. To give his customers a reason to stick with him over the long term and not defect to lower-fee competitors, Juan saw he needed to develop a new competitive edge. Reflecting on the fact that over the years he had often been asked if his employees could help customers with the many chores that go with putting on a party, Juan introduced a party setup and cleanup service. Positioning his new business midway between a high-cost traditional caterer and a janitorial service, Juan's allowed his customers to choose from a long list of helpful party services. These included preparty cleaning, renting and setting up tables, chairs, and other party equipment, as well as helping decorate a yard, patio, or inside space. In addition, Sparkle was equipped to provide coolers full of ice and beverages, serve drinks, provide Mexican-style hors d'oeuvres, and even do simple barbecue cooking. And best of all, almost before the party was over, Sparkle would make the mess disappear.

Sparkle's new, reasonably priced party service was an immediate success with Juan's cleaning customers. To drum up more business, Juan mailed flyers describing his new enterprise to Sparkle's roster of former cleaning customers. Almost immediately a number called him. And several, admitting that their new housecleaners were not reliable, rehired Sparkle to clean their houses. Able to charge higher rates for party work than he could for cleaning houses (people are in a good mood when it's celebration time), Juan was able to raise the pay of his employees, thus cutting down on turnover. But best of all, party work gave Juan a great chance to unobtrusively, but nevertheless determinedly, showcase his new service to everyone who attended the party, providing a steady stream of new customers. For example, all Juan's employees wore neat black shirts and jackets with the bright red logo "We Make It Sparkle" on the back.

You may wonder why, if the party business was more fun and produced a better profit, Juan hung onto the cleaning enterprise. Good question. Being a conservative man by nature, his first thought was to keep the cleaning business both to provide stable cash flow during the months when people entertain less as well as to find customers for the party business. But, as the party business continued to prosper and Juan got more and more calls from people who didn't even know he cleaned houses, he considered selling the cleaning service to his nephew and putting all his considerable energy into growing his more profitable new service.

However, before making the big change, Juan asked himself whether or not his party business was really positioned well enough to grow and prosper over the long term. After all, others, including his own employees, could form copycat businesses. But realizing that because there is a broad and deep consumer demand for help staging parties, Juan concluded that he could proceed by providing a consistent level of excellent service while regularly adding new and improved services types of party assistance. Accordingly, Juan decided to commit to his new enterprise full time.

Keeping Ahead of the Competition

Although some competitive edges will help insulate a business from competitive pressure longer than others, none will last forever. If your bookstore does a huge business each December, in part because it is the only one in town smart enough to provide free gift-wrapping, your edge is obviously extremely fragile.

Or look at Happy Feet, a store that seeks out and sells the most comfortable shoes on the market to an ever-increasing market of health-conscious middle-aged customers. The company puts great effort into building close relationships with local podiatrists, and clearly has a hard-to-copy market edge, certainly one that is more solid than that of the fashion-chasing shoe boutique next door. But sooner or later, competitors will find ways to poach Happy Feet's comfort-seeking customers, perhaps by undercutting its prices or offering a bigger selection or a more convenient location. To stay successful over many years, this means that Happy Feet, like all small businesses, will have to regularly deepen and broaden how it meets its customers' needs. Happy Feet might do this by broadening its selection—perhaps by importing walking shoes from other parts of the world. Another approach might be to create a store within a store to showcase reasonably comfortable shoes that don't look like grandma's galoshes. Some customers, at least, will want to include in their wardrobe at least a couple of pairs of shoes with a little style.

To stay profitable, Nolo has had to repeatedly figure out new ways to meet its customers' needs, and we've used a series of knowledge edges to help us succeed over the years. But before I tell you about a few of them, I have a confession to make. Like too many other businesspeople, I have sometimes assumed that because a particular way of doing business worked well for several years, it would continue to do so indefinitely. Wrong.

In the early 1970s, when Nolo was founded, the very concept of handling legal matters without a lawyer was radical or, if you prefer, deviant. Still, Nolo's first books, *How to Do Your Own Divorce in California*, by Charles Sherman, and *The California Tenant's Handbook* (now *California Tenants' Rights*), by Sherman, Myron Moskovitz, and myself, sold well. Fortunately for us, established publishers avoided the self-help law field, apparently reasoning that it made no sense to risk pissing off a famously litigious profession to publish books in an unproven market niche. Blessedly free of serious competitors, Nolo simply had to create and distribute quality self-help law information in order to build a loyal customer base delighted to have an alternative to hiring an expensive lawyer.

But as the years went by and Nolo successfully fought off the attacks of attorney groups attempting to suppress its publications, publishing self-help law materials became less risky. As a result, dozens of other publishers—from tiny start-ups to industry heavyweights with deep pockets and excellent distribution networks—entered the field. Many Nolo customers recognized that our carefully crafted, scrupulously updated materials were the best available, but people who had never heard of us were all too likely to purchase a competitor's book, especially if it cost a few dollars less and had a flashier cover.

As Nolo's original edge as the pioneer provider of self-help legal information lost traction, profits began to fall and we realized that to survive and grow Nolo badly needed to develop and exploit new knowledge. Starting in the mid 1980s, we accomplished this by pioneering the development of reliable, easy-to-use consumer legal software, including *WillMaker*, a program that allows users to quickly and safely make a will. Again, for a few giddy years, our new skill propelled us quickly and profitably forward. As one observer remarked during those times, it was a little like Nolo had invented a cure for the common cold. But, of course, no one keeps a corner on a highly desirable product for long. Our success with *WillMaker* promptly attracted a number of imitators, and our original gravity-defying profit margins began to fall to Earth.

And so again, predictably, Nolo needed to become smarter. This time, instead of just trying to introduce blockbuster new products (of course, like all publishers, we love a hot seller), we decided to fundamentally change how Nolo operated. Instead of continuing to follow our old approach, which can best be described as one-legal-problem-equals-one-

Nolo-product, we switched to a database publishing model. Using this new approach to produce a series of books and software programs for landlords and tenants, Nolo junked its old approach of signing up several different authors and expecting each to do duplicative research to produce their particular title. Instead we created an in-house database of landlord-tenant law for all 50 states, and had Nolo editors use it to create half a dozen publications in house.

Although moving to a database publishing model may not seem to be a particularly radical idea, it was truly innovative when compared to the customary trade paperback publishing practices followed by Nolo's competitors. Most conventional trade publishers produced their self-help law books in much the same hit-or-miss way they produced the rest of their large-format trade paperback titles. They simply had an acquisitions editor, often with no legal training, commission lawyer-authors who had little or no experience in writing plain-English books for legal self-helpers. The typical result was a poorly organized, jargon-filled book that provided little more than an overview of a particular legal topic before recommending the reader hire a lawyer. And because no data collection system was in place, the publisher's next books in the same legal niche were no better. In contrast, Nolo, by adopting a superior system of collecting and storing key information about the law, could more efficiently publish a series of superior products. Thus our detailed 50-state legal information about a landlord's responsibility to return a tenant's security deposit could be used in half a dozen books and software packages designed for land-lords or tenants.

But again, as I've emphasized, no sooner does developing key new knowledge provide a business with a competitive advantage than its value begins to slip. Nolo was poorly prepared when in the late 1990s, a big chunk of its knowledge edge was suddenly subject to aggressive attack by a gaggle of well-funded Internet sites, which promised instant access to free online consumer law information. As is true whenever any industry goes through a paradigm shift, Nolo had to quickly come to terms with the fact that its ability to produce superior print and software products was sure to become less valuable. To succeed in this new digital world, Nolo had to learn to leverage its large, plain-English legal database and create an easy-to-use website where consumers and small business owners could quickly find free, top-quality legal information and download or order our products at a reasonable price. Doing this meant Nolo had to rapidly change its deliberate publishing style to fit a speeded-up electronic marketplace—no easy task.

As Nolo hired programmers and Web designers and purchased a bewildering array of Internet-related hardware and software, it also had to dust off the best of its old knowledge. For example, Nolo's years of experience at defeating the legal profession's claims that publishing legal information was tantamount to practicing law without a license suddenly became newly valuable as bar associations studied ways to attack legal websites. Similarly, Nolo's understanding of how to efficiently keep our products up to date served us well on the Internet, where customers expected information to be updated almost constantly.

But, as if to prove the rule that competition often comes from unexpected places, as this book goes to press, Nolo is faced with a surprising new competitive development. Just as many of the venture-capital-backed sites that had so recently threatened to bury Nolo lost their funding and closed down, many federal and state agencies and courts have begun to provide free online legal information to the public. We've advocated just this sort of consumer legal access for almost 35 years—but that doesn't change the fact that we will again need to change our business to adjust to this welcome new development.

6

Innovate Now and Forever

"Even if you're on the right track, you'll get run over if you just sit there."

—Will Rogers

Look at a ten-year-old snapshot of Main Street in any American city or town and compare it to what you see today. I'll bet that many of the old businesses no longer exist and that most of the ones still there have expanded or updated their look. Probably just a few survivors still look much the same. Look again in another few years and most of the ones that didn't change will be missing. Downtown retail areas aren't the only business centers subject to relentless change. The same sort of winnowing will occur on the little white type of the directory board in the lobby of any office building.

Where are the missing businesses? A few will have moved to new locations, but the majority will simply be kaput. It's not surprising when you realize that by most estimates, 80% of business start-ups don't reach their fifth birthday. One big reason why many enterprises stagnate or even flatline can be summed up in this way: lack of innovation. Enterprises that build creative change into their very structure are far more likely to do well than those that look for a recipe for success and then hope to endlessly repeat it. And this, of course, is yet another reason why most paint-by-the-numbers franchise formulas quickly look as dated as your average Burger King.

The reason innovation is crucial to long-term success is simple: To establish and maintain a robust profit margin, you need to establish a true competitive advantage. (See Chapter 5, Get and Keep a Competitive Edge, for more on why this is true.) And assuming you are smart or lucky enough to accomplish this, you must keep your edge in the face of competitors who will inevitably try to copy it and customers whose thirst for the new and trendy seems almost endless. For example, if you establish a small graphic design business to help local businesses lay out advertising copy, you'll be competing with dozens if not hundreds of others who do much the same thing. And all of you will be selling your services to business customers, most of whom are price-sensitive, tight-fisted, and looking to hop onto the latest design trend. This means that to charge the premium prices you'll need in order to do well, you'll have to provide design work to your customers that's clearly more desirable than they can buy down the street (or increasingly over the Web). For example, if one year you are the first local graphics shop to offer a library of popular art deco design elements, chances are your competitors—who, after all, are similarly struggling to make a decent profit, will quickly offer similar motifs. To keep your edge, you'll need to be ready with fresh work, perhaps by turning to the creative design motifs of vintage appliances, including toasters, coffee pots, and stoves. Or maybe you'll seek inspiration in the wonderful world of 18th century Japanese art. Either way, one big key to economic success will be to almost maniacally innovate.

So when you consider starting a new venture or reconfiguring an existing one, think about not only whether your entrepreneurial edge is substantial enough to set you apart from the competition, but also about how you will be able to extend your advantage over time. To do this, you'll almost always have to build the determination to continuously innovate into your business culture from the start. If you don't, it's all too likely you'll develop the complacent habits that relegate so many once-promising businesses to the treadmill of hard work for little profit.

In my experience, innovation in the small business world occurs in three ways: invention, copying, and serendipity. Let's examine each to see how it might help your business.

Avoid Fad Businesses

Loads of entrepreneurs believe that the sure way to success is to spot a trendy business early, jump on it, and ride it to riches. In fact, some trust in this approach so firmly that they refuse to let repeated failure stand in the way of trying it again and again. Think of popcorn. During my lifetime I've seen dozens of popcorn-based businesses come and go, many of them in tourist or amusement districts, but a fair number at other locations as well. I've purchased popcorn covered with caramel, seasoned salt, cheese, garlic, powdered sugar, maple sugar, and even jalapeno peppers. Besides the manufacturers of the popping equipment and the owners of movie theaters, someone must have made money in the popcorn business. But compared to the number of people whose entrepreneurial dreams were crushed, the percentage is tiny.

There are at least three big reasons why trying to latch on to a fad business idea is likely to result in abysmal failure. First and most fundamental, by the time you spot the "can't miss" opportunity, more experienced businesspeople savvy enough to be ahead of the curve will be cashing out.

A second big reason to avoid fad businesses is that because they usually are simple to run, they are easy to copy. Almost as soon as croissants or fruit smoothies became popular, a thousand bakeries and juice bars began to serve them. As a customer, you probably barely notice when another opens or closes in your area. Why should you? Because these businesses are all much the same, there is little reason for you or any other customer to develop loyalty to any of them.

Third, because fad businesses tempt entrepreneurs to enter fields they care little about, they violate a fundamental rule of small business success: that you be interested in your business. (See Chapter 2, Choose a Business You Care About.) The result is that after a year or two, the chances that you'll become bored or burned out go way up.

Even if a red-hot new business looks to be enduring, it usually doesn't make sense to plunge in. That's because a truly huge change in the business firmament is sure to attract big competitors. A good example is the video rental business, where the rapid expansion of Blockbuster and other huge outfits in the 1980s and 90s quickly killed tens of thousands of mom-and-pop shops. Most small operators failed not because renting videos was last year's fad, but precisely because video rentals turned out to be a huge and lasting business. Much the same thing happened with while-you-wait oil changing and designer coffee boutiques. In short, unless you can locate a good location far away from the price-cutting chains (no easy trick), or develop some other clear entrepreneurial edge, big operators will almost surely use their economies of scale to drain most of the profit out of these hot businesses.

Paradoxically, rather than trying to win the race to the next big thing, it can often make more sense to look at business fields that were red-hot a decade ago. You might even find a field where so many underfunded businesses have folded that there is actually an opportunity for the survivors. Assuming it suits your personality and interests, you might be able to cheaply move in just in time to catch a second wave.

Invention

It's hardly a secret that Americans love new things. From digital camcorders and camera phones to MP3 players and programmable DVDs, much of our time is spent using tools and toys that didn't exist a generation or two ago. It's not only big inventions, however, that change lives and make fortunes. Think about the equipment in today's dental offices and compare it to what was in use a decade ago. Virtually every piece has been substantially improved or changed. Many of these state-of-the-art tools were thought up by dentists themselves who apparently thought it was more fun to invent things than fill another bicuspid.

Similarly, many of the services we now take for granted are either relatively new or are packaged or delivered in innovative ways. For example, most small businesses now outsource payroll preparation, equipment maintenance, graphic design, and many other tasks to automated specialists whose work is better, cheaper, and faster than that done in-house. Similarly, 21st-century electricians, plumbers, contractors, and most other service providers use many tools and techniques that didn't exist in Ronald Reagan's America. For example, a generation or two ago, hiring a housepainter usually meant living through a month of having a couple of men hang off heavy wooden ladders while swabbing away with short-handled brushes. Today the combination of lightweight ladders and scaffolding, power sanding and other efficient prep equipment, and better, faster ways to apply paint means the same job can be done in less than a week.

When new goods and services are introduced or old ones are improved, someone always profits from the attendant jump in productivity. The U.S. government hands out over 20,000 patents to independent inventors each year, a number dwarfed by the huge number of non-patentable but nevertheless significant innovations. Occasionally, an inventor is clever enough to both create and capitalize on a valuable breakthrough. But at least as often, much of the profit falls to others who use or market the unique product, service, or business method. For example, when *easy-to-customize* modular storage systems were first developed to organize closets and garages, interior designers who quickly understood and embraced these exciting new tools could charge hefty fees to customers determined to improve on closet designs that had changed little for several centuries.

I have little useful to say about the pure process of invention. Like art or poetry, "eureka" breakthroughs either occur or they don't—there is little most of us can do to turn ourselves into an Edison, Bell, or Shockley. But fortunately, to prosper in the small business world, you don't have to invent the light bulb, telephone, or transistor switch. In fact, most profitable innovations consist of combining or connecting two or more fairly mundane things. For example, in the 1990s a tiny website dedicated to buying and selling classic Pez dispensers figured out how to combine the fun of a local swap meet or garage sale with the global connectivity of the Internet. The result, of course, was eBay, now one of the world's most valuable corporations. Similarly, Amazon.com rode its patents on the simple but powerful concept of "One-Click Shopping" to create a hugely successful business selling a wide variety of new merchandise.

But it's not just large enterprises that profit by deploying existing knowledge in new ways. In your own neighborhood, many service businesses have very profitably found ways to provide traditional services in ways so efficient and attractive that their customers patronize them even though they charge a premium compared to many of their competitors. For example, near me, several opticians and eyeglass shops now work together, so in one stop you can have your eyes checked, order new glasses or contacts, and have them ready in 24 hours, something that was impossible just a few years ago. And an estate planning lawyer has given up her traditional office-based practice and switched to making house calls, an old-fashioned service her clients, many of whom are elderly, nevertheless regard as being highly innovative.

Often, the ability to look at familiar information in new ways is all the entrepreneurial insight needed to blaze a new and profitable small business path. When Ed Sherman and I started Nolo, we realized many millions of low- and middle-income Americans couldn't afford to hire high-priced lawyers to handle routine legal matters. We also saw that the few self-help law products then on the market were very poor. Putting this information together, we began creating a library of high-quality, plain-English legal materials that would allow ordinary people to safely and affordably take the law into their own hands.

Many new enterprises start when someone gets mad at how traditional enterprises operate and decides there must be a better way. This may be as simple as becoming disgusted with the quality of the coffee local restaurants provide and figuring how to serve a tastier brew. As you sip your morning latte at Starbucks, Peet's, or an independently owned purveyor of excellent coffee, it may seem like this hugely profitable innovation was a no-brainer. Not so. If you are old enough to remember how bad most American coffee tasted 30 years ago, you'll understand just how much insight and determination was necessary to create businesses that really can serve a great cup. And, of course, there are many other fields where dissatisfaction with the status quo was the fuel that drove innovation. For example, I patronize a shop that sells beautifully designed, handcrafted tile that got started in large part because its owners were frustrated with the unimaginative selection available at local building supply outfits.

Example:

Jill wanted to quit her job at ABC Travel and open her own travel agency. But airlines were cutting travel agent fees, and people were increasingly booking domestic air travel through discount websites. Realizing the last thing her city needed was one more struggling air travel booking agent, Jill decided she needed to do something different. As part of her planning process, she polled a group of affluent people who traveled frequently about the places they most wanted to visit. When she collected their answers, she saw that several destinations, principally in Europe, stood out. Deciding to call her business All About England and France, she focused on travelers visiting these two countries. Jill's new business quickly developed a reputation as being the most knowledgeable in her metropolitan area about travel to these places, and she quickly achieved a very solid profit margin booking a high volume of upscale tours and other vacation packages.

But within 18 months, several other travel agents began copying Jill's formula. Fortunately, anticipating this development, Jill had already improved her services. One way she did this was to ask her clients what they were most interested in doing, learning about, or participating in on their vacations. Seeing that bicycling, gardening, golf, and cooking were high on the list, Jill developed a number of preplanned itineraries emphasizing these activities. For example, working with English and French bicycle rental and touring companies, Jill was able to offer customers a dozen guided or self-guided tours complete with reservations at lively wayside inns and suggestions for places to eat and visit.

Copying

In big-business doublespeak, copying the ideas of other businesses is called "benchmarking," something that all major corporations routinely practice. For example, the owners of virtually every large entertainment and sports complex in America have for decades sent managers to Disney World to look for people-handling practices they can beg, borrow, or benchmark. Because most of Disney's business practices are right out in the open, learning from and even copying them is not only smart and cheap but, as long as competitors don't try to borrow the Mouse, Duck, or other copyrighted or patented characters or inventions, perfectly legal. And it should come as little surprise that Disney itself has borrowed innovative ideas from many other entertainment venues.

Copying, borrowing, or, if you prefer to be blunt, stealing is a particularly great way to innovate in the world of small business. America is a big place, and in many fields there are so many small operations that it can take years for best practices to permeate a whole business segment. For example, if you run a children's clothing store in Omaha, you may be able to check out a dozen similar operations in California and perfectly legally come away with several innovative business ideas no one in Nebraska has yet tumbled to. Similarly, if you own several bagel shops in Seattle, you would be nuts not to check out the New York bagel scene when visiting the East Coast. And if you picked up a couple of good ideas, you would really be *meshugeh* if you didn't quickly adopt them.

Copying the best practices of others should be a part of every new and established business's plan. Since it's free and easy, you may already do it on an informal basis. But to improve your chances of success, I advocate a disciplined approach of systematically studying the operations of excellent businesses in your field, particularly those that are not in your immediate area. Staying away from local competitors will not only avoid unnecessarily angering them (see Chapter 14, Embrace Your Best Competitors), but will also lessen the risk that you'll find yourself defending a lawsuit based on the claim you stole trade secrets. To locate businesses good enough to serve as role models, talk to suppliers and other knowledgeable people who work in a different geographical area. For example, if you plan to start a small ad agency in Bangor, Maine, you might call several business acquaintances who use similar agencies in the mid-Atlantic states. Ask them for the names of three excellent local ad shops in their area. If they can't help, maybe they know someone who can. Once you get a preliminary list, do some more checking (looking at websites often tells you a lot) to shorten it to a few successful businesses that are most like yours.

At this point, you'll need to decide whether it makes more sense to call the other business, explain what you are doing, and ask for help, or to anonymously study their operations. Depending on a number of factors, including whether you can arrange an introduction and how transparent the business is, either approach can work. For instance, it's surely a lot easier to learn a lot about a deli by walking in the front door a few times than it is to figure out what makes an ad agency tick by schmoozing with the receptionist.

Establish a separate notebook or computer file for every business you study, dedicating a section for each key business area. Depending on the field you are studying, this might include signage, marketing, staffing, website design, key products, and delivery methods. For example, if a business you study apparently gets lots of calls because of a super-clever Yellow Pages ad, you want to capture that information in your notebook so that when you return home, you can design an equally compelling ad.

Example:

Maureen has spent several years working as an electrician in a medium-sized midwestern city and recently passed the state electrical contractor's exam. Excited by the aesthetic and energy-saving possibilities of new lighting systems, Maureen dreams of opening a lighting store combined with a traditional electrician's business. Her idea is to give remodelers a one-stop way to buy new lighting systems and get them installed. Although in her city there are plenty of both lighting retailers and electricians, no business efficiently combines the two, in large part because lighting stores are afraid to offend electricians, who are a major source of customer referrals.

Maureen is convinced that customers will be enthusiastic about a one-stop operation. Although she concedes that her approach may alienate some independent electricians, who will send customers elsewhere, Maureen reasons she will gain far more than she loses by funneling lighting purchasers directly into her own installation business. And she's sure that once she provides these customers with quality electrical service, they will be likely to call her when they have future electrical needs.

Maureen enlists her Uncle Jimmy, who retired early with a big nest egg, as an investor. Although Jimmy is impressed with Maureen's reasoning, he has one big concern: Maureen can't point to any successful area businesses like the one she proposes. The positive side of this is that Maureen's business is fresh and innovative. However, Jimmy worries that since Maureen won't be able to learn from the good and bad practices of others, she'll likely make costly mistakes. Telling Maureen that Ecclesiastes had it right when he wrote, "There is no new thing under the sun," Jimmy gets on the phone and starts calling lamp manufacturers and wholesalers who do business across the country. Where, he asks, is there a business like the one Maureen proposes? He receives the names of a number of local lighting companies that are more or less similar to what Maureen envisions. Narrowing this list to three, all in other states, Maureen and Jimmy decide to take a few days to study each in depth. After two weeks of travel, considerable detective work, and meetings with several surprisingly friendly small business owners, Maureen and Jimmy return with several notebooks full of exciting information. They are convinced not only that Maureen's idea can succeed, but also that they now know exactly how to accomplish it.

Serendipity

Way back in the 1950s, in his groundbreaking book *Innovation and Entrepreneurship* (Harper Business), legendary business thinker Peter Drucker pointed out that many profitable innovations result from accidental or unexpected breakthroughs. He meant the kind of thing that occurs when you set out to develop a better variety of easy-to-remove packaging tape and end up inventing a revolutionary wallpaper that both sticks tight and is easy to peel off the moment you are sick of it. What's so special about Drucker's insight? After all, from the discoveries of penicillin and saccharin to the inventions of nylon and Velcro, it's obvious that chance plays a significant role in finding new ways to do things. Drucker really gets interesting with a second and more telling point: When businesses stumble on a new product or service, even one that could give them a significant competitive advantage, they often either fail to recognize it or even actively suppress it. That is, they keep fooling around with the tape and stick the wallpaper in the trash.

Example:

Leo Rac and Stan Frax are longtime partners in the Racafrax Glass Co., a nothing-special local glass supplier. It sells hundreds of types of glass to contractors for use in residential and small commercial construction projects, and also caters to do-it-yourselfers. A few years ago, Racafrax began to get more and more requests for several types of plastic, particularly for newer, unbreakable burglar-deterring types that could be substituted for window glass. At first, Racafrax sent these people elsewhere. Finally, after turning away more and more business, Leo and Stan began stocking a few of the most commonly requested types of window plastic, keeping them in an unused area behind the stairs they not-so-privately referred to as the Plastic Hole.

When plastic sales immediately turned out to be solidly profitable, helping Racafrax to have its best ever year, Leo and Stan were delighted that they finally had the financial wherewithal to expand and improve their facility. They bought and remodeled the next-door warehouse—something that allowed them to more than double their selection of glass. Despite their huge increase in floor space, they left the Plastic Hole in its same dingy spot.

Were Leo and Stan dumb? No question. Unfortunately, they were also typical. Like most business owners, they were slow to recognize and even slower to embrace an accidental business breakthrough, especially since doing so would have meant fundamentally changing their original formula.

Sadly, this head-in-the-sand approach often doesn't change even if the innovative business approach is more profitable than the original business. Drucker beautifully illustrates this point with a story of how after World War II, Macy's used huge profits from its suddenly red-hot sales of stoves, dishwashers, and other appliances to expand its lower-profit clothing business instead of its appliance department. And when this didn't work to restore clothing to its traditional three-fifths of Macy's sales, the company actually tried to push appliance sales down. The result was that aggressive competitors who understood that new affluent Americans were ready to fill their new suburban houses with appliances stepped in and captured the entire business.

Think about a half-dozen small enterprises you patronize. When was the last time your drycleaner, plant nursery, or beauty salon significantly changed the way it does business? If the answer is somewhere between "rarely" and "never," you can safely bet that the business is guilty of ignoring and probably even suppressing new information, and as a result is in at least the early stages of decline. In a world where change is an ever-present fact of business life, a more nimble competitor will surely appear and quickly grab market share. On the other hand, if a successful business you know has recently made positive changes to the way it looks, what it sells, or how it interacts with its customers, chances are its owner has learned to efficiently gather the innovative information necessary to build on the company's competitive edge.

In the big business world, innovation is often the product of many years of expensive research, as is obviously true for new drugs, computer chips, and jet engines. Fortunately, the information necessary to innovate in the small business world is usually far more available. Indeed, for the business owner with an open mind, good ideas that can be implemented at a reasonable cost are everywhere available. Unfortunately, as Drucker points out, too few businesspeople are prepared to recognize and act on the highly valuable information that is right under their own noses.

Here are several more examples of businesses that are ignoring information they should be embracing to improve their competitive position:

- A small-animal veterinarian who frequently gets calls from concerned pet owners after regular business hours, but can't be bothered to look into hiring another vet to run an evening clinic.

- A certified public accountant specializing in income taxes, who, despite being asked questions almost daily about planning to limit estate taxes, never reorganizes the business to provide customers helpful information and services geared to this topic.

- A prepress type shop located on a busy street that doesn't institute a free pickup and delivery service or otherwise improve access despite the fact its high-volume customers constantly complain about parking and ticket hassles.

- A consultant who helps city and county governments plan police, fire, and other public safety buildings, but turns down a number of requests to help plan newly popular disaster-response centers because they're outside her area of expertise.

- A haircutting salon in a city that is the destination for many Southeast Asian immigrants that doesn't seek out haircutters who speak one or more of the appropriate languages.

- A plant nursery which, when its normal fall bulb shipment sells out in two weeks instead of the normal eight, not only doesn't reorder, but next year increases bulb inventory by only ten percent.

Poor babies. By not gathering and acting on the information their customers are all but thrusting upon them, these businesses—all of which have lots of competitors—are turning their backs on ways to improve their profitability. But before you shed tears for them, take a moment to think about your own business. Now ask yourself this simple question. Do I have the innovative mindset to recognize and profit from valuable new information? If you say yes, quick, what are the three hottest areas of your business, and what are you doing to take advantage of their popularity?

Example:

Madge opened a gift shop, Something Special, in a small university city in the Midwest. Selling a wide variety of items, she barely broke even her first year. Given that Madge was a single mother with two teenagers to raise, this simply wasn't acceptable. Madge was about to put up a going-out-of-business sign when a customer came in and bought almost $1,000 worth of Native American crafts which were displayed on a couple of shelves at the back of the store. When the customer asked to be alerted when the next shipment came in, Madge reflected that sales of Native American artwork had been profitable and several other people had made similar requests. In short, after checking to be sure no one else in her extended area had captured this niche, she decided to put away her closing sign and convert half of the store to North American Indian arts and crafts. To make a long story short, Madge's new emphasis, aided by a savvy marketing campaign featuring programs and workshops hosted by many of the Native American artists, really worked. So much so that a year later, Madge renamed her new, prosperous shop Something Tribal, and dealt exclusively in indigenous arts and crafts.

Another great example of how to improve a business by paying attention to unexpected information involves the Holiday Inn in Cumberland, Maryland. As reported by Associated Press writer David Dishman, for years this motel bore the heavy burden of being built hard against a railroad line. When the hotel wasn't full, desk clerks, fearing that guests would be bothered by the 65 noisy trains that clattered past each day, assigned guests to the quieter rooms closer to the highway. Then one day a train enthusiast contacted Sales Director Karen Twigg to ask how much extra it would cost to book a room facing the tracks. Twigg could have politely said they were the same price, accommodated the man's request and gone on with her routine. Instead, she quizzed the caller about why he wanted to overlook the trains and then, realizing that he wasn't the world's only train enthusiast, decided to see whether she could profit from her new knowledge. She did this by starting a promotional campaign aimed at train buffs. "Make tracks to stay with us," Cumberland Holiday Inn advertised in train fanciers' magazines. This message was a big hit, and train-loving travelers from all over the world booked track-side rooms with a view of all those locomotives pulling their loads in and out of the CSX switching yard and maintenance shops.

One reason I'm so familiar with the tendency to suppress accidental discoveries is because, like most businesspeople, I've done it. One example involves Nolo's website, which we established in 1994. To attract users without incurring prohibitive advertising costs, we urged other Internet sites to use portions of our legal content free in exchange for providing a link to Nolo.com. Then one day an editor for a prominent website called asking for permission to place a significant portion of Nolo's Online Legal Encyclopedia on their site without a link back to Nolo. "Linking to other companies is against our policy," he explained. Seeing no benefit, our marketing rep said no thanks and hung up. Literally a few minutes later, the editor called back and offered to pay us an annual fee of $25,000 to use over 100 articles of our self-help law material. As you might expect, this time we cheerfully said yes.

Because this unexpected revenue had not been budgeted, it was essentially up for grabs. The marketing director opined that this was a lucky accident ("no one pays for content online") and suggested Nolo spend it as part of an effort to redesign its book covers. Since this was long overdue, we did. In the meantime, Nolo's Web marketing staff went about its usual business of trading Nolo content for links to our site. A few months later, much the same story repeated. Again, Nolo unexpectedly got a substantial fee for a content license. And again, Nolo management concluded this was a fortunate anomaly ("we wouldn't have gotten this money if the other site's negotiators were experienced") and spent the "windfall" to improve non-Web-related areas without changing the way we marketed our online content.

Fortunately, the third time we were offered dollars for content a few Noloids began asking why, if other businesses were willing to pay for online content, Nolo didn't actively pursue the business. To cut to the end of this little drama, licensing Nolo content finally did become a new and profitable Nolo endeavor. Interestingly, this in turn led Nolo to redesign its content creation process to create more products our licensees wanted to buy. Instead of simply publishing books and software in hopes someone would buy them, Nolo began to look for ways to create at least some of its plain-English legal information to order, thus locking in a profit before a word was written.

A Case Study in How Good Ideas Surface

Here is an extended example that illustrates how a troubled small business is likely to suppress the information it needs to survive and how, with patience, it can find and exploit it. I offer it in the hope that it will inspire you to take a fresh look at every aspect of your business, even the humblest. Over and over I've learned that big ideas can be found in the oddest places, sometimes even in the parts of a business everyone associated with it loves to hate.

Example:

Mack, the hardworking owner of Bright Spot, a small plant nursery, was forced to think about the future of his newish business for the most basic of reasons: It was failing. Mack, who had seemingly been born with a world-class gardening gene, had quit his job as a psychologist 18 months before to open a small plant nursery in an outer suburban area where there were already several larger and well-entrenched competitors. He believed that by specializing in two very popular plants—roses and Japanese maples—he would have the competitive edge needed to prosper.

Unfortunately, it hadn't turned out to be so easy. Despite bookkeeping help from his wife, Salli, who was a financial planner, his teenage son's and daughter's volunteer summer help, and not paying himself a salary, Mack's business still was in the red. Bright Spot's biggest problem turned out to be its small size. Customers wanting a larger selection of plants could patronize the two bigger nurseries, and price-conscious customers preferred to shop at the garden department of a big box store 15 miles away. Mark's seemingly clever insight that Bright Spot could succeed by specializing in just two hot plant areas turned out to be flawed. In large part this was because the two larger nurseries immediately responded to his competitive gambit by installing their own specialty rose and Japanese maple boutiques. By using profits earned in the rest of their business, they were also able to steeply discount prices. To fight back, Mack expanded his selection of other plants and held frequent sales. Although these strategies brought in customers, neither contributed a speck of black to Bright Spot's bright red bottom line.

Finally, on Labor Day, when his business was mercifully closed, Mark convened a meeting of his family and his three key employees. After handing around his latest lousy financial statement, Mark asked for honest feedback. Could Bright Spot ever earn a decent profit? Or should Mark put it out of its misery and go back to work?

At first no one said a word, each trying to avoid being the first to say that Bright Spot was simply the wrong business in the wrong place at the wrong time. Finally, Ed, Mark's 15-year-old son, tried to put a positive spin on things. "Dad, I know we're not selling enough plants, but like I've been telling you, my part of the business is in great shape. I've gained ten pounds and can bench 270."

"Ed, you agreed to help carry the heavy stuff to peoples' cars," Mark snapped. "I wish you would stop complaining."

"C'mon, Dad, I was trying to say something nice. And you have to admit I've lugged tons of dirt. Probably 70% of the work I've done this summer involves fetching and carrying those heavy bags of soil."

Curious, Salli asked, "Do people really buy that much soil?"

"Oh, yeah, Mom. I've ended up spending most of my time as Dad's dirt boy, hauling the stuff to people's cars."

"Why do customers buy so much?" Salli asked. "Isn't bagged planting mix mostly used in small outside containers?"

"Nah—people who get frustrated trying to break up the rocky soil around here spread it right on their gardens. Or they end up digging out the hard stuff and replacing it with new soil that's easy to work."

"Can't people buy bags of soil cheaper at the shopping center?" Salli asked.

"A little bit, but remember they have to drive another 15 miles to do it, and on a Saturday morning, who wants to ..."

Salli interrupted, "If that's really true, I suggest you look at how you can sell more dirt."

When Mark ignored her and began to explain several problems that were preventing him from making a profit on the roses, Salli interrupted again. "Mark, I'm serious. Let's talk about the dirt. Ed, tell me more about what you have been doing."

Ed explained that in the spring, the nursery had carried only two types of soil, each in bags piled behind the fertilizer shed to the side of the small sales building. After dragging the bags all the way in on delivery day and then right back out the rest of the week, Ed had begun piling it closer to the front gate. More customers now spotted the dirt, and sales improved. Then Bright Spot had begun carrying both finer and coarser grades of soil, plus some fancy stuff with chicken poop mixed in. Sales went up again.

Next Salli—who you'll remember is a financial planner—asked about the profit margins on the dirt business. It didn't take her long to figure out that although soil and soil amendments amounted to only 20% of Bright Spot's sales, they were among its few profitable items. After all, you don't need to water bags of dirt every day and it never dies on you. Armed with this info, Salli began a campaign to convince Mark to reorganize the operation into what she and Ed started calling the "family dirt business."

Fortunately, since there was a large fenced area behind the nursery, this proved fairly easy. After investigation revealed that no special permits were needed, Mark ordered truckloads of different types of topsoil and piled it high. Now customers could buy it in bulk and bag it themselves to save money or, for a few dollars more, purchase it prebagged. Mark also made a deal with

Fred, a guy with a small dump truck, to do affordable home deliveries.

When the new service immediately proved popular, Mark added various types of bulk mulches and began experimenting with related product lines, such as ornamental rock and big planters that were a little nicer than those available at the mall. Somewhere along the way he met Mikey, a retired iron worker who used an acetylene torch to create oversized garden sculptures that he was happy to have Mark sell on consignment. Although retailing Mikey's creatures wasn't highly profitable, their presence turned the dirt yard into a fantastical destination for small children, pleasing their parents and bringing in more customers.

What about the plants? Mark soon decided he could give up the unprofitable pretense of being a full-service nursery. Instead of trying to bring in customers by holding money-losing sales, he returned to his original idea of concentrating on Japanese maples and roses, especially varieties not easily available elsewhere. Although at first Salli counseled that it made no sense to continue to plow dirt profits into these marginal businesses, this time it was Mark who turned out to be prescient. Not only did the dirt yard increase plant sales by bringing in lots of potential customers, but also before long the larger nurseries realized that Bright Spot wasn't going to be forced out of business by aggressive price-slashing, and returned prices to normal levels. This gave Mark the opportunity to raise his prices to a profit-producing level and to establish Bright Spot as one of the best specialty nurseries in the area. Within two years, his nursery business was almost as profitable as his dirt yard, and in response to customer requests he added an immediately profitable line of antique fruit trees.

Making Innovation a Continuous Process

If the innovative ideas behind your business turn out to be on target, and your enterprise is otherwise competently run (and sometimes in the short run, even if it isn't), you will enjoy a period of success. Now your task is to keep innovation happening, so that competitors can't immediately catch up to or even leapfrog your new approaches.

Although this sounds easy, it isn't. As the owner of a small business, you will daily be pulled in many directions. Customers must be satisfied, employees organized, supplies ordered, and bills paid, to mention just a few. And in the midst of all this, you must still plan to improve your business. While at first you might think the biggest problem would be having time to come up with creative ideas, the opposite is more often true. For many entrepreneurs, ideas, it turns out, can be as numerous as pumpkins in October; it's picking the best ones and carving them to perfection that's difficult. And once each is implemented, you'll also need to be able to track its success or failure. That's because you'll never have time to nurture the best ones if you aren't equipped to recognize and shuck off the losers.

When thinking about how to improve your business, start with three key principles. First, if your business is already successful, you'll want to improve it incrementally, not fundamentally reinvent it. This way, you both minimize jeopardizing your success while at the same time take steps to extend your entrepreneurial edge before it begins to erode. For example, if yours is a small software company whose profitable specialty is designing database software for lumberyards, it probably doesn't make sense for you to try and apply your innovative inventory-tracking ideas to retail stores or other businesses you don't fully understand. Better to focus on innovative ideas to make your software absolutely essential to your lumber industry customers. If you do decide to expand, focus on modifying your software to meet the needs of closely related businesses you already have a good feel for.

Second, focus on ideas that can be implemented promptly. In the small business world, the investment of time or money to get something going two or more years from now is almost always more than you can afford. Better to focus on innovations that can be implemented immediately. If you are right, they'll produce income now and in two years. And if your idea doesn't work, you can quickly scrap it and move on to something else. For example, the owners of the Cumberland Holiday Inn might conclude that while immediately redesigning their operation to cater to rail buffs makes great sense, opening more railroad-focused motels does not.

Third, focus on the real needs of your target market, not on your own hopes and dreams. When asked—and believe me, it's always wise to ask—customers often request the most basic improvements, not clever breakthroughs. For example, a lawyer, house remodeler, or landscaper who adopts a policy of returning all phone calls the same day may do more to please customers and clients than they would if they developed a laundry list of new services. Similarly, a coffee shop that serves better grades of coffee and tea may score more points with breakfasters than if it went to far more trouble to create a whole new menu.

Example:

Madge, the woman who was smart enough to turn her failing gift shop into a successful purveyor of Native American arts and crafts, distributed a questionnaire to a number of her best customers requesting feedback as to how she could better serve them. A number of responders suggested she not only carry arts and crafts from North America, but also stock folk art from other parts of the world, including Nepal, Tibet, South East Asia, and Central America. Worrying about spreading herself too thin, Madge nevertheless decided to expand her inventory to include folk art from all the Americas. Although doing this involved the cost of renting a small adjoining space, Madge's new initiative was profitable from the start.

Gather as Many Good Ideas as Possible

To identify ideas that fit these three criteria, I suggest you start by adopting this principle: Everyone with a stake in your business success should be involved in the innovation process. Fortunately, since most ideas are free, it will cost you very little to set up a process to facilitate this. But since business-changing ideas rarely show up on schedule or in easy-to-recognize ways, bringing as many as possible to the surface will take both creativity and stubbornness. For example, if you operate an organic grocery, you'll want an idea-gathering system that encourages the high school kid who uses a cute little wheelbarrow to load heavy orders into customers' cars to tell you if customers frequently ask where they can buy one. This doesn't mean you'll ultimately decide to sell wheelbarrows—just that you want to capture this information.

Here are some suggestions that may help you design an information-gathering system.

Brainstorm

An approach I find particularly useful consists of setting up one or more brainstorming sessions with people who care about your success. Depending on whether your business is still in its start-up phase or is well-established, participants might include investors, family members, and close friends with deep business experience, as well as current or prospective employees and key contractors or suppliers. Most of these people will have ideas to improve your business. And the great thing about the American tradition of participatory democracy is that you need only ask to find out what they are. Of course, some of the suggestions you collect will be wildly impractical, others far too costly, and a fair number just plain kooky, but there are also likely to be at least a few excellent ones.

Groups of from six to eight or at most ten people work best. Arrange to get your group together in a quiet place for several hours. To make sure all participants are well informed about your business, provide in advance financial projections, marketing information, and other helpful background materials.

Prepare by placing an easel holding a big pad of white paper at the front of the room with an important question written at the top using a dark marker. Something like "How can ABC Ventures become more profitable?" works well. Designate as group leader someone who can write clearly, has a good sense of humor, and is comfortable in front of people. It's usually best if you don't assume this role, since your presence at the front of the room may intimidate some participants.

The facilitator, acting as master of ceremonies, should begin by making it clear all ideas are welcome and that there is no such thing as a stupid suggestion. It's also a good idea if the facilitator coaches people to be brief, explaining that the exercise works best if you first collect as many ideas as possible and then later discuss the most viable ones. For example, if you plan to open a firewood business, the first person might say "Advertise in the PennySaver," the second "Offer summer discounts," the third "Pay salespeople commissions for larger orders," and the fourth "Paint the delivery truck a distinctive color and list all the types of wood we sell."

Don't insist people speak in order.

Some facilitators may be tempted to go around the room and ask participants speak in turn. This is a mistake. People who know it will be their turn next often worry about what they'll say instead of listening. Better to just ask people to speak when they're ready. If for any reason participants are slow to get started or seem guarded in their responses, the facilitator can almost always loosen people up, writing "market to shy people" or "give away food"—ideas that might even work in the right context.

No matter how seemingly silly, boring, or counterproductive an idea may at first sound, the facilitator should record it without argument or editing (except to summarize long-winded statements). Again, a big key to freeing people up to tap into their creativity is to convince them there really are no bad ideas. For example, if someone you plan to hire to work in your new greeting card shop starts to explain why she thinks it would make sense to also run a takeout coffee bar, don't laugh and ask for a more serious suggestion. Just write on your white board "sell coffee." Who knows—if there is nowhere in the neighborhood where customers can get a decent latte, a card and coffee shop might just work. Once participants trust that all contributions really are welcome, it's likely that suggestions will come fast and furiously. After a half an hour, your sheet might look something like this.

How Can ABC Ventures Become Profitable?

✓ Sell goods at cost—mark up services

✓ Pay employees sales commissions

✓ Free customer parking

✓ Raise starting pay—retain worker loyalty

✓ Deliver on Sunday

✓ Target affluent young adults

✓ Go online

✓ Sell coffee

✓ Provide a money-back guarantee

✓ Deliver in the evening

✓ Stay open Sunday

✓ Buy XYC Inc.

✓ Advertise in Spanish

✓ Search for strategic partners

✓ Open at two locations

✓ Sponsor kids' sports teams

✓ Recruit workers of all racial backgrounds

✓ Create a clever Yellow Pages ad

How to handle a "bingo!" moment.

Occasionally during a brainstorming process someone's idea will seem amazingly spot-on. Everyone in the room may even want to drop the game and discuss it. Because interrupting a brainstorming session—especially one in its early stages—chokes off other ideas, it's usually a mistake. But, as with all rules, there are exceptions. Especially if lots of ideas are already on the white board and the group is winding down, it may be a good idea for the group to bore into one that seems truly exciting.

In my experience, it takes less than an hour to extract all of a group's good ideas on a particular subject. Especially if things are going well, you'll want to give people a short break and then ask them to consider a second question. This time you'll probably want to focus on a narrower issue, again providing the group with as much useful data as possible. For example, if your small spa offers a number of different massage and exercise packages, and you want ideas on how you can better market the most profitable ones, you'll want each participant to have information about your sales volume by package, profit margins, hours of peak usage, and so on.

Depending on your business, here are some areas you might want to probe:

- How can we identify our best potential customers?
- How can we market more effectively to more people at an affordable cost?
- What additional products or services can we introduce?
- How can we better distinguish ourselves from our competitors?
- How can we increase sales and profits?

Chances are your brainstorming sessions will produce at least several excellent ideas you haven't already thought of. And if you are lucky, you'll get one or more provocative new wrinkles that truly improve your business. But it's also possible that your brainstorming group won't produce ideas that are likely to substantially improve your prospects. Assuming you assembled an able, energetic group, this may be a signal that your foundation business concept needs rethinking.

Get employees involved

Your employees undoubtedly know a great deal about your business. And many of them probably care nearly as much about its success as you do. In addition to including key employees in your brainstorming sessions, here are some efficient ways to solicit their good ideas.

- **5/15 reports.** Periodically ask everyone in your company to spend no more than 15 minutes writing down their suggestions for improving the business. You, in turn, should be able to read each report in five minutes. Reports can be kept confidential if the writers want it that way—otherwise, share the ideas with everyone.

- **Notebooks.** Give every employee who deals with the public a notebook (paper or electronic—it makes no difference) and ask them to list all customer requests and suggestions.

- **Email conferences.** If your business has an internal email system, establish a new idea conference, where employees can post and read suggestions. To keep things fresh, it's best to time-limit each conference. For example, on April 1, you might ask employees for their ideas on improving customer service, giving them a week or two to respond. Then on May 1, you could ask for ideas about new products and services.

Recognize employees for their good ideas

To encourage employees to stay interested in generating ideas to improve your business, and at the same time avoid jealousy or the feeling that one employee may be claiming too much credit, it's a good idea to do three things. First, publicly recognize the person (or people) who contribute the good idea. Second, spread the credit around as widely as possible. For example, if someone in your warehouse figures out a better way to track inventory, you might celebrate by taking the hero of the day and a group of coworkers to lunch. Of course, you will also want to remember the clever employee the next time the opportunity for raises or promotions comes around. Third, establish a bonus pool, with appropriate awards made monthly or quarterly. For example, if your monthly bonus pool was $1,000, you might in the first month award all this to the two employees who codeveloped a significant way to cut costs. But the next month, you might make three different awards to people who suggested innovative ways to market a new service. For good ideas on how and why to establish a bonus pool, grab a copy of *Ideas Are Free: How the Idea Revolution Is Liberating People and Transforming Organizations*, by Alan Robinson and Dean Schroeder (Barrett-Kohler).

Get customers involved

If yours is an established business with repeat customers or clients, these folks almost surely want to tell you things. Too bad that so few businesses encourage them to do so and that many find ways to resist or even reject customers with good ideas. For example, recently when I was working out at a gym, I overheard the manager discussing with a contractor the layout of a new stretching room. The conversation was public, and another member (let's call him Craig) politely asked if the new room could contain wider mats. When the manager didn't seem very responsive, Craig pointed out that big men like himself who didn't easily fit on the existing mats used two mats so as not to bump neighboring stretchers. Craig's point that small mats actually resulted in fewer—not more—people using the stretching space was so good that several other members immediately spoke up to agree. Too bad that after listening for a very short time the manager interrupted to say that the size of the mats wasn't his decision, but he was pretty sure the owner was buying more of the small ones.

"No big deal," you may be thinking. After all, most people won't switch health clubs based on the size of their mats. Don't be so sure. When I glanced at the window of another local exercise facility, I saw it was advertising a new yoga area. Although I didn't bother to check the new place out to see if the stretching area was better designed, Craig might.

Not only is it wise to listen to good ideas your customers bring to you, it also makes sense to solicit them. Depending on your business, there are a variety of appropriate ways to ask for feedback. Often the traditional method, asking interested customers to complete a brief suggestions form before dropping it in a box or mailing it back in a pre-stamped envelope, works best.

But it's a mistake to ask for suggestions unless you are prepared both to implement the best ones and tell your customers you acted on their feedback. If you take those two steps, you'll not only increase customer satisfaction (the mats really are wider), but will also reinforce the trust you want them to place in your business (Craig and the others will feel greater involvement with and loyalty to a business that pays attention to them).

One good way to let people know that their suggestions aren't being ignored is to periodically list ones you have implemented. For example, when the customers of Pam's independent drugstore stuffed her new suggestion box with good ideas, she created a small display area next to the suggestion box listing a number of the ideas and what she had done to implement them.

Take time to think about your business

Although it's always rewarding to get your employees and customers involved in suggesting ways to improve your business, it's at least as important to engage the creative juices of your single most important employee. That's you—just in case you have been too busy lately to remember.

Your first thought may be, "Oh, no. I already obsess about my business. The last thing I need is to spend more time worrying about it." Forgive me, but even if your business is a mighty success, you do need to think about how you can apply new and innovative information to keep your edge and stay ahead of competitors. Fortunately, done right, this is very different from lying awake at night replaying familiar problems and hassles for the 200th time. Just the opposite; to open your mind to fresh ideas, you need to put day-to-day hassles aside.

I often do this by going for a long walk or jog. Getting more oxygen to my brain, combined with the relaxation of the spirit I experience when exercising, allows my mind to pop out lots of fresh ideas. Once this process begins, I focus my thoughts on one aspect of Nolo's business—for example, our online site or our publishing strategy. On good days, when ideas flow like a river in spring, my next step is to find a peaceful spot where I can capture these thoughts in quick notes.

You may already have your own favorite method of brainstorming. Whether it involves going for a bike ride, listening to music, or picking the brain of a creative relative or mentor, the key is to make enough time to do it on a regular basis. Allowing yourself to be too busy to think creatively is always a mistake. If you doubt this, consider for a moment about how much of your working time is spent doing relatively unimportant tasks that won't contribute to your bottom line.

Taking a few days or even a week off is an excellent way to make time and energy to think about strategic issues. Unfortunately, when I suggest this strategy, many entrepreneurs say something like this: "I haven't even had a decent vacation in years—there is just no way I have the luxury of taking a week off." If that's your first response, seriously consider changing your business. A person too busy to take a couple of days off is almost always overextended and all too frequently operating a business that is barely profitable.

Choose the Best Ideas to Implement

Choosing the best of a basketful of innovative ideas is usually no easy task. But in a world where ideas are usually cheap and implementation is often expensive, choose you must. One good approach is first to systematically rank your best ideas by awarding points on a one-to-five scale to the ones that best fulfill your key criteria. For example, if your primary goals are to improve customer access, increase sales, and to tell more potential customers about your business, you would award points on a one-to-five scale in each of these areas. Once this is done, adjust your rankings based on how much each idea costs. One excellent way to do this is to double the point total of ideas that can be implemented at the lowest comparative cost while halving the points of the most expensive ones. In my experience since you'll never really know which ideas will work until you try them, it's usually wise to try as many of the top scorers as possible.

Example:

Amos, who has been laid off from his job maintaining computers at a large corporation, decides to accept his father's offer to take over the family TV repair business and see if he can breathe some life into it. He uses several methods, including a brainstorming session with employees and suppliers, to come up with new ideas to try to achieve his four big goals: increase sales, improve marketing, improve customer access, and reduce employee turnover. To decide which he should implement first, Amos creates the following grid. He then rates the ideas he collects one to five as to how likely each is to further his larger goals.

Idea	Increase Sales	Improve Marketing	Improve Customer Access	Help Keep or Recruit Talented Employees	Total
Paint the truck	1	3	0	0	4
Institute a 401K plan for employees	0	0	0	4	4
Stay open longer hours	2	1	4	0	7
Fix computers as well as TVs	5	3	0	4	12

Amos's final step is to factor in how much each idea will cost to implement. Realizing that painting the truck will cost very little, but the other three ideas will be expensive to implement, Amos changes the totals as follows:

Paint truck	8
Institute a 401(k) plan	2
Open longer hours	3½
Fix computers	6

Not surprisingly, based on these results, Amos decides to add computer repair services and repaint his truck to say Big Screen TV and Computer Installation & Repair.

■

7

Target Your Customers

"I don't know the key to success, but the key to failure is trying to please everybody."

—Bill Cosby

In the magazine and newsletter business, it is common to begin a marketing campaign by hanging an oversized target on the wall as a focus for a brainstorming session. In a process that is well described by Cheryl Woodard in her book, *Starting & Running a Successful Newsletter or Magazine* (Nolo), you start by listing your most likely subscriber groups near the center of the bull's-eye. Then, in the middle rings of your target, you enter your pretty good prospects. Those who just might subscribe are relegated to the outer edge. For example, the publishers of a home furnishings magazine might list people shopping for a new house near its target's bull's-eye, the soon-to-be-married in the next ring, and those whose kids have just graduated from college—and may have a few extra dollars to refurbish the house—in an outer circle. Similarly, a publisher of a consumer product guide might be eager to reach reference librarians who are regularly consulted about how to find consumer information, and less eager to market to college students, many of whom are still trying to perfect the art of asking their parents for more money.

Although you are probably not planning to start a periodical, the idea of identifying your best customer groups in this way makes great sense. Only when you can convincingly describe who your best prospective customers are and why they will want to patronize your business can you sensibly create a marketing plan to reach them. So if you plan to open a dental lab making crowns, bridges, caps, and other oral paraphernalia, you should be able to list near the center of your target the specific dentists or groups of dentists you believe will use your services. In addition, you should be ready to explain why they will do so. What utility or value will you offer to convince area dentists to prefer your service?

Similarly, if you will open an aerobics and dance studio, you should be able to identify the folks you are pretty sure will enthusiastically don their leotards for your master classes, as well as the baggy-clothing set you hope to coax into your early morning weight-loss session. And you should be prepared to detail your marketing message—that is, why, once these people find out about your classes, they will prefer them to others.

Unfortunately, many businesses have only a hazy idea of their markets and how to reach them. They follow the open-the-doors-and-hope-for-the-best marketing approach, which of course goes far to explain why so many promptly fail.

Typical of this approach might be a new restaurant that places a few ads in free local newspapers, does some leafleting in neighborhood office buildings, places an early-bird special sign in the window, and buys into several two-for-one coupon books. A couple of these initiatives might make good sense if they were part of a coherent marketing plan aimed at budget-conscious diners who live or work close to the restaurant. But in the absence of such a focused plan, this approach is likely to do more harm than good. For example, if this restaurant owner hopes to attract a more affluent dinner crowd later in the evening, two-for-one deals and cut rates to early diners are likely to amount to a kiss of death, because many upmarket customers equate low prices with poor quality.

Given the fierce competition in the restaurant business, only establishments that figure out exactly who their customers will be, why these people will prefer the restaurant over others, and how to successfully reach them will have much chance of success.

Now and then, of course, businesses that don't do their marketing homework are nevertheless lucky enough to succeed for some reason the owner had never thought of. But then, as my father used to remark when, despite his refusal to practice, he occasionally sank a 15-foot putt, "even a blind squirrel finds an acorn once in a while."

Be Specific

Ready to identify your most likely customers and explain why they will prefer your business to others? Although this may sound easy, I've found that most small business owners can't do it. For example, here is a short list of sadly inadequate marketing statements.

Business	Inadequate Target Statement
Clear Zone car-detailing service	People who want beautifully maintained cars
Happy Pup dog daycare center	Working people who don't want to leave their dogs home all day
Divorce Yourself legal document preparation service	People who have legal problems and don't want to go to lawyers
Persimmon children's clothing store	People who want to buy clothes for kids
ClipZone hair cutting salon	Women who want an up-to-the-minute haircut

Each of these descriptions of the target market is so general that it's close to useless. To see why, let's take a closer look at Happy Pup's claim that its market consists of working people with dogs. Well, it's a start. But here are just a few facts it doesn't allow for:

- The great majority of working people can't possibly afford Happy Pup's going rate of $25-$40 a day for dog daycare.
- Just because a dog owner works doesn't mean someone else in the family isn't available to care for Bingo.
- Old dogs sleep a lot and may be content to stay home alone.
- Other area dogsitting services are available—why should dog owners choose Happy Pup?

In an effort to identify likely customers, let's now assume Hillary, Happy Pup's owner, works through the disciplined targeting exercises discussed later in this chapter. Her result is this more detailed profile: "Affluent, working people with active dogs who want to provide them the highest quality of care." Because this statement takes into account the owners' ability to pay and desire to provide their dogs with excellent daycare, it's a big improvement. But several crucial marketing factors are still missing. Hillary's biggest omission is her failure to consider location. Assuming most people won't drive more than five to ten miles out of their way to drop Bingo off, it's obvious that Happy Pup should concentrate its marketing efforts on affluent owners of younger dogs who live or work fairly close to Happy Pup's facility.

When it comes time to prepare a marketing message for this group, Happy Pup will need to include an explanation of why dogs really are pleased by its facility. Do they get more exercise? More attention from the staff? Are there other ways in which Happy Pup offers a better service than its competitors?

Now it's your turn. Considering the following three key marketing principles, identify your most likely groups of customers.

- **Need.** People who have a pressing need for your goods or services, even if that need is occasional or intermittent, are obviously more likely to patronize your business than those who don't.

- **Price.** In some markets (discount hair cutting or fast food, for example), people often make decisions based on who offers the lowest price. But in many others, people are more likely to patronize the business they believe provides the best value, regardless of price. A shoe store that sells well-made, but higher-priced shoes may do better than a low-cost competitor, and the drycleaners seen as the most trustworthy in town may be regarded by many customers as providing a better value, even though it charges more than many competitors.

- **Access.** If cost and quality are equal, customers will usually follow the course of least resistance, patronizing easy-to-access businesses and avoiding those that are tough to get to.

Get out a big hunk of paper, draw a bull's-eye, and list your best prospects closest to the center. If possible, get help from business-savvy friends, family members, and employees. At this stage, don't complicate the exercise by simultaneously trying to figure out how you'll reach the people you target. No question, that next step is crucial—but for now, just identify the groups or individuals who are the most likely to buy what your business sells and be ready to explain why each of these groups will prefer your business. Later, it will be time to develop a plan to reach them.

Example:

Sandy, a fast-pitch softball coach, opened a batting cage to teach hitting to young women softball players. With softball's fast-growing popularity, Sandy hoped she would draw enough students to allow her to quit her day job. During the prime spring months, more girls tried to book lessons than she could accommodate. But during the rest of the year, the flood of students slowed to a trickle. On a Tuesday night in October, Sandy was lucky to give two half-hour lessons.

To attract more off-season students, Sandy decided to engage in a marketing campaign, a subject about which she knew substantially nothing. When Sandy first tried to describe her target audience, the best she could come up with was "girls and young women age 8 to 18 who want to play better softball and who live within 20 to 30 minutes driving distance of my facility." Realizing she had described her existing market—the one she already knew wasn't producing enough year-round business—she resolved to do better.

After some thought, one of the key groups she wrote in her target's inner circle was "serious players age 12 to 18 who play tournament softball on club teams much of the year, who live within an hour of my facility, and who are advanced enough to appreciate that my teaching methods are state-of-the-art." Although there were far fewer young women in this "travel ball" cohort than there were little league or high school players, Sandy believed they (often with parental encouragement) were highly motivated to improve their skills. If she could reach them with the message that she was a super teacher and could help polish their skills to a "college scholarship" level, they might sign up for lessons year-round.

Sandy also made several other entries close to her marketing bull's-eye. One was for high school and club softball coaches who might want to rent her cage—or the extra space in the back of her facility—during bad weather months to run their own hitting clinics. Although neither of these initiatives would directly help Sandy's teaching business, they would significantly reduce her overhead costs. Finally, Sandy listed young baseball players in one of the outer rings of her target. She wasn't sure high school boys would take lessons from a woman, but she thought younger ones with older sisters who she had successfully coached well might. And if they did, and noticeably improved their performance, their friends would follow.

Like Sandy, once your target is complete, it's time to move on to step two of your marketing plan. How do you reach the people near the center of your bull's-eye? The best approach depends on the field you are in and the number of people you need to reach. A physical therapist and a floor refinisher will adopt very different types of outreach plans. But there is a common element to all good small business marketing plans. You must empower, motivate, and encourage the customers your marketing efforts recruit to recommend your business to others. (See Chapter 8, Market Your Business Creatively.)

Example:

Sandy's decision to market her services to serious softballers over a much larger geographical area paid off. She began by calling the 30 or so coaches of the club teams within a 40-mile radius of her facility and offering to run free weekend hitting clinics for their players. When a number jumped at the chance, Sandy was able to show off her indoor training facility and sophisticated teaching techniques. Almost immediately a number of players who participated in the free clinics signed up for private lessons. As their hitting quickly improved, it didn't take them long to tell their athlete friends about how much Sandy was teaching them.

Fueled by this positive word of mouth, larger numbers of committed athletes from more distant areas began to sign up for regular lessons. Before long, Sandy was almost as busy during winter as she was in the spring, and was able to support herself coaching full time.

Go After Both Novice and Experienced Customers

In developing your targeted marketing plan, realize that the potential customers of many businesses tend to fall into two categories: people who have had experience—sometimes lots of it—with businesses like yours, and those who are new to the field. For example, if you open a mid-priced shoe store, all of your customers will have patronized similar shoe retailers and will have a pretty good idea of what to expert. To impress them, you'll need to exceed these expectations. By contrast, if you start an upscale vintage clothing boutique in an area where shopping for used clothes has always meant going to Goodwill or the church jumble sale, many of the people you hope to attract will never have dealt with a store like yours. Just your presence will offer potential customers a unique retail experience. But to succeed, you'll have to convince them that paying just a little extra for your cutting-edge experienced clothing can be simultaneously frugal and exciting.

All of this is just another way of emphasizing that you'll have a very different job attracting and satisfying newbie and experienced customers. For example, if yours will be the third Indian restaurant in town and at least one of the others is good, many of your initial customers will know enough to hold you to a high standard. By contrast, if yours is the first in your area, your challenge will be to attract and educate a clientele that knows little about the food you offer.

If you haven't thought about potential customers in this way, you may be tempted to ask which group is preferable. Is it easier to convince the uninitiated to try something new or to market to a group of experienced—and possibly jaded—customers? There is no one answer for all businesses. In some instances it may be appropriate to go after both experienced and novice customers, but doing so will always involve different strategies. You'll need to develop a marketing plan specifically designed to reach whichever group your business targets.

Coffee is a field where this has been famously done. Forty years ago, Americans drank uniformly terrible coffee whether they bought it in cans and made it themselves or ate out. Only a relatively few coffee drinkers, who had spent time in Europe and the Middle East, where coffee quality was far higher, even knew what they were missing. Then, specialty coffee stores, that sold richer, more varied coffee and coffee drinks in European-style shops, began to pop up. One of the first was Peet's, a tiny Berkeley, California, company. Like Peet's, many of these new-style shops started in university towns where there were at least small pools of experienced customers. At first Peet's and the other coffee shop innovators didn't reach much beyond their small audience of coffee aficionados. But then, gradually, largely by word of mouth, more and more people became converts to better coffee sold in a more pleasant retail environment. Eventually, of course, the combination of an improved product sold in stylish coffee bars changed the habits of millions of American coffee drinkers, and created huge numbers of new ones.

Although it's probably overly optimistic to think that you'll come up with a similarly world-changing business, it often does make sense to consider ways you can create loyal customers by improving the quality of familiar products or developing better ways to market them. Customers who perceive that you offer a more valuable product or service are highly likely to both patronize you repeatedly and tell others of their discovery.

Example:

Roman dreamed of opening his own gourmet takeout pizza shop. Knowing, of course, that virtually every American already eats pizza and that there were dozens of competitors in his area,

Roman realized that to succeed, step one was to produce a pie so good that longtime pizza lovers would brag about it. To this end, Roman spent months visiting and sometimes revisiting the best independent pizza shops in several states. Every time someone told him about another super place, he made it a point to taste their crust and analyze their toppings. Coupled with his own experience, seeing what worked in the marketplace convinced him to develop a line of deep-dish thick-crust vegetarian pizzas very different from the mega-meat pies featured by local franchised operations. As part of doing this, Roman created his own group of a dozen pizza lovers to act as his tasters. Convening the group half a dozen times, Roman presented dozens of variations of his basic recipes until an enthusiastic consensus developed as to which pie really was best.

But Roman worried that in a hyper-competitive business, creating a uniquely mouthwatering pizza wouldn't guarantee success. What if not enough people bought it to cover his costs? Identifying time-challenged two-worker families as a crucial slice of his target market, Roman decided to focus on making it easy for people to get his pizzas.

To this end he borrowed two innovative marketing ideas he thought would be successful for the neighborhood shopping street location he planned. The first consisted of a half-baked pizza that could be bought hours ahead of time and finished in a home oven. Second, on busy nights Roman decided he would cook a steady stream of his most popular pies before he received orders. That way when the flood of last-minute orders threatened to cause delays, he could say, "Today's two special pies are ready now. Otherwise there will be a 30-minute wait." In short, by focusing both on creating unique pizzas and on meeting the needs of pizza eaters who are pressed for time—both early birds and night owls—Roman gave experienced pizza eaters a reason to patronize his restaurant and at the same time expanded his potential market.

Don't Forget Your Current Customers

No matter what your field, if you are preparing a marketing target for an established business, the words "current customers" should almost always be listed near the bull's-eye of your target. That's because with a very few exceptions, such as businesses that market to tourists or help people with onetime problems (divorce, tubal ligation, and cremation come to mind), your existing customers are the easiest to reach. Although it may seem obvious that the customer list of a successful business is a golden asset, many, if not most, small businesses ignore it. Instead of making special offers to their existing customers and working to develop more attractive goods and services, they concentrate their marketing efforts on the more difficult task of trying to locate new ones.

How do you find out how you can sell your current customers more or different products? Simple: Ask. If you stay in close communication with your customers and make it easy and fun for them to tell you about their needs, they will. Business owners who depend on just a few customers can often best do this in person. Businesses with a larger customer roster will often prefer to periodically send customers a short, easy-to-fill-out form asking for suggestions about new and improved services. When Roman asked his pizza-eating customers, the response he got boiled down to "gourmet salads." As a result, using only the freshest ingredients, Roman promptly created a spinach, mixed green, and fruit salad and happily found that he could actually mark up the salads more than the pizza.

Example:

When her dad died, Mandy took over his business, which pumped out vacation-home septic tanks in a resort area. Soon she got a call from Janet, a customer whose main home was in a city several hours distant. Could Mandy take some cat food with her and feed the feral cat that was living under the porch, Janet asked?

Not only was Mandy happy to do this, she was even happier to prepare a questionnaire to all her septic tank customers, asking them whether there were additional things she could do when she visited their properties. When quite a few responded yes, Mandy developed a service she called Property Check. For a modest fee she would work with the homeowner to develop a list of every-thing the homeowner wanted checked. Each time Mandy visited the property, she promptly emailed to the owner a list of all items checked and any problems discovered. Before long, Property Check became so successful that Mandy hired an assistant to drive the honey wagon and concentrated on developing more new services for absentee owners.

Say thank you.

If your customers are kind enough to fill out a feedback form or otherwise suggest ways you can introduce new or better goods or services, always thank them. A brief note is a good way to do this: Including a small gift is even better.

Here are just a few examples of businesses that profitably concentrate on existing customers:

- A dentist who, after fielding a number of questions from patients with snoring and other sleep problems, decides to educate himself on the mouth guards and other devices that can help restore even breathing and a good night's sleep. When he tells his patients about his new specialty, a number ask for help. In addition, as word of his sleep work gradually spreads, he is able to attract new patients to what quickly becomes the highest-profit and most interesting part of his practice.

- A used bookstore that decides to stock 750 new titles in the subject areas most popular with its customers, including biography, science fiction, and mystery. Displayed on attractive racks near the front of the store, these books are immediately popular with used book customers who occasionally splurge on a new title.

- Sandy, the softball coach we met earlier in this chapter, creates a small retail area to sell several of the swing-training devices she uses and recommends. Offering them, along with high-end bats, hitting nets, instructional videos, and other hitting paraphernalia, she nets over $1,000 per month from her existing customer base.

- A small-business lawyer develops a specialty in helping clients cope with and, if necessary, fire problem employees. In addition to letting clients know he is available to help with crisis situations, the lawyer tells his existing small business clients that for a very reasonable fee he will help them create an employee handbook, a necessary first step to help guard against frivolous employee lawsuits.

- A restaurant in a popular tourist area fills an underused space near the cash register with locally produced mustards, jams, hot sauces, and other gourmet specialty items. The products are sold individually and also in boxed collections ready for mailing. Just produce your credit card and the addresses of family members and friends, and the restaurant will do the rest. The program is so popular the restaurant sets up a website to handle repeat orders.

Although the wisdom of developing and marketing new products and services to existing customers may seem obvious, it can be difficult to accomplish since to work in the long run you need to provide a product or service of real utility. I can vouch for this out of my own experience. For many years, Nolo's self-help law customers asked us if we could recommend lawyers. Often they didn't want to hire the lawyer long-term, but only to get the answer to a fact-specific question or obtain advice in a complicated legal area beyond the scope of Nolo's materials.

One day at a marketing meeting, someone asked for about the thousandth time why Nolo was trying so hard to find more customers for its self-help law products, but ignoring people who wanted to solve their problems with limited help from a lawyer. In the middle of repeating the answer I had given for years—"Most lawyers are hostile to self-helpers and won't help them on a question-by-question basis"—I realized that it had been years since Nolo had taken a fresh look at this area. And in the intervening years, at least some lawyers had become more open to working with self-helpers who wanted to purchase limited legal advice.

With our eyes newly open, Nolo decided to form a relationship with the ARAG group, a prepaid legal insurance company whose main business consisted of providing legal help to people who worked for large corporations. As part of ARAG's employee benefit program, plan lawyers answered legal questions by phone. Now, under Nolo's arrangement with ARAG, Nolo's Internet customers can call a lawyer in their own state (or specialist area) and for a very modest fee discuss their legal questions or problems. For Nolo, offering this new service to our customers has been solidly profitable from the beginning. Too bad it took us so long to take our marketing blinders off and introduce a new product our customers had actually been requesting for years.

■

8

Market Your Business Creatively

*"If you hype something and it succeeds, you're a genius;
it wasn't a hype. If you hype something and it fails,
then it's just a hype."*

—Neil Bogart

Once, when speaking at a workshop for people interested in starting a small business, I met a man who was optimistically planning a new venture, despite the fact that he had suffered a long string of failures. After listening politely to my remarks, he pulled me aside, lowered his voice, and said that after many years of making mistakes he had finally figured out what he needed to do to make his new venture succeed. After a dramatic pause, he all but whispered, "Plenty of money for advertising."

I was tempted to sit the fellow down and explain why I had reached just the opposite conclusion. But seeing that his eyes had the glint of the true believer—and remembering I was late for my daughter's softball game—I decided to save my polemic for another day. Here it is.

What Advertising Can—and Can't—Do

There are at least half a dozen reasons why spending significant money on advertising rarely pays off for a small business. But before I give you the whole list, let's start with two big cautions.

The Biggest Problems With Advertising

The first big drawback is that spending all or most of your promotional budget on advertising risks stifling more imaginative initiatives that can attract more long-term customers at a far lower cost. Much like giving a teenager a fat allowance and then wondering why she doesn't get a job, once the monthly ad buy is made, too many business owners lack incentive to work hard to get the word out in other ways. Why should they bother? Their ads are already out there attracting all the customers they need, right? Unfortunately, it's rarely that easy, even for large businesses with huge ad budgets. It's virtually never a winning strategy for small outfits with very limited marketing budgets.

Example 1:

Ted is an early retiree lucky enough to have received a generous compensation package from his former employer. With money in his pocket and his kids grown, Ted is ready to fulfill his lifetime dream of opening a small bookstore, which he calls Academy Books. Before the doors are even open, Ted signs an expensive contract with a weekly newspaper to run a large display ad in the next 12 issues. When Ted writes the check and hands over the simple ad copy, he feels good—he's taken a big step towards getting word out about his new shop. After two months, when the ad doesn't seem to be producing enough customers even to pay for itself, let alone help Academy sell enough books to earn a profit, Ted calls the newspaper to express his concern. Joy, the ad salesperson, explains to Ted that ads work best when they run for an extended period and that she thinks Ted's copy needs "more zip." So with Joy's help, Ted designs a zippier ad, signs a second contract, and continues to hope for the best. When sales don't improve much, Ted begins to worry that Academy Books will never succeed.

Example 2:

Instead of only buying advertising, Ted decides that he needs to target readers who live and work close to his shop and find low-cost ways to reach out to them. Accordingly, Ted arranges a meeting with Ann, the owner of WakeUP, a neighboring coffee bar, and proposes a series of joint promotions. These include having WakeUP place a small display of Academy bestsellers in the coffee shop and having Academy give every book purchaser a 50-cents-off coupon redeemable at WakeUP. In addition, book lovers who attend one of Academy's frequent author readings will be able to order coffee or tea delivered right to the bookshop.

When several of these and other promotional ideas work well to increase both WakeUp's and Academy's sales, Ted and Ann ask Molly, the owner of Molly's Place, a nearby restaurant, to join their local marketing group. Now, on the evenings when Academy Books schedules readings by particularly popular authors, Molly's Place provides a fixed-price buffet supper to super-fans willing to come early and pay a few extra dollars to break bread with the author before everyone adjourns to the bookshop for coffee and the reading. Eventually these evenings become so popular that the local public radio station asks to do a live broadcast from the bookstore. To express their appreciation and support public radio, all three businesses contribute thank-you gifts for listeners who participate in the station's pledge drives. For example, if you join at the $100 level, you receive a free half-pound of coffee at WakeUP, 20% off your next book purchase at Academy Books, and a free dinner at one of Molly's book lovers' buffets.

Obviously, there are lots of differences between the marketing approaches in these two examples. But the most important is that in the second, Ted uses his energy and common sense to design low-cost ways to let readers in his target group know about his business. In Example 1, he simply pays a local newspaper to try to do the entire job for him.

My second caution is that before you can use advertising intelligently, you must have realistic expectations as to what you hope to accomplish. Advertising may bring people into your business, but it doesn't make them buy anything, and it certainly doesn't encourage them to tell others about you. Too often advertising attracts fickle customers. After all, people who will try out your business because you advertise a sale or other special deal will try your competitors for the same reason. By contrast, positive recommendations from satisfied customers to people like themselves are much more likely to build customer loyalty, the real engine that will drive your future growth.

True, like churches that recruit Easter and Christmas worshippers and then try to turn them into regular churchgoers, you'll hope to turn people who respond to your ads into loyal customers. But it's my guess, based on experience, that if you used the same funds to better meet the needs of your faithful followers, those people would take care of recruiting others.

Other Downsides of Advertising

The notion that prosperity will envelop your business like the winter's first heavy snow if only you can design a brilliant ad and place it in just the right spot is largely a myth. In the small business world, where saturation advertising is unaffordable, it's more likely that your ads will produce a brief flurry of interest—sparse and quick to melt away. Here's why.

Money spent on advertising isn't available for more important needs. In a perfect world, a small business owner would have enough money to pay for an ad campaign and other business priorities. But in the real world, where the vast majority of start-ups are short on capital, it's almost always more sensible to spend most of your scarce dollars on improving the core competencies of your business than on advertising. First, invest in the quality of your goods and services, provide easy and affordable customer access, and work to attract and keep top-quality employees and contractors. Only if you have money left over should you even consider spending it on advertising.

Your message probably won't get through. As you well know, Americans are bombarded by thousands of ads each day, many of them part of big-dollar, multilevel saturation marketing campaigns conducted by huge corporations. In this ever-present ad cacophony, your small business ad is likely to be drowned out, which helps explain why, if you do plan to advertise, it makes sense to try an offbeat humorous approach. For example, as reported by the Associated Press, when coffee served by Fireside Books of Palrorer, Alaska, got poor reviews, the owners David Cheezem and Melissa Behnke "just sort of ran with it" and began selling t-shirts printed with "good books, bad coffee." Because this made people laugh, the store followed on with a "bad coffee poetry contest" and even sells "Real Alaska Ugly Coffee" beans. As Cheezem points out, "My feeling about marketing is there's so much hype everywhere, I'd rather be self-deprecatory. Get people curious, they can find out for themselves."

People distrust ads. I regard most ads to be at best half-honest and many to be first cousin to consumer fraud. Given that I'm obviously not alone in my negative attitude, you need to recognize that your ads may discourage—or even drive away—a significant percentage of your existing customers. To see how this works, imagine you spot a new restaurant that looks so inviting that you consider booking a table when your in-laws are in town. A few days later you receive a card deck in the mail that includes discount coupons for rural home sites, a backyard spa, a car repainting service, and several two-for-one meal offers from local restaurants, including the one you just discovered. Is your first thought "Hooray, I can get a great deal at a terrific restaurant"? Or are you more likely to decide to pick a different eating place? If you would make your reservation elsewhere, give a thought to how other types of ads might similarly repel your prospective customers.

In the rare instance when advertising does produce lots of customers, your business may not be able to handle the rush. Once, when I badly needed an electrician, I did something a little unusual for me and responded to Reliant Electric's large advertisement in the local weekly paper. But when I called, they told me their waiting list was two weeks. I relate this little story because it illustrates an all-too-frequent problem with advertising. If an ad does produce lots of customers—perhaps by promising a special deal—the business often can't cope, and many people have a negative experience. Certainly I'm not likely to call Reliant again, especially since Ben's Electric, the outfit recommended by the knowledgeable friend I called when Reliant couldn't handle my business, showed up the next morning, and fixed my problem at a reasonable cost.

Further reading on advertising and marketing.

Some of the points I make in this chapter come from my experience at Nolo. But I learned many others from an inspirational little book Nolo publishes and which I had the good fortune to edit, called *Marketing Without Advertising*, by Michael Phillips and Salli Rasberry. It's become a sort of in-house marketing bible here at Nolo. I suggest you read its greatly expanded discussion of advertising and its alternatives. Like all Nolo publications, it's available at Nolo.com. Or check it out of your library—that way your marketing efforts will be off to a truly cost-effective start.

How to Use Limited Advertising Effectively

Some types of ads, including those in the Yellow Pages, in the services section of a pennysaver newspaper, and in special-interest media, such as publications and websites aimed at parents, sports enthusiasts, or dog lovers, can be effective at letting people know about your business. They work precisely because, unlike most ads, they don't try to reach a broad audience. Only a few people will ever see them—but those people are likely to be receptive. Although the wisdom of planning to have customers find your ad, rather than hoping your ad finds a customer, may seem obvious, it is the opposite of the standard shout-from-the-mountaintop advertising approach followed by most American businesses.

To "narrowcast," not broadcast, your promotional messages, the best approach is to list your products or services where potential customers are likely to look for them. For example, if you own a summer horse camp, buying a classified ad on an equestrian website may pay for itself many times over.

Here are some places where listing-type ads may work:

- Auction websites such as eBay, and single-interest sites where goods and services are listed by category or keyword.

- Publications aimed at visitors or new residents. For example, list your big-city restaurant in a guide given to guests at local hotels.

- Publications or websites of nonprofit organizations or other groups popular with people you want to reach. For example, if you're a child care provider, place an inexpensive ad in the newsletter published by a working moms' group.

- Special interest journals. For example, an architect who specializes in designing fire stations might place a small monthly ad in journals read by city, county, and state planning officials.

- Trade publications and struggling local media outlets. Although quality media outlets keep their editorial and advertising departments completely separate (putting an ad in *The New York Times* won't buy you an inch of coverage in its news pages), others are far less scrupulous. Like it or not, in many fields, the best way to ensure regular editorial coverage in a particular publication is to purchase an ad contract. Usually there is no need to ask for any quid pro quo in terms of coverage—in most cases you'll get it.

Example:

Emiko lives in Metropolis, a good-sized city that is a popular international tourist destination. Reasoning that because the city-operated tourist office is small and shabby, there is a golden opportunity for a private business, she opens Metropolis Today in a downtown storefront. She provides free maps, walking tours, and restaurant lists, but also sells tours, event tickets, and other tourist-focused goods and services, including Metropolis-branded clothing, books set in Metropolis, and even a line of hand-painted Christmas ornaments depicting Metropolis scenes. Realizing that because she is targeting tourists and other visitors, it will be very helpful to have regular articles written about her new business in the weekly tourist newspaper distributed free at area airports, Emiko buys an ad package. A few weeks later, the newspaper writes an extensive feature about her innovative new enterprise and, even more important, adds Metropolis Today to its Good Tourist Info list, which appears in every issue.

Before you commit to any ad campaign, even a modest one, test it. Experiment with language, layout, and, most important, different publications. For example, instead of running the same small ad promoting your tai chi classes in the bodywork section of a free weekly paper for two months, run several different ads for two weeks each and keep track of which draws more customers.

How to Write a Good Ad

Pull out a pennysaver magazine or the Yellow Pages and turn to a popular category such as Roofing or Plumbing. Read a bunch of ads and circle the ones you feel best speak to your type of customer. If you are selling primarily on the basis of a low price, you'll likely identify a number of ads that effectively and loudly say cheap. One popular way to do this is to quote a competitive price and then further sweeten the deal by offering a "dollars off" coupon.

But if, as is more likely, you want to market to customers whose main goal is to find a reliable, high-quality provider, then you'll want to find ways to emphasize these attributes. Here, assuming they fit your facts, are several ways to do this:

- How long have you been in the business or the trade?

- What relevant education or experience do you have?

- Do you provide references or offer a guarantee?

- Is your business family-owned?

- Can you respond to customers' needs on a priority or emergency basis?

When you identify the key marketing elements you believe will best speak to the customer groups you want to reach, write a draft. Use the simplest, most direct language you can. Then, unless you are an experienced writer, enlist a friend or family member with excellent language skills as your editor.

Getting Customers to Recommend Your Business

As discussed above, I believe that "How can I create a winning ad campaign?" is the wrong question. Better to ask, "How do I create a business so compelling that my customers will recommend it to others?"

Think about how you and your family decide where to buy goods and services. What process did you go through the last time you chose a house painter, gardener, lawyer, or dentist? Also think about the last few times you went out to eat or attended a movie. I'll wager that in many, if not most, of these instances the recommendation of a trusted friend or acquaintance, not an ad, helped inform your decision. I'll also bet that another source of the information you used to make at least some of these purchasing decisions came from media people you trust. For example, you might have picked a movie or restaurant in part because it got high marks from a critic you respect, or called a contractor whose name appeared on a local consumer group's "highly approved" list.

It will help reinforce the point that advertising is usually not the best and most cost-effective way to reach new customers if you now make a mental list of five local small businesses you regularly patronize and respect. How often have you recommended each of these enterprises, or at least told someone that you patronized them? If your answer is "regularly," it's obvious that these businesses are doing so many things right that you, and probably many other satisfied customers, promote them for free.

Here are some key attributes of businesses that people are eager to tell their friends about.

Quality. Provide excellent goods and services that meet, or preferably exceed, those offered by your competitors. To be sure you really do this, set up a system to benchmark your offerings against those offered by competitors. For example, is your eyeglasses shop really the cleanest, best stocked, and most accessible in town? Does your staff deal with customers more promptly, pleasantly, and knowledgeably than do other stores' employees?

Keep it clean.

A small, but nevertheless significant, slice of the public makes many purchasing decisions based on how clean a business is. For example, I have several friends who won't patronize a good-sized list of local restaurants because they aren't spotless. Similarly, a member of my family only buys one brand of gas, based on her belief that their restrooms are usually the cleanest. Fortunately, since insisting on the highest standards of cleanliness doesn't cost much, and it really will distinguish your business from its sloppier competitors, it's an easy way to create a marketing edge.

Freshness. We humans are fickle. If a flashy new shop opens, many of us will give it a try and, if we like it, abandon our old patronage habits. It follows that, especially in fields where style is a key element of a business's overall presentation, you need to guard against the possibility that your customers will become bored and will drift away to trendier providers. Often the best way to do this is to regularly refresh the look and feel of your business. For example, if your tile shop looks like something out of the 1980s, you're in trouble if a competitor with a cool new look opens down the block. Lots of homeowners who want a state-of-the-art kitchen or bathroom are likely to patronize the new outfit, even if both of you stock many of the same products. If, on the other hand, you update the look of your shop and regularly improve its stock, you may discourage other shops from opening nearby or, even if one does, hold onto most of your customers. (In Chapter 6, Innovate Now and Forever, I discuss in more detail why it's essential to build continuous innovation into your business.)

Put change on automatic.

From waiting areas and conference rooms to signs, store windows, websites, and stationery, all of your business's public spaces, displays, and logos should be updated on a regular basis. Don't wait until they look a bit tatty to make a change. Adopt and stick to a schedule to change, renew, and redecorate.

Helpfulness. Customers want to know how to use your goods and services efficiently. The more honest, easy-to-understand information and handholding you provide, the more likely they are to purchase. For example, a plant nursery that offers classes on how to grow abundant vegetables will sell far more tomatoes than one that simply displays the plants. Similarly, a lumberyard that provides lots of how-to advice will sell lots more of almost everything than one that assumes customers know what they're doing.

Providing good information doesn't result only in increased sales. It can be another great way to motivate customers to recommend your business to others. For example, a doctor whose practice is built around educating patients about eating a healthy diet, exercising, and other ways to care for themselves may actually see these patients less. But people who feel their doctor is committed to helping them lead healthier lives are almost sure to refer others. Similarly, a lawyer who fills the waiting room with top-quality legal information (including self-help materials describing tasks people can do for themselves) will get more referrals than one who displays copies of last year's *Field & Stream*.

Example:

Real estate brokers Ira and Carol Serkes, of Berkeley, California, own a good-sized panel truck that they make available free to their clients for local moves. And when the truck is not being used as a small moving van, it's available free to community and charitable groups. As it rolls around town, the van prominently advertises the Serkes' real estate business. But since Ira and Carol are simultaneously providing a needed and appreciated service, their moving ad is seen in a positive light.

Customer recourse. Everyone wants to feel they are in good hands when they patronize a business. Providing high-quality goods or services, of course, is a big part of accomplishing this goal. Another important part is letting customers know that should anything ever go wrong, you can be counted on to put it right. Backing your products with a no-hassle, money-back guarantee is one excellent way to convey both of these messages. Customers intuitively know that sloppy operators can't afford to stand behind their offerings this way, and their comfort level with your business goes up—meaning they will be more likely to recommend it to others. For example, at Nolo, we offer a money-back guarantee if you're not satisfied with any of our products, no matter where or when you bought it. As a result, our customers often compare us favorably to other publishers—and especially to the legal profession.

Easy customer access. Lack of parking is one of the biggest reasons I avoid a business. Failure to return my phone calls in a timely manner is another huge turnoff. And, of course, there are many other ways poorly run small businesses place roadblocks in their customers' paths, including confusing voicemail systems, out-of-date websites, and inconvenient business hours. One business I know actually maintained an unlisted 800 number, apparently afraid that if it was readily accessible, too many customers would use it. Enough said, I hope. It's always wise to spend thought, creative energy, and, if necessary, money on improving in-person and electronic access to your business.

Responsiveness. Many people in your business's network, including customers, suppliers, employees, freelancers, and others you encounter regularly, will be delighted if you ask them to suggest improvements. Unfortunately, few businesses take the time to ask or have the mindset to listen. If you are one of them, take your head out of the sand and find appropriate ways to encourage feedback. And once you get it, be ready to act on the best suggestions.

Example:

Earlier in this chapter, I mentioned that when I was put off by an electrician whose ad I saw in the local paper, I got a recommendation from a friend and called Ben's Electric. Ben not only did a good job repairing several broken outlets and fixtures, but as he left, he asked if all my other systems were working well. This jogged my memory about my wonky front doorbell, and I asked Ben if he could replace it. He replied that he didn't install new doorbells, but would be glad to help me with other purely electrical problems.

A week later, Ben called me and said that because I wasn't the first customer to ask, he had decided to install doorbells. He had picked up several catalogs from an electrical supply shop and would be happy to show them to me at my convenience. I was not only pleased to get my doorbell replaced, but to deal with someone willing to listen and respond to my needs. And I was even more pleased when I next encountered Ben six months later, when he thanked me for helping nudge him into offering what had turned out to be a profitable service.

Don't ask for feedback unless you are serious about making changes.

I used to patronize a neighborhood restaurant that somehow survives despite its lousy coffee. When the owner placed a suggestion box on the counter, loads of people quickly pleaded "better coffee," "fix the coffee," "kill your coffee," or something similar. After a few weeks, when the coffee didn't improve, I asked a waitress about it. She replied, "The owner says there is nothing wrong with the coffee and since that was the main complaint, she doesn't plan any changes." I don't know about other customers, but now I go out of my way to eat elsewhere.

Getting Free Publicity

Media exposure for your business is often free and surprisingly easy to get. Radio and TV stations, magazines, online sites, and other types of media need piles of new content daily. It follows that with a little imagination, many businesses can figure out ways to get free—and often far more valuable—coverage than they could ever buy. A greengrocer who distributes weekly "freshest produce" tips to local media outlets and is frequently interviewed on the subject is one illustration. A financial planner who regularly appears on a local radio talk show called "Saving for Retirement" is another.

Providing consumer advice is only one way to get free exposure. If there's something special about your business—and there should be—the local media, at least, may want to report on it. And don't be discouraged by the belief that your business isn't newsworthy. With a little creativity, every business has an interesting story to tell.

Example:

Marty and Karen run a K-8 private school, Meadowbrook. They get most of their new pupils through referrals made by parents of current and former students. But when they decide to rent an adjoining building and double the size of the school, they fear that word of mouth won't fill up all the new desks quickly enough.

One way to try to do this would be to run newspaper ads. But Marty and Karen know that excellent schools generally don't need to advertise, although they may buy listings in specialized publications aimed at parents. Because advertising might put the school in the company of schools with lesser reputations, it might even disappoint the parents of current students. What are the alternatives?

One is to go out and get the school some favorable media coverage. To do this, Marty and Karen start by creating a press package. On a single sheet of paper, they list Meadowbrook's innovative educational programs and other things they believe make the school special:

- Meadowbrook's commitment to improving all students' language skills by teaching Latin and French beginning in the sixth grade

- Meadowbrook's decision to teach math one grade level ahead of the local public schools so that Meadowbrook kids will be better prepared for the rigors of advanced-placement high school math courses

- Meadowbrook's program of encouraging social interaction among older and younger kids (something Marty and Karen feel has been largely and sadly lost in most schools), by having middle-schoolers work with younger kids both in and out of the classroom, and

- Meadowbrook's budget week in Paris, open to all eighth-graders who pass a French proficiency exam

The next step in creating a press package is to use their short list as the framework to explain how Meadowbrook's unusual programs result in a top-quality learning experience. Marty and Karen flesh out each of the items on their list and add supporting facts, including how well Meadowbrook students score on standardized tests and the high percentage who go on to succeed in high school and college. Finally, they obtain favorable quotes about Meadowbrook from prominent local educators.

When the materials are finally done, Marty and Karen send them to Marybeth, the education reporter for the biggest area newspaper. Marybeth is immediately interested in the highly unusual Latin program and wants more information about how and why it helps Meadowbrook students develop superior language skills. In fact, she concludes it's such a novel approach she uses it as the centerpiece for a very favorable feature story about Meadowbrook's innovative but rigorous learning environment. Within days, the school receives more new student applications than there are slots available, allowing Marty and Karen to drop their proposed ads into the recycling box and spend the ad money on repainting two classrooms.

Don't invite media scrutiny if you have something to hide.

Unless your enterprise really is well run, media coverage is not the best way of getting publicity. Because negative stories sell just as many newspapers as positive ones, reporters won't shy from printing or airing any not-so-glowing aspects of your business. Also, before you invite the press in, give a thought to your reputation in the community. As discussed in Chapter 14, Embrace Your Best Competitors, reporters are likely to check your business out with prominent people in your field.

Figuring out how to get media coverage is only one way to get your business's name out without advertising. Here are some others.

Sponsor nonprofit activities. Supporting youth sports or arts groups, as well as community-based health, education, or environmental activities, to mention just a few possibilities, helps your business make friends. Often, for a surprisingly small dollar amount, you can receive good publicity from associating your business with a good cause at the same time you and your employees feel positive about helping your community. For example, when a deli sponsors "Two Legs for Four Legs," an annual 10K run with proceeds going to a local animal rescue center, many people in the community hear about it.

Participate in local events. Street fairs, cultural and historical celebrations and parades, little league parades, and dozens of other community activities afford you effective and fun ways to promote your business. Encourage your employees to add a dash of creativity to the usual plain-vanilla presentation and you can reach lots of people for a low cost and have fun doing it.

Example:

Dr. Price, a children's dentist, sponsors the Walruses, a local little league team, whose symbol is, no surprise, a huge tusk. Each year, when the Walruses are invited to march in the parade, Dr. Price makes a huge plaster-of-Paris walrus tusk. The day before the parade, the third-graders on his team decorate it, using paint, sticky paper, colored band-aids and other fun stuff.

On the big morning, the tusk is placed on the bed of Dr. Price's appropriately decorated pickup truck, which then leads the team dressed in their walrus tusk team t-shirts in the parade. The result is that the kids, as well as Dr. Price and his staff, who supervise the decorating process, have a great time. And if, in their march along Main Street, Dr. Price recruits a few new patients, so much the better.

Become a source of trusted information. It can be an extremely valuable business asset to be known as a source of high-quality unbiased information. For example, a plumber, optician, or veterinarian who publishes and updates a series of free handouts designed to help people troubleshoot predictable problems and, if possible, solve them on their own, will soon gain respect among customers, peers, and the local media. This positive reputation will grow in direct proportion to how unbiased the information is.

Marketing to Your Target Audience

Whatever methods you decide on to promote your business, you've obviously got to aim them in the right direction to get the maximum benefit.

To do that, you should first identify as many discrete groups of potential customers as possible, then rank them with those most likely to patronize your business at the top. (This process is explained in Chapter 7, Target Your Customers.) You'll not only want to concentrate your marketing efforts on these top-ranked groups, but you'll do best if you feature the goods or services most in demand, not less-desirable products you are trying to get rid of. For some types of businesses—for example, a hardware store that sells to casual consumers, serious do-it-yourself remodelers, and professional contractors—ranking customers and the products each group is most likely to purchase means engaging in a fairly complicated, data-heavy process. For others, including consultants and other businesspeople who provide a niche service to a relatively small clientele, it will be easy to list the few groups of potential customers at the center of the customer target.

Go with the winners.

Too many businesses, big and small, feature the wrong products —ones that used to do well, but are now fading, or items someone mistakenly ordered too many of. Far better to concentrate most of your marketing efforts on your biggest winners, while dumping the losers at or below cost. Think of it this way—it's far easier to sell an extra 10,000 tickets to a popular ball game than it is to sell 5,000 more when the last place team is in town.

Example:

Here is a marketing target for an accountant who specializes in providing services to authors, musicians, inventors, and others who sell intellectual property.

Once you have identified your most likely groups of customers and what they are most likely to buy, you are ready to figure out how to reach them as effectively as possible. If your universe is relatively small, as would be the case for the accounting business discussed above, your best approach is usually a personal marketing effort. For example, if a half-dozen agents represent most of the well-known authors in your area, getting to know them personally and educating them about your expertise would be a good start. After all, a prominent agent who appreciates that you understand all the tax ramifications of the many ways royalty deals can be structured (and even better, if you are available to advise the agent on structuring deals), is in a great position to recommend you to many others. Similarly, local publishers and support groups for inventors, musicians, and writers are excellent venues through which to get the word out to many potential clients.

If your potential customer universe is both bigger and more diverse, you will want to consider more public ways to market your goods or services. Again, depending on the type of business, these might appropriately include:

- Events. A sporting goods store sponsors a 10K run; a restaurant heads an annual food-for-the-homeless drive.

- Tie-ins. An orthodontist sponsors a kids' soccer team; a plant nursery becomes leads an effort to restore the town's neglected rose garden.

- Coupons. A music store works with a classical music radio station to distribute discount coupons to listeners.

- Free media. A general contractor who runs a house inspection business self-publishes a small book and quarterly newsletter explaining such topics as what to look for, how not to get ripped off, and how to make needed repairs as frugally as possible. He widely distributes these for free through local real estate offices, lenders, and at several annual home-buyers' fairs. This helps establish his credentials with local media outlets, where he is regularly interviewed and quoted.

9

Hire and Keep Good People

"I not only use all the brains I have, but all I can borrow."

—Woodrow Wilson

Use these techniques even if you don't have employees.

If yours is a one-person business, you may be tempted to skip this chapter. Please don't. Sole operators depend on many personal relationships—with suppliers, vendors, and freelancers—and the best techniques for working with these people are very similar to the ones that successfully motivate and manage employees.

A highly competent and truly enthusiastic employee can be at least three times more valuable than a person of average skills. Yes, this is a huge difference, but it's one we all recognize. Think for a moment about whose line you queue up in at your local supermarket. If you're like me, you prefer being number four in the best checker's line to being number two in the worst one's. And, of course, the more skills and training a job requires, the greater the spread between the work of an average and excellent employee. While it may be difficult for the fastest checker to scan groceries at more than twice the speed of the slowest, an excellent software designer, architect, or salesperson can perform many times better than a sub par performer. Of course, it follows that to retain and motivate and star performers, you need to appropriately reward them. Fortunately, you should have the economic wherewithal to do so, since even if you double the pay of an employee who is several times more productive than average, you still come out far ahead.

Your goal should be to hire and retain truly excellent employees—not reasonably competent ones. I know from experience why it is so important to do this. Nolo has grown and thrived for almost 35 years in large part because of the efforts of the capable, productive, and creative employees we have attracted. There are several key reasons why we have been able to assemble such an excellent staff. Certainly one of the biggest is that people are drawn to Nolo's mission to help people with legal problems who can't afford or don't want to patronize lawyers. But at least as important, Nolo has learned to do two key things. First, we follow a thorough recruitment and hiring process designed to sift through many applicants and pluck out the best people. And second, we pay lots of attention to the positive management techniques designed to keep day-to-day workplace enthusiasm high and employee turnover low.

Nolo wasn't always good either at hiring or managing people in ways that would help them succeed in our workplace. In our early years, our employee recruitment practices were often haphazard and management nonexistent. Sometimes we hired the best friend or roommate of an existing employee rather than searching for the best candidate. Often we were lucky and hired wonderful people who, despite the lack of training, figured out how to get the work done. But occasionally, we ended up with a real dud—someone whose poor work habits or lack of skills subtracted significantly from both Nolo's overall productivity and our ongoing feeling of group well-being. Clearly, our lives would have been easier and our bank accounts fatter if we had learned earlier to hire smarter, manage better, and to more quickly cut loose our disappointments.

Before getting into the details of how to create your own excellent hiring and management processes that will net you a happy, hardworking, and creative workforce, let me focus on several common hiring errors. For some reason, hiring is an area where a great many new entrepreneurs make exactly the same mistakes.

Don't Hire Casually

Too often, small business owners, hire friends, relatives, friends of friends or sometimes even people whose main credential seems to be that they are standing on the doorstep when another body is needed. Although some of these people may make wonderful employees, you'll almost always do better to create and stick to a structured hiring process. If, after careful background checking and consideration of all other candidates, a friend, relative, or acquaintance emerges as the best choice, great. (More on this in "Avoid Nepotism, Not Relatives," below.) But don't make the decision without clearheaded analysis.

In fact, a huge advantage of establishing a well-thought-out hiring system is that it helps you avoid being pressured into giving jobs to problem relatives and friends. Once the word is out that your business is hiring, all sorts of relatives, friends, and acquaintances are likely to beg for jobs for themselves, for their kids, and sometimes even for an under-performing employee they are trying to get rid of with minimum guilt. If you can honestly say that hiring decisions are made by a hiring committee that has strict instructions to screen every candidate thoroughly, you may not hear anything more from your angry niece Kathryn or your feckless cousin Roger. Without such a system, all the dodging and weaving in the world may not keep them off your payroll.

Example 1:

At a family gathering, you mention your decision to hire a financial manager. The next day your brother-in-law calls to forcefully recommend his close friend Elizabeth. Ten minutes later Elizabeth faxes her résumé and then calls to ask for a meeting. Since, at least on paper, she has the qualifications you are looking for, you agree to interview her. Impressed by Elizabeth's energy and your brother-in-law's thrice-repeated recommendation, you hire her after making only a cursory check of her references. Only later do you learn that Elizabeth (who your brother-in-law never tells you he continued to date even after he met your sister) is in the throes of a midlife emotional crisis and is about to be fired from her present job because she has trouble getting along with other employees.

Finally, six months later, with your books in a mess and your stress level off the charts (and the growing suspicion your sister married an idiot), you fire Elizabeth. Alleging that you have not reasonably accommodated her mental problems, Elizabeth promptly calls a lawyer who threatens to sue you for violating the Americans With Disabilities Act. Your own lawyer says that although Elizabeth doesn't have a decent case, it will cost you at least $25,000 to prove it. After much teeth-grinding, you accept his recommendation to settle for $10,000.

Now let's take a look at this same scenario, but this time add a hiring committee that has real power to make decisions.

Example 2:

When your brother-in-law calls to push his protégé, you truthfully reply that a hiring committee, not you, makes all the decisions and that you never try to influence it based on personal consider- ations (you probably won't even need to admit that you are a member of the committee). Now when Elizabeth calls, you politely respond that you don't talk to candidates outside the committee process. Elizabeth submits her application, as do half a dozen other seemingly qualified candidates. When you conduct a careful background check of each, several, including Elizabeth, are eliminated. In her case, a phone call to a person your sales manager knows, who worked with Elizabeth two jobs ago, is all it takes to uncover the fact she's a high-maintenance employee.

Avoid Nepotism, Not Relatives

Many business commentators advise against hiring any family members, even when they are more qualified than nonrelatives. In my experience, this approach makes little more sense than it does to hire every relative who asks for a job. A significant number of small businesses wouldn't exist, let alone thrive, without the positive energy, hard work, and sacrifices of loyal family members.

What you do want to avoid is nepotism—undue favoritism towards relatives. That, of course, is not the same thing as hiring competent people you happen to be related to and treating them fairly. And don't make the mistake of thinking that when family members are hired favoritism is inevitable. Often, just the opposite is true. Especially when a business is in its start-up phase, it's common for relatives to work harder for less pay and benefits than do nonfamily employees.

To hire competent family members while avoiding the corrosive effects of nepotism, separate the perks of ownership from those of employment. That is, pay people who are related to you (and yourself) exactly the same as you would anyone else doing the same job. Apply the same evenhanded approach when setting schedules, assigning work, and handing out criticism and praise. Take pains to be sure relatives are really being paid and promoted fairly, not based on how close their branch is to yours on the family tree.

Don't Hire Problem Employees

In my experience, about one in 20 American workers comes straight from hell and a like number hail from the same neighborhood. Other employers may make a more or less charitable guesstimate, but anyone with workplace—or for that matter, human—experience will surely agree that rotten employees do exist, and that hiring even one to do an important job risks poisoning your entire workplace.

In *Anna Karenina*, Tolstoy famously wrote, "Happy families are all alike; every unhappy family is unhappy in its own way." The same point can be made about workplaces. Happy ones usually have much in common, including high productivity, a shared sense of purpose, and a reservoir of goodwill large enough to help your business skate over the inevitable bumpy ice. On the other hand, a toxic relationship with even one key employee can make your workplace miserable in myriad ways.

Rather than focusing on the many things bad employees may do wrong—lying, stealing, intimidating others, doing poor work, and trying to cover up mistakes come quickly to mind—let's focus on how you can avoid making bad hires. You'll make a great start if you simply avoid hiring people in the following three categories.

People With Lots of Jobs in a Short Period

Especially for applicants in midlife, a history of frequent job changes is a strong signal that you are considering an applicant you don't want to hire. Every smart employer does two things: goes to great lengths to retain bright, hard-working employees who get along well with others, and tries to get rid of the misfits. It follows that people who have lots of jobs in a short time are likely to have repeatedly proved themselves inadequate. Sure, excellent employees do make career and job changes for good reason, but they rarely do it often. Most people who change jobs frequently fall into one of five undesirable categories:

- They do poor work. Often they put in long hours—often over-long hours, but they simply don't have the discipline, focus, and smarts to do a superior job.

- They are chronically insecure. Often they fight needless turf wars, trying to steal credit, shift blame, or otherwise needlessly and endlessly pissing off their coworkers.

- They steal or are otherwise highly irresponsible.

- They are chronically unhappy (often because personal problems lead them to seek something the workplace can't provide).

- They have substance abuse problems.

People Who Come With a Qualified Recommendation

As I'm sure you know, every job applicant who has ever prepared a résumé attempts to paint as positive a picture as possible. This usually includes a list of respected people prepared—and, frequently, even rehearsed—to provide a glowing recommendation. It follows that if a job applicant's former college teacher or ex-boss provides only faint praise, something is almost always seriously wrong with the person. Often the recommender is trying to avoid fibbing while at the same time trying to be loyal to the applicant.

Listen closely to catch someone who overpraises an applicant's few good qualities while trying to avoid discussing others. It isn't always easy to pick up on key omissions, but with practice and patience, your skills should improve. It's a little like hearing the national anthem sung without one verse—since you expect all the words to be there, you must pay careful attention to notice that a few key ones are missing.

Another common technique employed by recommenders who know a job applicant has serious weaknesses is to simply avoid directly answering a key question. For example, assume you ask, "How did Tammy get along with her coworkers?" Instead of saying "very well" or "mostly well, perhaps with a short list of minor exceptions," suppose Tammy's former boss says, "Tammy is a very bright person who cares so much about what she does we actually found she did best when we gave her a lot of independence."

C'mon, it was a simple question. The fact that you got a politician's non sequitur should tell you all you need to know about Tammy's poor interpersonal skills.

Also listen for someone who tries to put a positive spin on an applicant's negative quality. Say, in answer to the same question about how well an applicant gets along with others, a former boss says, "Joe is an amazing self-starter—an energetic person who regularly gets way out in front of everyone else and can be impossible to catch." Again, pink, if not red, flags should be flying. It's all too likely you are being politely warned that Joe is a loose cannon who, despite having a load of energy and good ideas, is difficult for others to work with.

How to Ask Questions That Will Get You Honest Answers

The more specific your questions, the more likely you are to get valuable information. For example, instead of asking "Was Betty a good employee?" you would do better to ask "How exactly did Betty perform compared to others doing the same work?" Similarly, if you just ask "How did Hector do under pressure?" you'll want to follow up and request an example of how the applicant coped with a specific urgent situation.

To make sure you get all the information you need from a person who knows the applicant, prepare a list of ten or so questions. Some of these, such as asking for the dates during which the applicant worked with (or otherwise knew) the recommender, will always be the same. But others should be modified to fit the job.

If, in the course of checking an applicant's reference, you are told something that seems just a little off, it's up to you to follow up and ask the tough questions necessary to get at the truth. It's my experience that if I spot a missing or qualified part of a recommendation and politely insist on being told the whole story, I'll get much, if not most, of it. Or put another way, when pinned down, many recommenders won't lie.

Example:

Edna, just out of college, applied for a copywriting job with QuickTime, a five-person ad shop. Gordon, QuickTime's owner, called Francis, the college professor Edna listed as a personal reference on her résumé. Before Gordon could even ask a question,

Francis, who seemed pressed for time, quickly said that Edna was bright, intuitive, and a quick study and that he recommended her. Only after a couple of other people at QuickTime read Edna's résumé did someone spot that it had taken her more than six years to graduate. Gordon again called Francis, but this time he insisted on answers to a short list of focused questions, one of which was, "Why did it take Edna two years more than normal to graduate?" When Francis replied that for all her brilliance, Edna sometimes had trouble meeting deadlines, Gordon decided she would not be a good fit at a company that constantly faced them.

People You Don't Like

No matter how faithfully you check a potential employee's educational background, personal skills, personal history, and other key attributes, it's important to understand that the things you won't find out about the person are likely to be at least as important as the things you'll learn. It follows that it's always wise to pay attention to your gut reaction about the person—at the same time that you guard against discriminating against people "not like us." If you, or one of your key employees, have a good reason for experiencing strong doubts about a supposedly diamond-encrusted applicant, it's best to keep interviewing.

How to Hire Top People

Enough worrying about how to avoid mistakes. How do you actually go about hiring excellent employees you can afford? Start by fully accepting the fact that consistently hiring well is a disciplined process with few shortcuts. It usually involves at least seven steps.

Define the Skills You Need

Whether you want to hire someone to set up and run a website, write press releases, clean up hazardous chemicals, restore furniture, or make sandwiches, you need to clearly define the skill set you are looking for. For example, writing compelling press releases requires a person with excellent English composition skills and an understanding of marketing. It's not a job where you want a good salesperson who doesn't know the difference between a comma and a semicolon—or an English major who has no concept of how to pitch an idea. Similarly, if you run a sandwich shop that is super-busy two hours a day, you need sandwich makers who can do a good job super fast. Someone who sees each sandwich as a work of art that must be deliberately put together and presented will be of use to you only if she works for a competitor.

Establish Your Pay and Benefits Package

It's a waste of time to interview people until you have established or announced an appropriate pay range and a list of benefits, and are prepared to answer potential employees' questions about the possibilities for advancement. If you are casual about any aspect of this crucial step, you'll almost always waste time by interviewing people you can't afford to hire, or worse, agree to pay an applicant more than you need to. And remember, as discussed above, paying highly productive people well normally saves money in the long run.

Find the People Who You Don't Have to Train

Your goal is to match productive employees to needed tasks as closely as possible, not necessarily to hire brilliant people. The fact that a potential employee graduated from an Ivy League college, has composed a sonata, or understands knot theory is irrelevant if you want someone to manage a store, sell furniture, or repair computers. And although larger businesses can afford to train inexperienced workers, you don't have this luxury. Your goal should be to hire people who already know how to do the job.

Even if you had time to train people from scratch, it would rarely be a good use of your time. Especially when your business is new, you will personally have to cope with far too many tasks you are ill-equipped to accomplish efficiently. Depending on the field you are in, you may need to choose and order inventory, deal with key customers, keep the books, make sure the quality of your product or service remains high, and do a dozen other things. Unless Clark Kent is your cousin and will lend you his blue and yellow suit, you are unlikely to have the ability or temperament to do all this work well, which also means you'll be ill-equipped to teach others. I know I still feel sorry for people who received boxes of books I packed during Nolo's first year, and even worse for those whose orders were packed by the well-meaning but memory-challenged high school student I hired and tried to train to replace me. But if, instead of simply hiring a warm body, you replace yourself with a person who already knows how to competently perform the needed task, your business should quickly become more productive.

Hire people who can handle the job on their first day.

In Nolo's early days, I frequently made the mistake of hiring intelligent people not trained for the tasks I was asking them to do. I assumed that because the job didn't seem all that hard, they would quickly learn while they worked. Mostly they didn't. Gradually I learned that in the absence of a well-thought-out training and mentoring program, it's a mistake to assume an inexperienced employee will quickly and efficiently figure out how to do a new task. Only when I finally began to insist that new hires be able to do their job from day one, did Nolo's productivity begin to increase.

To find superior people for a decent but still affordable salary, start by identifying appropriate groups of high-quality employees others may overlook. If you don't, you'll usually find yourself sifting through the people left over after more established and better-funded enterprises have done their hiring. Here are several groups in which you may find excellent, affordable employees.

- **People who have been recently laid off by high-quality employers.** When large corporations downsize or move jobs overseas, they often cut big groups of workers with little attention to individual competence. At least some of these well-trained, often well-connected folks will be open to finding steady work in the small business sector, even at reduced pay. For example, a salesperson who represented a major player in your field and got to know buyers at a number of major accounts could be a godsend for your niche start-up. So when you hear about mass layoffs at a big local company, quickly fax your job announcement to their human resources department. You could get very lucky.

- **People who need a flexible work schedule.** Parents with child care responsibilities, people who care for aged parents, part-time students, and part-time retirees are among the many people looking for time-flexible employment. For example, Nolo employs many highly skilled lawyers whose commitment to raising their young children means they are unwilling to cope with the big-firm rat race. Many larger businesses can't or won't bend their rigid work rules to accommodate these people; if you can, you'll increase your chances of hiring a top-notch person at a reasonable salary. Listing our legal jobs at college placement offices and with parent-support organizations are among the best ways to reach these highly skilled job seekers.

- **Recent immigrants who are learning English or speak with an accent. Look especially for people who have a strong educational background or good on-the-job training in their native country.** Nonprofit groups that work with immigrants are often an excellent source of referrals.

- **People with the skill to do the job, but without the formal education or professional certifications typically required.** For example, at Nolo we need editors with excellent writing skills who are knowledgeable about the legal system. Some of these people have active law licenses, but since we don't deliver individualized legal advice, this isn't essential. We can increase our applicant pool by considering people who are knowledgeable about the law but who have not passed a bar examination—for example, a consumer educator or experienced paralegal.

Give All Candidates a Practical Test

If you're hiring a store clerk, you need someone who can quickly and competently operate your pay-point cash and credit systems. If you're a delivery person, you need a driver who can safely operate your truck and navigate through the area you serve.

At Nolo, we have developed skills tests for a number of our jobs. For example, two experienced legal editors treat every editorial department application as if it were a formal test. They grade each letter and résumé for clarity, organization, and grammar. Only if the applicant scores well do we move on to the next stage, which involves asking the person to come to Nolo to take a more formal test, which usually consists of editing a couple of pages of garbled syntax. Similarly, people who will check over computer code are asked to sit down at a computer and swat some bugs. Occasionally the person who comes across best at an interview also does best when confronted with the real tasks to be done but, at least as often, a less verbal person shines. If you don't thoroughly test job applicants, you may end up hiring the talkers, not the doers.

Check References and Nonreferences

It is essential to talk to people who know the applicant's work, but are not listed on his or her résumé. Fortunately, finding these folks can be surprisingly easy. Look carefully at where the applicant has worked, volunteered, or gone to school, and think about who you know who might have known the applicant in one of these places. If you can't come up with a direct connection, think about people in your extended business or social network who might be able to help. More often than not, the folk wisdom that holds everyone in the U.S. is linked by no more than three phone calls turns out to be true.

Don't set much store by what a current employer says. In an age when many employers are terrified to fire problem employees, lest they be sued, it has become popular to get rid of even the rottenest of apples by helping them find a new job. To do this, many employers provide sub par and even some terrible workers with positive references. This explains why it's usually not only a waste of time—but often counterproductive—to talk to anyone in authority at a company where a job applicant currently works. You're far more likely to get an unvarnished story by talking to a previous employer, who is far less likely to be motivated to shade the truth.

Of course, there are exceptions to the rule. For example, when a job applicant leaves a job for an obviously good reason, such as to move across country with a spouse or as part of a major career change, a current employer may give the straight scoop. But even then you'll want to get a second and third opinion, preferably from people not listed on the applicant's résumé.

Example:

John plans to open a company to refurbish museum-quality antiques. To succeed, he needs an experienced sales manager who can work easily with his anticipated clientele of collectors, gallery owners, and museum curators. After listing the job in several industry publications, John gets an application from Evie, a woman with both an MBA and ten years' sales experience at a prominent auction house specializing in antiques. Concerned only that Evie seems almost too perfect to be true, John remembers that José, a business acquaintance, used to work for the auction company. José, it turns out, doesn't know Evie, but offers to call Ann, an executive at the auction company, who does. When Ann whispers that Evie is great on the days she is sober, John sensibly decides to keep looking.

Include Coworkers in Interviews

People who will work closely with a job applicant have as big a stake in detecting and eliminating slackers as you do. Whether your business is fixing cars, publishing a newsletter, or selling salami, make sure that at least some of the people who will work with your new hire participate in the interview process. Employees who have participated in selecting a new employee are far more motivated to work well with that person than with a new person who suddenly parachutes into their work group from on high.

Learn from job applicants.

No question, interviewing a number of job applicants can be an exhausting task. One way to make it better is to assume that at least some of the applicants have information or skills you or your company doesn't have. Structure your interview to bring this information to the surface, and you may be pleasantly surprised to find that even some job applicants you don't hire can teach you how to improve your business.

Schedule an Early Review

For all but the most senior jobs, you'll want to make it clear that the employee will receive an evaluation after the first 30 to 90 days of work. If someone turns out not to be a good fit, it's far easier to make a change early on rather than after the person has settled in. But if you adopt this approach, do not describe the employee as temporary or probationary, since this might imply that the person attains the right to long-term, if not lifetime, employment after the initial period is over.

Know and follow employment law.

Federal and state laws prohibit discrimination against job seekers and employees for many reasons, including race, religion, natural origin, age, and sex. This is as it should be. But employment laws also contain needless technicalities that can easily trip the honest but unwary. For example, if you ask for an applicant's college graduation date, you have probably violated age discrimination laws, since this can be seen as a stealthy way to determine the person's age. Fortunately, it's relatively easy to learn how to stay out of trouble by understanding and adopting good hiring and employee management practices. *The Employer's Legal Handbook*, by Fred S. Steingold (Nolo), is an excellent primer for small business owners. Also check out the free information in the employment section of Nolo's online legal encyclopedia at www.nolo.com.

Keeping the Great People You Hire

If you've got a boring, poorly organized, or joyless workplace, don't bother trying to hire highly talented, energetic, and productive people—they won't stay long. In fact, hiring them may even be counterproductive if they defect to a competitor or start their own competing businesses.

Even laying aside these fears, you don't want to lose experienced employees. Just as it will take many small business owners three to five years to really hit their stride, top-notch employees, even those who can do skilled work from their first day, will become more valuable every month they work for you. Not only does building a veteran workforce mean you'll get more mistake-free work done, but each of your long-term workers will build a valuable mental database of useful information about your products or services, customers, coworkers, and suppliers. As long as these people continue in your employ, this knowledge remains at your service. If they move on, you lose everything they know.

For example, at Nolo we hire legal editors, most of them lawyers who can explain legal rules in plain English (a rare combination, admittedly), to edit and often write our new titles. Even though we use a rigorous screening and testing process to hire highly skilled people who can immediately do good work, we've found that, on average, it takes about 18 months before a new editor can do the job without at least some mentoring from a more senior editor. And it typically takes even longer for a new editor to gain enough knowledge about a wide range of Nolo products to fully catch up with their more experienced peers. It follows that Nolo has a huge interest in hanging on to people who go through this extended apprenticeship.

To fully appreciate how valuable it is to keep good employees for as long as possible, think about your own relationships with local businesses. If you are like me, you enjoy dealing with the same competent people year after year, and can become frustrated when familiar faces (or even familiar voices) are replaced by new ones. It's no fun to deal with someone who is obviously learning on the job. More than once I've gone elsewhere when I realized that, as a longtime customer, I knew more about the task than the poorly trained novice employee who was trying to do it.

So how do you go about keeping an extremely productive employee working for you as long as possible? At a time when most Americans will have many jobs during their working lives, the key is to focus on the words "as long as possible." For example, if you run a take-out food business, you may achieve a real victory if you keep the college kids who work the counter and drive the delivery vans for a year. On the other hand, you may be able to hang on to your bookkeeper and night manager for a decade or more. The point is that if you can keep the best short-termers for a year or two instead of six months and provide a career path that will keep top-notch long-termers loyal for many years, you'll get a huge gain in productivity.

Treat—and Pay—People Fairly

"Fairness" is the best one-word prescription for keeping employees loyal to your business. Workers who believe your business can be trusted to treat them equitably are likely to be loyal; those who feel they are in untrustworthy hands are almost sure to move on. Thus the absolute size of a person's pay packet will have less to do with loyalty, than will their subjective belief that are being compensated fairly. This explains why investment bankers, corporate lawyers, and executives who make six- or even seven-figure salaries are at least as likely to quit in a huff as is a truck driver, tile layer, or office worker.

And, of course, it isn't only money that's important to retain good workers. It's also critical to establish and follow a set of employment policies that are understandable, consistent, evenhanded, and which, above all, your employees regard as being fair. What do I mean by fair? Basically, that your business uses objective criteria—not your whim or pique—to hand out rewards and punishments. For example, if you promote your lazy cousin over a long-term, experienced employee, you risk convincing everyone in the company that you can't be trusted to be equitable. But if you adopt a merit-based system of promotion and stick to it, even though it means your cousin doesn't get the promotion (and may even be laid off), you go far towards reassuring all employees that they will be treated fairly. True, your aunt may snub you at the next family gathering, but that's a price you'll have to pay to run a business your employees will respect.

When it comes to pay, employees normally use three key factors to judge whether they are being fairly treated:

- **How much similar jobs in your area pay.** Especially for highly productive people who receive $10 to $12 per hour or less, it's essential to pay more than your competitors do. If you don't, those penny-conscious employees are sure to feel slighted and move on, with the predictable result that you'll quickly be left with a stable of the slow, difficult, and depressed. Unfortunately, most small employers never grasp this lesson. Thus in most businesses the sales clerk who works twice as fast as the norm gets the same pay as the others. Again, as emphasized at the beginning of this chapter, it's far better for employee retention, overall productivity, and workplace happiness to significantly raise the pay of your most productive employee and look to hire more like her.

- **How much others with comparable skills are paid in your company.** Your employees will have no trouble accepting substantial pay disparities as long as in their eyes they reflect real differences in skill, training, seniority, and job responsibilities. But dissatisfaction will quickly surface if employees conclude that one person or group receives substantially better pay or perks for no honest reason—or worse, for a bad reason. This is not the place to tackle the details of complicated pay equity issues, such as differing pay rates for different departments, individual vs. across-the-board raises, and overtime for some job categories and not others. But it is important to grasp just how essential it is even for employers with just a handful of employees to create logical, understandable, and defensible pay policies and modify them only when objective new factors require it.

- **How much the boss's pay and perks are.** As I discuss in detail in Chapter 10, Drive a Modest Car, even if your business becomes highly successful, it's important that you not offend your employees by showering yourself with money and perks. True, you can try to pay yourself lavishly and try to keep it secret, but unless you are married to your bookkeeper, it won't be easy.

Purpose

As discussed in detail in Chapter 1, successful small businesses are almost always imbued with a sense of purpose. Their owners understand and respect the fact that most of their employees and contractors yearn to find meaning in their work. There are several tried-and-true methods to help your employees believe in the value of their work. But no amount of cheerleading will work unless your employees believe you really do run a high-quality operation. For example, if you claim your café serves the freshest baked goods in town but your employees know you occasionally slip a few day-old muffins in with today's batch, you'll need to change your ways before you'll get any traction trying to convince them your business is special.

But assuming you do run a quality operation, helping your employees create and participate in a larger vision will go far towards cementing their loyalty. I'm reminded of a veterinarian who not only ran the cleanest, most efficient animal care operation in town, but also carved out the hours necessary to allow employees to participate in a variety of free animal rescue and support activities. As a result of this altruism, the vet attracted a terrific crew of animal-loving employees, people who were so pleased to be part of a committed business that many of them stuck around for years.

You may be thinking that while your business is meaningful to you, it doesn't have an obvious and easy-to-communicate larger purpose. Nonsense. Just as it's up to you to create a superior business along the lines discussed in Chapter 1, Build a Meaningful Business, it's your job to help all your employees see that their individual roles are important. Whether you run a gas station, flower stand, or a gene-splicing boutique makes no difference as long as you communicate your sense of purpose to the people you work with. Here are some examples of how this can be done.

- A small manufacturer that hand-makes custom wooden windows using only the highest grades of wood and the best woodworking techniques teaches its employees how to educate customers as to why this results in a far better, more long-lasting product than can be purchased at a big box building supply store. To this end, the company develops a video showing employees carefully making the windows and before-and-after shots of installations.

- A business that imports large glazed clay planters from Thailand all but adopts the Thai villagers who make the pots. Not only do customers learn where and how the planters are made, they have a chance to make a small contribution to a fund to benefit the village school where workers' kids are educated. Although the company itself makes the largest contribution to the fund, it is administered by employee volunteers on their own time. Each year the business pays the most senior employee who hasn't already made the trip to go to Thailand and spend a week hanging out with the pot makers.

- A real estate broker not only helps people buy and sell their houses, but encourages its agents and employees to take time to help buyers get acclimated to their new neighborhood. Among the business's initiatives is a get-to-know-the-neighborhood booklet (also available online) in which employees tell new-comers their favorite places to shop, recreate, and play. One feature that often draws critical acclaim is called "How to spend a perfect day within a few miles of home."

- A neighborhood restaurant not only serves an innovative break-fast and lunch menu, but publishes a small cookbook containing 100 favorite meals. The book, created with input from employees (and containing plenty of pictures of the whole crew), is sold both at the restaurant and at several local bookshops. With costs of production underwritten by the restaurant, all profits go to purchase food for the homeless.

- A local body and fender shop works in a variety of ways to promote auto safety. Each year the garage runs a raffle to raise money for a safe driving course taught at a local high school and several senior centers. Several employees of the garage who have been appropriately trained are given paid time off to help give the courses.

Mentor New Employees

Some businesses do almost everything right during the hiring process: they reach out to good people, interview them, screen them, test them, and hire them. And then, after some cursory training, they assume that the new employee knows all aspects of the job. Especially if you follow my advice and hire a skilled person, this approach can work, after a fashion. But a sink-or-swim philosophy can also leave new hires feeling adrift. Thinking that they are expected to be fully competent in all aspects of the job, they may be hesitant to ask questions, and as a result be prone to making mistakes. They may also feel that the company doesn't care much about their personal growth or their contribution to the business.

You can avoid or at least reduce these problems by making sure that every new employee—no matter how experienced—has a mentor, someone who helps guide the new person's development within the company. A mentor isn't necessarily a supervisor, but should pay attention to both the new hire's progress and any problems that crop up.

Mentoring doesn't have to be a formal process, as long as an experienced person is asked to look after the new employee. It can be a great help with making sure that new hires are comfortable in the company and get the training and feedback they need to do a good job.

Making people welcome and comfortable is more important than you might think. Although you probably regard your small business as a friendly place, it's probably also a very busy one, where employees don't always have time to reach out to new folks. That's why it's so valuable to have a mentor who can answer questions, provide background about how the business works ("institutional knowledge"), and see that the new employee is getting the tools, time, and information necessary to do the job.

Good training is all about the employee, not all about the employer.

At Nolo we believe it's our job to help every employee improve her skills to the point that should she ever leave us to find a new job, she'll be prepared to take a step up. One way we do this is to have everyone who trains a new employee keep the focus on the trainee. Do this by having the trainer ask, "What does the new person need to learn, not what do I need to teach?"

Appreciate Your Employees

It's simple, really: Employees strive to do even better when they know their hard work and creative contributions are noticed. Those whose good work isn't acknowledged are likely to look for jobs where they feel their efforts will be better appreciated.

Whether you have 5, 55 or 105 employees, I strongly encourage you to develop your own employee appreciation program. But to make sure your program really will be welcomed by your employees, it's best to create it with their input. If you don't, you risk adopting a plan that will be ignored or, far worse, resented—for example, if your well-meaning plan to recognize creative work by paying bonuses is seen as a cynical ploy to make your overworked employees put in extra hours.

Example:

Jan decided that a great way to reward hard work and increase sales was to create a salesperson-of-the-quarter award, with the winner getting a trip for two to Hawaii. Consulting no one, she called a company meeting and proudly announced the detailed rules of this new program. Too bad that Jan hadn't realized that the rules she announced favored the three salespeople with the best territories, and in consequence angered several others who worked in less productive areas and saw the whole program as a backhanded way to tell them they weren't producing enough. Even worse, Jan didn't create a parallel award for the office staff and other support personnel who processed the orders, shipped the goods, collected the bills, and did other essential work to allow the sales staff to succeed.

Fortunately for Jan, a longtime employee soon marched into her office to forcefully explain that everyone, save the three already highly compensated salespeople, was offended by her plan. Reluctantly acknowledging her mistake, Jan cancelled the program after the first three months and set up an employee committee to recommend a way to use the same amount of bonus money to provide incentives to everyone. To Jan's surprise, the committee proposed that whenever the entire business exceeded its quarterly sales goal, $1,500 would be used for a dinner party at a nice restaurant to which everyone in the company and their spouses or significant others would be invited. These events turned out to be so welcome that everyone, from the senior employees to the high school kid who helped with filing, began paying close attention to weekly sales totals.

In addition to involving your employees in helping you create appropriate ways to appreciate them, let me suggest a second principle that has served Nolo well. When thanking people for good work, be as inclusive as possible. Don't recognize or reward just the most visible person or even the person who has led a particular effort. Acknowledge everyone who contributed to the good work you are recognizing and honoring. For instance, in the example above, the thing that really made Jan's reward program fun was that it included everyone, even the high school kid, who proudly brought the boyfriend she normally complained about.

Finally, it's best to keep your appreciation efforts simple and sincere. Often a public thank-you at a company meeting or via email, or a nice lunch with a key person or small group is more welcome than a chance to participate in a more complicated rewards program. A big reason for this is that many rewards programs are designed (or at least are perceived to be designed) to influence or even manipulate employees' future behavior, rather than to simply acknowledge their good work. While crafting clever incentive plans to coax employees to work harder or smarter may occasionally work, they are just plain awful ways to recognize and appreciate good work. Just think about how good you feel if a spouse or friend says something like, "Thanks for cooking such a great meal—I really appreciated it." And how you would feel if the same person said, "You know, if you would just cook this well for the next two weeks, I'd take you out to dinner."

Further reading on rewarding employees for good work.

A number of publications contain good ideas on how to recognize employees' good work. One I like, *1001 Ways to Reward Employees*, by Bob Nelson (Workman), provides a comprehensive list of awards, rewards, and other techniques to let employees know that their contributions are important. While few of them will fit your business exactly, reading this little book should jump-start your thinking.

Have Fun

Not enough businesses encourage their employees to enjoy themselves. Some sobersided owners simply don't understand the value of creating an environment where employees have permission to enjoy themselves. It's as if they really believe the old saying, "If work was supposed to be fun, it wouldn't be called work." Other entrepreneurs act as if they believe fun is subversive and will undermine productivity.

To cut through this neo-Puritanism and quickly understand how actually encouraging workers to enjoy themselves can be a powerful motivator, consider Southwest Airlines, which in most years is the world's most profitable air carrier. In addition to charging low prices and providing reliable, if somewhat spartan services, Southwest is surely the world's largest corporation that actually encourages its employees to enjoy themselves. Cabin attendants tell jokes, ticket agents dress up in holiday costumes, and even pilots have been known to tell one-liners. How effective is this unique company culture? Almost alone among all the world's major airlines, which are constantly beset by strike threats from angry unions, Southwest enjoys relatively harmonious relations with its employees. And its customers are so loyal it was the only large U.S.-based airline not to reduce flights after the horrors of September 2001.

Just how well Southwest's work-with-a-smile policy works to create a positive bond with both customers and employees came home to me a couple of years ago when I happened to fly Southwest on Halloween. Entering the Albuquerque, New Mexico, airport, early that morning, I walked past half a dozen other airline counters to get to Southwest. Several ignored the day entirely, while others displayed a sparse sprinkling of tacky dime-store decorations. United, for example, could muster only cutouts of three pumpkins, one ghost and two mangy black cats that looked like they had been stuffed into a closet since last year. My five-year-old grandkid could have done better in half an hour.

Then, towards the end of the row of counters, I spotted a cornucopia of color and creativity totally transforming the ticketing area. Although the sign was partially covered by a huge pumpkin, I knew it had to be Southwest. And not only were walls overflowing with handcrafted displays, behind the counter everyone was decked out in colorful costumes.

As you might expect, Southwest's employees dressed as Elvis, Captain Hook, and Diana Ross were enjoying a high-spirited morning, a feeling that was immediately transferred to their customers. Instead of looking anxious and impatient, customers in line were smiling, pointing, and talking to each other. And when they finally got to the front of the line to check their bags, everyone had something nice to say to the people behind the counter. A few minutes later, as I walked smiling and almost relaxed towards my plane, I understood once again why Southwest's decision to encourage its employees to do their jobs seriously and well, but also to enjoy themselves at work, is one important reason why it is so successful.

Okay, I'm sure you get my point that fun and enthusiasm will increase productivity, not subtract from it. But even if no more widgets are made, or whatchamacallits sold, encouraging people to smile can help create camaraderie and long-term loyalty to your business that are all but impossible to replicate in other ways.

Since workplace environments vary so much, no one can give you a 100% effective list of ways to encourage employees to enjoy themselves. But fortunately, writing a prescription for fun isn't necessary. All you need do is send the occasional message it's okay for employees to enjoy themselves, and then get out of the way and let it happen. Often the best way to do this is to loosen up a bit yourself. For example, if on St. Patrick's Day, you come to work dressed as a leprechaun, people will likely get the idea.

Here are a few of the things that I've found work to establish an upbeat workplace tone. Like many smart approaches to life, many are as simple as they are commonsensical.

Food. Sharing food is probably the most basic way to build community. If you occasionally bring in some treats (homemade is best), others will, too. Be sure that when this happens everyone in your business has a few minutes to enjoy the gift. If this means that you sometimes spell the person who answers the phone, do it with a smile.

Birthdays. Families celebrate one another's important milestones. Businesses smart enough to treat the people who work for them as part of a workplace family do, too. Keep a calendar of employee birthdays and remember to do a few little things (balloons and a cake may be corny, but they always work) to honor the birthday person. In businesses with more than a dozen employees, combine birthdays and have one party every month or two.

Hats, shirts, and other tchotchkes. At Nolo we have a long tradition of occasionally giving our employees Nolo t-shirts, baseball caps, coffee mugs, and other little gifts. (Our "Don't Feed the Lawyers" t-shirt has become so popular we've also sold over a thousand in our retail store.) Recently, we distributed press-on tattoos featuring our logo shark. Everyone—most especially our younger employees—was delighted.

You're doing fine if employees wear their company shirt.

I can pretty well judge the mood at Nolo by how many of our employees voluntarily choose to wear the Nolo logo shirts, caps, vests, and other paraphernalia we periodically pass out. If I don't see many for a week or two, I know something is bothering people.

Wall decorations. Taking the trouble to put framed prints or other tasteful decorations on the walls is a great way to tell both employees and customers that you take pride in your workplace. This costs very few dollars, but is well worth it in many ways. For example, if an impressed visitor tells your employee, "Wow, it's really nice here, you're lucky to work in such a cool place," obviously you have received a huge dividend on your investment.

Parties and picnics. Now and then it's a great morale-builder to invite everyone to a fun off-site party or other social event. There are many ways to do this, from the ubiquitous summer picnic and winter holiday party to all sorts of less-usual events. For example, at Nolo we usually hold an annual Play Day. We close the entire business for a day and all go to a local park to hang out with each other (no spouses or kids are allowed). A committee of employees helps design the day's activities. Often each Nolo department comes up with a wacky game for everyone to play. For example, our design group might divide the rest of the company into eight teams, giving each a pile of objects including colored paper, string, glue, a couple of vegetables, and a golf ball. Each group is then given ten minutes to create the funniest book cover. Of course, there are silly prizes for the winners.

Other popular Nolo events have included the Pet Parade. Held in the parking lot as part of a lunchtime potluck, everyone is invited to show off their willing pets, from dogs to doves and cats to iguanas. Of course, there are many goofy prizes for stupid pet tricks, pets that look most like their owner, and so on. One year, my three-legged tortoise won a prize for taking the longest to jump over a three foot barrier. (We waited ten minutes before saying "what the hell" and awarding the prize.)

And our famous No-Talent Show. Like many businesses, Nolo has talented painters and filmmakers working in our warehouse, musicians in customer service and accounting, and dancers in the marketing department. For fun, though, we prefer to occasionally level the playing field and encourage every ham in the company to participate in our No-Talent Show. Last time, a big favorite was a chorus line of body-part wigglers— employees who could twitch ears and noses, and turn double joints inside out.

I'm sure you get the idea, so I will spare you the details of our Halloween party, holiday gift exchange, and other events, some of the best of which are spontaneous.

■

10

Drive a Modest Car

"Success has made failures of many men."

—Cindy Adams

In a small business, where you and your employees will almost inevitably work together, you have a choice: Conduct yourself as a team player who demonstrates respect for the judgment of coworkers and leads by example, or as the big boss who rules by edict and doesn't pull a fair share of the load. It's my strong belief that everyone associated with your enterprise will be happier and your business more productive if you adopt the posture of leader, not dominator. Without attempting to list all the psychological reasons why this is true, it should be enough to point out that American traditions are democratic and majoritarian, not autocratic and imperious. At all levels of our society, leaders who work hard and are in touch with ordinary people command loyalty and respect.

Those who dress up in a fancy uniform and mount a white horse often find themselves riding alone.

Drive a Modest Car

In the United States, the formal class structures common even in other affluent nations are absent, and even the rich claim to be part of the middle class. But many affluent people buy expensive things they don't need in part to signal that they are nevertheless somehow above the herd. And the more luxuries they flaunt, the more it annoys many of those who are less affluent. This desire to one-up the Joneses is so much a part of our national psyche that advertisers repeatedly depict the smug suburban homeowner who purchases a new car, snowblower or, even better, grass seed and then sits back to watch the neighbors seethe with envy. Exaggerated? Certainly, but nevertheless we all notice the kind of cars our friends (and especially our foes) drive, how fancy their houses are, and whether they adorn themselves with expensive clothing and jewelry.

It isn't just social acquaintances who judge each other by their possessions. For better or worse, your employees, suppliers, and even your customers will also pay close attention to the goods and toys with which you surround yourself. And again, given America's deep puritan and egalitarian roots, the more ostentatious you are, the more harshly they are likely to judge you. Should you doubt this, ask yourself which of the two business owners briefly profiled below is more likely to be popular with coworkers:

- **Fred.** Flies first class, drives a big Mercedes, wears a $3,000 watch, and owns lots of flashy electronic toys and top-of-the-line sports equipment. Fred always eats at pricey restaurants and makes no secret of his stock market successes and how much he spends on exotic vacations.

- **Fredericka.** Flies coach, drives a Honda Accord, wears a sensible watch and wedding band, and plays golf at the local public links. Fredericka eats wherever the food tastes good, sometimes leaves work an hour early to volunteer with one of several community organizations she is involved with, and keeps both her investment successes and how much she spends on her holidays to herself.

If your answer is Fred, go buy that 12-cylinder Jaguar you have been lusting for and skip the rest of this chapter. If you work very hard at your business, treat your employees well, and have a bit of luck, you may overcome the seeds of resentment your showy behavior is sure to engender. But, if you prefer Fredericka, you're already on the right track towards understanding why it makes sense in the workplace, at least, to curb your more ostentatious habits.

Now let's add a few facts. Assume that Fredericka takes home a larger paycheck than Fred does, and that she quietly spends some of her money on luxuries—a second home in the mountains, foreign travel and a rare book collection. Who wins the popularity contest now? Again, of course, it's Fredericka, something that won't change as long as Fred drives that big Benz and brags about buying Microsoft in '89. Point made, I hope, that it's conspicuous consumption—not financial success—that rankles.

One morning when this book was about to go to press, I opened the newspaper and a prominent headline jumped out at me from the first page of the second section: "S.F. schools chief treats herself to sporty $33,000 Chrysler." The story detailed how the superintendent of San Francisco schools had just bought, at school district expense, a brand-new sports sedan. She described it as "middle of the road"—but the article also quoted the proud car salesman, who said the car was "as loaded as you can get" with fancy options. The story then went on to note that the heat had recently been out at a San Francisco elementary school for a month.

The superintendent's large salary ($200,000 plus) hadn't been newsworthy. But her car, complete with a detailed description of its leather upholstery, sunroof, and other goodies, was. Just imagine which page the story would have run on had the superintendent bought a $50,000 car at taxpayers' expense.

If you still doubt the huge negative message your ostentatious behavior can have on your employees, walk around any business park or commercial neighborhood until you find a perfectly detailed, new luxury car in a reserved parking spot next to the front door. (Given the large percentage of self-important business owners, this shouldn't take long.) Hang around for a few minutes until an office or service worker enters or leaves the building, and say something like, "Cool car, huh?" Chances are good the person will shrug and make a sour comment about the boss. And why not? It's no fun to work for someone whose car cost three times your yearly pay.

Employee disdain for a boss's flaunting of wealth can manifest itself in many ways. For example, a number of years ago I sold a small business to a woman (let's call her Jane), part for cash and part for a promissory note to be paid off in monthly installments. When neither the May 1st check nor an explanation appeared by midmonth, I called Jane, only to be told she was out of the office. When a second call was similarly fruitless, it began to dawn on me that I might have a collection problem. But since I had enjoyed decent relations with Jane in the past, I was not yet ready to adopt an aggressive "pay me now or I'll repossess your desk" posture. That quickly changed when I received a surprise call from Ellie, Jane's secretary, who said, "I know I shouldn't tell you this, but Jane can't pay you because she took money out of the business account to redo her Mercedes—she got a new paint job, expensive tires, new leather, the works. It set her back $6,000. That's the real reason why she won't take your calls."

When I investigated, I learned that Jane's divorce and child custody battle had taken a turn for the worse and she simply wasn't able to concentrate on running the business. Apparently she had spent the money she owed me on her car to try to cheer herself up. Acting quickly—and with Jane's somewhat reluctant agreement—I was able to take back the business and resell it while it still had considerable value, giving an appropriate amount of the receipts to Jane to reflect her ownership interest. But for Ellie's call, I probably would have wasted months trying to cajole Jane to pay up, time during which the value of the business would have surely declined. I've always wondered if Ellie would have tipped me off if Jane had spruced up a Honda or Ford.

When Jerry Brown was governor of California, he insisted on driving an old Plymouth and living in a budget apartment instead of the governor's mansion. Similarly, a few business owners go to extreme lengths to demonstrate their humility. This is overkill. There is no need to buy your clothes at The Goodwill Store, work in a broom closet, and drive a used Kia to send the people you work with the message that you aren't a spoiled brat. Like the citizens of California, many of whom eventually concluded that the *Doonesbury* comic strip had a point when it portrayed Brown as "Governor Moonbeam," your employees want and expect you to act like the boss, not an entry-level employee. As long as you avoid "it's all about me" behavior, you'll be fine. Here are a few tips that should help you do this:

- Choose an appropriate office and furnish it in a businesslike way. Save the oriental carpet, fancy furniture and TV-stereo combo for your living room.

- Share secretarial and other office help with others on an as-needed basis. Avoid the urge to hire an unneeded private secretary whose main job is to make you feel like a big shot and keep others in their places.

- Park in the lot or garage with everyone else, not in a "CEO" slot next to the front door. If parking is tight and others have reserved spaces, you obviously should, too, but if you are often out of the office, consider sharing with another employee.

- Roll up your sleeves and participate in periodic workplace cleanup efforts.

- Get your own coffee and snacks. If you insist, people will probably fetch and carry for you, but every one of them will think less of you for making them do it.

- Buy and use equipment such as computers and phones that are appropriate for the work you really do, not to window-dress your ego.

- Always address and refer to employees by their names. Never use disrespectful terms like "sport," "stud," "honey," or "babe."

Lead, Don't Dominate

If your employees regard you as a decent human—and not just the big boss—they will be far more willing to share their thoughts about how to improve the business. Probably many of their "brilliant ideas" won't be that great. Some will be self-serving, others will be things you thought of and rejected years ago, and still more just won't make much sense. That's okay—chances are lots of your ideas aren't so wonderful either. But now and then an engaged employee will come up with a true gem, something so valuable that it will make listening to dozens of mediocre ideas more than worthwhile.

Treat all ideas—even ones that are obviously nonstarters—with respect. Employees who see others' suggestions belittled or dismissed will be unlikely to make their own. You also need to develop a process to capture good ideas. This is discussed in detail in Chapter 6, Innovate Now and Forever. That chapter also explains the importance of making sure you recognize, appreciate, and reward good ideas that really make a difference.

Example 1:

Liam answers the phone and schedules service calls for Goodlight, a local electrical contractor. Because he talks to customers all day, Liam learns a lot about their needs and desires and sees that Goodlight is out of touch with some significant new developments in the market. Liam considers talking to his boss, Peter, about how introducing two new services might really kick up profits. But ever since the company began to grow Peter has barely seemed to have time to nod hello. Still, wanting to share his insights and ideas, Liam thinks about asking Peter for a short meeting. Then he hears through the grapevine that when Jen in customer service tried to suggest changes in the phone system, she was laughed at. Liam doesn't bother to talk to Peter. Six months later, when a competitor opens, Liam applies for and receives a job at considerably higher pay, in part because at his interview, Mia, his new boss, is impressed by several of his innovative ideas. When Mia implements the first one to immediate success, she not only gives Liam full credit within the company, but also a meaningful raise.

Example 2:

Now let's change this story a little and imagine that despite Goodlight's success, Peter's personal style remains a little more homespun. Not only is there a suggestion box in the employee lounge, but recently a display recognizing the best suggestion of the previous month was added. The day after Liam has his big idea, he drops it in the box. The next day, he encounters Peter helping repair a door on one of the delivery trucks. Peter invites Liam for coffee and asks him to present his idea in more detail. Impressed, a few days later Peter convenes a meeting with several key employees to which Liam is invited. The result is that Goodlight introduces what turns out to be a highly profitable new service.

A few months later, when annual profits turn out to be a little better than expected, Peter announces at a company meeting that everyone in the company will receive a small bonus. In addition, he thanks Liam for his creative idea. Later, privately Liam receives a decent raise and a promotion. After word of this gets around, Liam is not the only Goodlight employee who resolves to try to come up with more good ideas.

Once good ideas are captured, it's time to implement them. When it comes time to make the decisions necessary to do this, be sure you include key employees in the process instead of setting down the law, Moses-like. New policies and procedures carried out with the input of the people who will have to cope with them day to day are not only likely to be more successful—but they are far less prone to be sabotaged. Remember, employees who don't buy into new way of doing things can always find ways to subvert them.

No question, it's easier and certainly quicker to issue an order or impose a decision than it is to listen, reason, and help build consensus. But in the long run, it's far more efficient to establish and respect a consensus-building management structure. Or put another way, a business that is viewed as being all about you won't be as successful as one your employees see as also being about them.

I don't suggest that you make your workplace a perfect democracy where all decisions are equally shared. Leaving aside the fact that it's your business and you have the biggest financial stake in its success or failure, it simply takes too long for everyone in the kitchen to discuss how much sugar to put in the brownies. Although I've seen a very few cooperatively run businesses do well, I suspect their success has come despite the fact they elevated democratic decision making to a first principle, not because of it. Far better to run your enterprise with a strong purposeful center and at the same time welcome and respect employees' opinions and treat employees themselves with dignity.

Adopting a Good Decision-Making Process

The relentless pressure to do business at Internet speed often discourages people from following a careful decision-making process. Even important determinations are sometimes made too quickly, when you are angry or in a bad mood or without input from key coworkers. Acting too fast without gathering all the facts and the opinions of key employees can severely damage your business. Your goal should be to arrive at the best—not the fastest—possible decision. To this end, you want to encourage a creative problem-solving process designed to bring out important information and capture the best ideas of your employees.

Although how decisions are made will be very different in companies with 5, or 25, or 55 employees, here are some elements every good decision-making system should include:

- **Sleep on it.** Fight the pressure to make split-second judgments, and always insist on a reasonable amount of time to consider your options. The weeks, months, and sometimes even years it takes to recover from a truly bad decision are always far longer than the few days it commonly takes to make a good one.

- **Involve others.** People affected by a major business decision, including employees, contractors, and investors, should have a chance to air their views before the decision is made. As noted above, not only does this often make far better solutions, but just as important, it raises the level of trust in your leadership, something it always makes sense to bank so that it will be available to draw on at times of crisis.

- **Support the final result.** After an open, candid decision-making process, once the decision is made, you're in a good position to insist that the time for singing in different keys is over.

Credit Is Cheap—Spread It Around

Flaunting possessions and adopting an authoritarian management style aren't the only ways small business owners find to needlessly bug their employees and, as a result, decrease their enterprise's chances of success. Hogging credit for the business's achievements is another huge and common faux pas. Just as professors are sometimes guilty of putting only their names on research done largely by their graduate students, owners of successful small enterprises are prone to act as if they alone made the business a success. Few things are more disappointing and insulting to employees who have worked hard and creatively to help build the company.

At Nolo, we try mightily to foster a culture in which leaders go out of the way to acknowledge everyone's contributions. If this means that our company meetings sometimes sound like a roll call of every Noloid's achievements, so much the better. People work harder and enjoy it more when they know their efforts are acknowledged and appreciated. Here are just a few of the things we routinely do to foster this attitude:

- The credits page of each Nolo book lists the names of everyone who worked on the book, not just the author, legal editor, and any contributing legal expert. For example, the names of the people who did the layout and design, proofreading, cover design, and index also appear.

- Senior editors don't hog the cool media appearances. All legal editors, even brand-new ones, are encouraged to do TV, radio, and press interviews including, if appropriate, the big national ones about their legal specialties. For example, not long ago, a young Nolo editor was chosen to appear on the "Today" show because she knew the most about the law of name changes, the subject of the interview. Despite the fact that her only previous

TV appearance had been at age 13, accompanied by her wonder dog, she did great. And perhaps best of all, the dozens of Noloids crowded around our office TV saw that knowledge about a subject, not one's title, determines who gets to be media star of the day.

- When a perk pops up, the people whose work was instrumental in making it happen reap the rewards. When the Nolo website was nominated for a prestigious Webby Award for best Law/ Government site, the hard-to-get tickets to the awards ceremony were offered first to the Noloids who worked on the website day to day, not senior managers. (We won, by the way.)

- At company meetings, through companywide emails and at Nolo parties, we try to recognize hard and creative work throughout the company. So when our warehouse crew ships a big order in record time, it's common for everyone to hear about their great job.

- Kind words about Nolo from outsiders are routinely shared throughout the building. Bulletin boards adjacent to the employee lounge and in our online retail store feature newspaper and magazine articles about Nolo and its products. And our customer service department regularly forwards customer emails to every-one in the company. That way, if a customer says, "Your book on immigration law saved me $10,000 and my sanity. Were it not for you, my parents never would have gotten their green cards," everyone in the company is thanked—which is as it should be.

Given that your business is sure to be very different than Nolo's, these examples may not be directly relevant. But again, I hope they'll get you thinking about how crucially important it is to encourage a culture of "we," not "me." If, when the limelight goes on, you can learn to routinely step aside while pushing someone else forward, you've made a good start. But to really help people feel appreciated, you'll need to go beyond fancy words and often superficial "employee of the month" type programs to show people you really do value them. In addition to paying decently, rewarding superior work, and providing good benefits, especially health care for all employees, adopting a simple stock option or other employee ownership plan can be the best way to literally put your money where your mouth is. That way your employees really do know that your business is about them, not just you.

Thanks can be as important as money.

No question, paying people fairly is a key way to retain employees' loyalty (see Chapter 9, Hire and Keep Good People). But compensating people decently, or even giving them a bonus or raise, as welcome as either of these always is, isn't a substitute for publicly thanking them. Oddly, many small business owners don't seem to understand this. It's as if they think that standing up and saying "Adam, Mary, and Wayde did a wonderful job," somehow diminishes their own contribution, when of course just the opposite is true.

Don't Become Lazy

For a small business owner to build a strong ladder of employee respect, another rung is essential: your own continued hard work. Especially when your business begins to prosper, you must continue to work diligently. Working too little is rarely a problem owners experience when a business is in its start-up phase; in fact, it's more likely that you'll overdo it. (See Chapter 11, Don't Work Overlong Hours.) But once a business becomes comfortably solvent—especially if affluence comes suddenly—a fair number of entrepreneurs go through a quick and unhappy transformation from hard-working ant to showboating butterfly.

It is easy to understand why the workaholic owner of a suddenly successful small business may want to take a little time to flit among the flowers, golf balls, sailboats, or motorcycles. But understandable or not, going walkabout for any extended period is always a mistake. Few, if any, of your employees who have worked so hard to help your business succeed will have a similar opportunity, and many will almost surely begin to resent you. And no matter how successful your small business has become, it's not big or established enough to stay that way long if you withdraw your attention at the same time key employees become disaffected.

Taking off an afternoon or even a day to indulge a favorite hobby or just to spend time with your family or by yourself can be good for both you and, by extension, your business. But redirecting a significant amount of your time and energy to nonwork activities is not. If you no longer want to stay involved in the day-to-day management of your successful business, you may be able to reduce your managerial role by delegating these tasks to others, while concentrating on another important part of your business, such as new product development. But if there really is no part of your business that truly interests and engages you, your best bet is probably to sell it. That way, you allow the business to move under committed new leadership while you have the freedom to do other things. Later, should you be ready to recommit to being a business owner, you'll have the financial wherewithal to start fresh.

Example:

Ted started Sunshine Electric, a business installing rooftop solar panels that allow consumers to generate at least some of their own electricity. For the first couple of years, business conditions were tough, and Ted paid his two installers, Emily and Angie, very modest wages. Some weeks he couldn't pay himself at all. Then when power prices spiked, the business took off. Over the next 18 months, Ted was able to triple Emily's and Angie's pay, hire 20 more installers, and pay himself a very generous salary despite the fact that he cut back to working two days a week. In Ted's view, at least, everything was going great until the day Emily and Angie both quit and announced they were starting their own business. Ted went ballistic, called them ungrateful and swore he would never speak to either again.

Finally, six months later, when Ted ran into Angie and Emily at a supplier, the three former buddies agreed to call a truce and sit down over a pitcher of beer. When Ted said he had no idea that Emily and Angie had been unhappy enough to quit, they told him that when the business was on short rations and the three of them had worked shoulder-to-shoulder, they felt fairly treated despite their low pay. But when Sunshine hit the jackpot, and Ted quickly transformed himself from a hardworking guy with dirty jeans into a very part-time boss with clean hands, a shiny new Lexus, and lots of vacations, they had felt slighted. The big raises didn't change the fact that they no longer felt that everyone was in the same boat. Had they been given (or even been permitted to buy) a small ownership stake in Sunshine, they would probably have hung in there over the long term. But without it, being a wage slave, even a well-compensated one, to an absentee boss, just didn't cut it.

11

Don't Work Overlong Hours

"Busiest men find the most leisure time."

—Proverb

Virtually every article or book profiling a successful entrepreneur prominently mentions that he or she routinely works a 60- to 70-hour week. Since, in my experience, loads of prosperous entrepreneurs work far less, I've concluded that the American media has predetermined that the ability to go without weekends is a big key to attaining riches—and that people who don't conform to this stereotype simply don't get profiled. Realizing that the press loves to write about people who suffer to succeed, I suspect many savvy businesspeople exaggerate how hard they work. If so, they are part of a long tradition— Ben Franklin admitted in his autobiography that he regularly left a candle lit in his Philadelphia print shop so passersby would think he was toiling into the wee hours instead of, in fact, being snuggled cozily in bed.

As with other enduring American folk myths (rich people retire happy, virtue is rewarded, inventors are heroes), the notion that working 9 to 5 twice each day will all but guarantee entrepreneurial success is bunk. It's at least as likely that people who work overly long days on a regular basis will be less successful than those canny enough to keep their work and personal time in better balance. In a world full of cheap labor but short on intellectual capital, it rarely pays to try to substitute hours for smarts.

Although there can be all sorts of reasons why a particular business-person chooses to work too much, one of the biggest is the belief in a direct relationship between the number of hours worked and financial result. But profits flow from businesses that effectively meet their customers' needs—something you can almost certainly do without missing dinner with your family every night.

Example:

At Nolo, we subscribe to a number of daily, weekly, and monthly legal newspapers and magazines. It's obviously key to our continued success that all of our legal editors stay up to date on their specialties. That's why for years we circulated all the publications and all looked at them. Then one day someone suggested a new system by which one person reads for the others, flagging only those articles that were important. As a result, the total time spent reading legal journals dropped from 20 to two hours per week, with no loss of efficiency.

The Importance of a Sane Schedule

Many business owners, of course, would love to work less—but fear that if they did, they would quickly go broke. They are almost always wrong.

Most businesses that really meet a customer need offer many opportunities for an owner to be more productive in less time. Except for starting or buying a business that soon bores you into disinterest, it's my experience that owner overwork is the biggest reason why potentially successful businesses close. Working too many hours for too long is bad for your health and the well-being of your family—two things you absolutely need to nurture to have a chance of thriving long-term. Fortunately, in most instances overwork isn't necessary; by learning to concentrate on the activities that count most, most entrepreneurs can achieve excellent results in up to a third fewer hours. If, despite the obvious perils of working too many hours, you conclude that your business would otherwise fail, you need to face the fact that your enterprise is not financially viable. Except possibly during a fairly short start-up phase, your business should produce a solid profit in a reasonable number of hours. If you can scrape by economically only because you work 60 to 70 hours a week, year after year, you are not really in business at all. Instead, you have hired yourself, at a rotten wage, to do a task no one values enough to generate a decent profit.

The Danger of Burnout

Most well-run small businesses become more profitable—often far more profitable—as they age. Often this is because experienced owners figure out how to take advantage of money-making opportunities that present themselves along the way. And as years go by, a well-run business that provides a quality product or service and maintains its competitive edge will be recommended by an ever-increasing pool of customers, almost automatically increasing profitability. (Chapter 8, Market Your Business Creatively, discusses why positive word of mouth is one big key to success.)

In short, growing a successful business is like running a marathon, not a hundred-yard dash—to go the distance you must adopt a work schedule that allows you to pace yourself. Many small business owners who fail to understand this quickly burn themselves out working far too much and quit after a few years, in some cases just when their businesses are poised to make good money.

Example:

Sal and Patricia, each the 30-something mother of young children, began a business, Z-Pot, importing and wholesaling large glazed pottery planters from Southeast Asia. They almost immediately began making a solid profit wholesaling their unique wares to about 25 nurseries and half a dozen indoor gardener shops. In addition, they opened their own retail outlet to profitably dispose of overstock and slightly damaged goods.

But after two years of running both Z-Pot's wholesale and retail businesses, while trying to keep on top of their growing family responsibilities, Sal and Patricia both felt exhausted. Patricia's husband, whose own career was also going well, began to strongly suggest that their family life would improve if Patricia sold her share of the business and stayed home with the kids for a few years.

Not wanting to give up the business entirely, but recognizing their problem, Sal and Patricia decided to hire a salesperson to operate the small retail operation. When, after a few months, it proved difficult to hire and keep a trustworthy employee to run what was essentially a cash business, the two women reluctantly decided to close it and concentrate all their energy on the core wholesale operation. Although they missed the additional income the retail outlet had generated, both appreciated the extra time.

And then an exciting thing happened. Because Sal, who handled the sales side of the business, had more time and energy to call on prospective customers, Z-Pot landed several large new nurseries, with the result that profits actually increased. To get rid of slightly dinged-up inventory, they held a yearly blowout sale. Although this meant selling some pots at or even below cost, they did so cheerfully, knowing they had reorganized their business for long-term success.

For me, working 35 to 40 hours per week with the occasional week or two off is about right. It lets me stay focused and interested in my writing and editing responsibilities and approach them with drive and enthusiasm. And it also gives me enough time and energy for personal and family needs. To get enough highly productive work done in this comparatively short period, I must first understand that all tasks are not of equal importance and focus on the ones that I personally need or want to do, something I actually find easier to accomplish when I have limited time. Occasionally, when I get behind and a deadline looms, I work extra hours. But I've learned time and again that if I do this for anything beyond a few days, my sense of personal well-being begins to erode, and my output of quality work quickly drops. In short, when I'm tired and grumpy, I don't get many good words written no matter how many hours I spend gripping my pen.

It may be that I'm not typical and that many people have a greater capacity to work long hours. Perhaps, but when I look around at friends whose small businesses have done extremely well over a number of years, I see no one who consistently works more than a 50-hour week, and many who average fewer than 40. The few who regularly put in ten-hour days compensate by working fewer days per week and taking at least a month's annual vacation. In other words, virtually every successful small business owner I know has adopted a work schedule that provides them plenty of time to have a life. And I don't believe I happen to hang out with a lazy or pampered group, but rather that the ability to create a business that very effectively meets the needs of its profitable customers, not the determination to work many hours, is the real hallmark of a successful businessperson.

Interestingly, when I talk to these successful people about how much they work, many immediately say that although they're not at work long hours, that doesn't mean business isn't on their minds. Several report coming up with their best, most creative business ideas when they're swimming laps, tossing a Frisbee to the dog, or just taking a walk—away from the emails, phone calls, meetings, and other distractions that crowd days at the office, store, or factory. One friend puts it like this, "Busy work—doing any one of thousands of little tasks at the office—doesn't improve anything important about how my business operates. Just the opposite. To have time to focus on important initiatives, I have to stop spending all day at the office dealing with an endless list of things that don't really count. When it comes right down to it, I need to take the time necessary to figure out how to better meet the needs of my customers. If I can do that, both my business and I will thrive even if I only work 30 hours per week.

Keeping Your Priorities Straight

Ask retired businesspersons you admire to tell you what they learned about keeping work, family, and personal time in perspective, and I'll be very surprised if you are told "If I had to do it all over again, I would have worked lots more." It's far more likely that they'll advise you to spend more of your life's energy developing personal interests, protecting your health, and spending time with family and friends.

Doing good and profitable work is important to leading a satisfying life, but it should never be all-important. As the old saying goes, "All work and no play makes Jack a dull boy." And if too much work makes your life one-dimensional, when you retire and work stops, you won't have a life.

Another way to think about how to fit your work into the type of life you would like to lead is to make a list of the things you really care about. Mine would go like this:

- stay close to my family (including being willing to interrupt my workday as needed)

- spend time on personal interests and develop new ones

- stay physically active and otherwise protect my health

- spend time with my friends, and

- do work I enjoy and which pays well enough to adequately support me and my family.

Assuming your list is even a little like mine, work is only one item. This should really be all you need to know to understand why working so many hours that you leave inadequate time for other priorities is a poor way to lead your life. Of course, if work, work, and even more work were the only way to ward off starvation or keep a roof over your head, it might be your only choice. But in 21st-century America, people usually work too much, either because of their own obsessive natures, or to make up for the fact that their businesses do not connect well with their customers' needs. Too bad that neither of these reasons forms the basis of a good business plan.

Planning to Work Less and Make More

If you already work too many hours on a regular basis—or fear that a new enterprise you're planning will push you in that direction—how can you cut back without significantly reducing your income? The answer is to understand the importance of delegation, and why, for most entrepreneurs, it's not just a personal necessity, but an opportunity to improve their businesses.

The Power of Delegation

At the Acme Sandblasting Co., the New York City company my grand-father Frank "Stuke" Toors owned and ran during most of the first half of the last century, Stuke personally knew how to do almost every job in the business. He could make cost estimates for jobs, close a deal, machine a spare part, splice a rope, write payroll checks, and even collect overdue bills. A few days before he retired, at 75, he shed his three-piece suit, donned a respirator and some work clothes, and climbed a scaffold to prove he could still blast grime off a big expanse of granite.

Stuke was typical of the jack-of-all-trades American businessman whose heyday lasted from the end of the Civil War through World War II. In a far less bureaucratic, rule-bound, and technologically sophisticated world, these people really could cost-efficiently do a great many tasks themselves. This is no longer true. Contemporary entrepreneurs who try to run the whole show usually make a big mistake. As Adam Smith famously noted way back in 1776 in *The Wealth of Nations*, the principle of the division of labor is a huge engine driving increased productivity. Or put more directly, there is almost always some specialist who can accom-plish all but your core business tasks better, and ultimately cheaper, than you can. One good example involves preparing the payroll, something that for a modest fee can be farmed out to a highly automated specialist, freeing your staff from the time-consuming payroll-preparation ritual my grandfather's business performed every other Friday afternoon.

Of course, it costs money to hire others to accomplish routine tasks. But because sensible delegation frees up your time to concentrate on the high-value aspects of your business, it produces long-term profits. And, by definition, this is even more true for entrepreneurs who run one- or two-person businesses and must purchase most services from independent contractors and vendors than it is for larger outfits with many employees. If, for even a moment, you doubt the wisdom of working with others, consider that without the phone company, your Internet service provider, and package delivery companies, you would probably need to spend every waking hour just trying to deliver essential messages. Fortunately, because these companies are at our beck and call for a very reasonable cost, you can efficiently delegate your communications tasks for a fraction of what it would cost to personally deliver your messages.

Unfortunately, when it comes to many other business tasks—from bookkeeping to equipment maintenance and repair to graphic design to human resources management—the wisdom of delegation is less well understood. In a nutshell, that's a big reason why so many Americans persist in wrongly believing long hours and high profits go together. People who work overlong hours often do so precisely because they fail to grasp the crucial difference between routine work and high-value work.

Example:

Jeff is an architect whose firm, J&D Associates, designs big buildings such as schools and hospitals. Although he is a gifted draftsman, Jeff's real skill is his ability to inspire people who have different agendas to agree on design issues. Given that the success of every

J&D project—as well as the firm's reputation—depend on gaining the support of many powerful stakeholders, including neighborhood groups, school or hospital administrators, building contractors, and trade unions, it's easy to see just how crucial Jeff's special talent is to J&D Associates' success.

Fortunately, both Jeff and his partner, Dale, a more introverted type who enjoys sitting in the office and designing the buildings, understand that Jeff's time is best spent coaxing everyone to sing the same tune, not sitting in front of a computer dealing with the details of building design. If this means Jeff and Dale have to hire an additional draftsperson to get all the plans done on time, it's a small price to pay for keeping Jeff focused on the high-value job he does so well.

What Do You Do Best?

Before you can delegate well, you need to understand the things you do that contribute the most black ink to your bottom line. Only then can you aggressively look for ways to get someone else to do the other bits. So your first step is to identify the tasks you must really do yourself, as opposed to the large number you handle either because no one else is available, you believe you can't afford to hire help, or for some other less-than-convincing reason. For example, if you are a website designer, and customers are attracted to your small design company because of your imaginative graphics skills, it makes sense for you to concentrate on the creative process. Don't spend your energy interviewing candidates for the administrative assistant's position or renegotiating the lease—things that need to be done, but that won't affect your relationship with key customers.

Example:

Hallie owns MusicWorks, a new and used CD store. Most of the profit comes from the sale of used CDs, because they can be bought cheaply and marked up a far higher percentage than can new CDs. But the used music business has a big Achilles' heel: There is virtually no market for most of the product people bring in for sale. Hallie's business won't last long if she buys *Bobbie Blue Bland Live at Reno, Fess Parker's Greatest Hits,* or tens of thousands of other titles nobody wants.

That's why, on the days she works, Hallie personally buys and prices used CDs from 10 until noon and again from 2 to 4, rejecting at least 90% of what she's offered. It also explains why Hallie hires a manager and assistant manager to open and close the store and supervise the college students who cover the sales counter, restock shelves, and do other routine tasks. Although her shop is open from 9 a.m. to 10 p.m., seven days per week, Hallie works only from 9:30 to 5, Tuesday through Saturday, and takes time to go jogging in the middle of the day.

When Should You Do It?

Many enterprises, including creating arts and crafts, designing websites, and writing books, allow their proprietors to work flexible hours. If you have substantial control over the hours you'll work, you'll want to carefully assess which part of your workday is most productive. As a writer and editor who also has important administrative responsibilities, I know from long experience I produce the bulk of my writing, editing, and content design work between 8:30 and 11:30 in the morning. And, especially when I get some exercise in the middle of the day and drink a cup of coffee, I often experience another burst of creative energy in the middle of the afternoon. All told, this means I only have about 20 to 25 hours per week in which to work at peak efficiency. It is extremely important that I actually use them to produce or scope out new products, relegating as many of my administrative duties as possible to other times.

Similarly, a dentist who feels best and works most efficiently in the middle of the day should schedule root canals and other difficult high-profit work at this time, while handling more routine tasks in the early morning and late afternoon. And it makes sense for a programmer who writes code best in the middle of the night, when "it's quiet enough to think," to reverse the clock.

But if you run a restaurant, tutor kids, or operate a flower stand, to mention just a few time-sensitive businesses, you'll do most or all of your daily trade in a relatively few predetermined hours. To succeed, this means you'll need to dovetail your personal work schedule with the needs of your business. Ideally, you'll find considerable overlap between your most productive hours and the times when your business absolutely needs you to be on deck. If your times of peak productivity don't substantially over-lap with these critical hours, it's a huge indicator that you are in the wrong field. No matter how much a food-lover dreams of opening a fancy supper club, if she wakes and sleeps with the robins, she'll almost surely do far better to try a café serving breakfast and lunch.

Don't work when you don't need to.

Look at the possibility of cutting back your hours during times when your business isn't particularly profitable. For example, if you own a café that does 40% of its business at lunch and another 40% after 5 p.m., do you really need to be open all afternoon just to pick up a few extra customers? Or would you be better off locking the door and taking a nap, spending time with your kids, or doing something else to restore your energy for the evening rush?

Often it takes both a determined commitment and real creativity to sensibly adjust one's work hours to produce a saner schedule. Sadly, many business owners must experience a family emergency or health crisis to face up to the need to make a change. But fortunately, this isn't a requirement—there are almost always loads of ways for a determined person to work less and make more. One of the best is to eliminate customers who aren't profitable. Serving a significant number of money-losing customers is a huge problem for many small businesses. Identifying your losers and taking steps to either turn them into profitable customers or finding a way to diplomatically fire them will immediately free up the time to recruit more lucrative replacements.

Example:

John drives a cab in a suburb where throngs of residents commute by train to a nearby city. This means John is super-busy from 6 a.m. to 8:30 a.m. and again from 4 p.m. to 8 p.m.; during these times, he can typically fill his cab with three or four regulars for each train, earning as much as $50 per hour. During the rest of the day,

John not only has fewer customers, but because he typically drives one person at a time, earns significantly less, sometimes as little as $15 per hour. Even though John is often tired and irritable as a result of his 14- to 15-hour days, he believes he can't cut back and still earn enough to pay the mortgage and all the other bills of a growing family.

Fortunately, John's wife Peg finally proposes a way out of the time trap. If John will stop driving from 9 a.m. to 3 p.m. each day, devoting two hours to shopping and preparing meals, and taking off the rest, Peg will get a second cab permit and drive the family's other car from four to seven during the peak evening commute. Grandma agrees to stop by each day to be sure the kids are safely in the house and doing their homework by 5:30. The result is that by shifting work to the most productive times, family income goes up significantly, while the total hours expended to earn it drop substantially.

How to Delegate

Many small business owners readily agree they need to learn to delegate tasks that someone else can do better. But they put it off. One man who puts in 12-hour days at his Internet-based sports memorabilia business and whose wife had recently threatened him with divorce told me, "I know I need to cut back, but I just can't spare a dime to hire help right now." When I explained that learning to delegate is even more important for a tiny struggling operation than it is to an established and profitable enterprise, he asked me to how to go about it. Here's what I told him.

There are two keys to making a delegation plan work. First, you need to find people who can do the task as well as you can and at less cost. Again, if you understand Adam Smith's basic point that productivity increases and costs drop when work is divided into a series of tasks, with a specialist assigned to accomplish each, you'll also understand that this shouldn't be difficult. No question, if you are a perfectionist who has trouble letting go of even the simplest tasks, learning to delegate can be a big hurdle. But perhaps it will help get you started if you are able to concede that there really are people in the world at least as competent and careful as you are. (See Chapter 9, Hire and Keep Good People.) Whether the person you hire is an independent businessperson or an employee is not important. What is crucial is that you know the job is in excellent hands so you can let go of it. And this is just as true if you are hiring someone to do routine tasks, such as keeping an office running smoothly, or work that is crucial to your business's success, such as making important sales calls.

The second key to profiting from delegation is to put at least some of the time you save into more profitable activities. For example, if finding new clients for your financial planning service is the activity that will most positively affect your bottom line, you'll want to delegate routine tasks such as bookkeeping, using time saved to sell more. That way you win three times: revenue goes up, your total work hours go down, and the jobs you delegate get accomplished better.

Example:

Tina owns and runs East Mountain, a rural yoga center that offers weekend and week-long retreats. Like many small business owners, Tina finds herself stretched too thin, trying to deal with the many workaday details of running East Mountain's business and at the same time paying enough attention to her core job of spending time with guests and teaching many of the classes. Finally, realizing that something has to give, Tina makes two lists: one of the time-consuming tasks that wear her out without really making much difference to East Mountain's success, and a second list of the tasks that really are important to attracting clients. The routine jobs include meal preparation, bookkeeping, and designing promotional materials; the ones that are most important to customer satisfaction are teaching excellent and innovative yoga classes and spreading the word about East Mountain's unique yoga programs.

Tina's next step is to find good people to accomplish the noncore tasks at a price she can afford. When it comes to designing brochures and doing the bookkeeping, it proves relatively easy to find affordable independent contractors to take over. Unfortunately, hiring someone to do all the meal preparation turns out to be prohibitively expensive. So, instead, Tina decides to hire a cook to coordinate dinners only, relying on workshop participants willing to trade work for a tuition reduction to prepare East Mountain's simple breakfast and lunch offerings. To cover the additional costs of hiring others, Tina decides to devote 20% of the hours she saves to teaching two more classes per week and 50% to increasing East Mountain's marketing activities (the other 30% she saves for herself).

Tina's increased marketing efforts include writing articles for interested media, preparing periodic press packages highlighting East Mountain's new and noteworthy offerings, and, most of all, using email, regular mail, and the occasional phone call to stay in close touch with former students, yoga teachers, and others in the yoga network. As a result, business increases by 40%. This, in turn, allows Tina to raise her rates by about 20%, with the result that East Mountain is more than able to cover its additional labor costs.

12

Learn to Live With Luck

"Fortune brings in sound boats that are not steer'd."
—William Shakespeare

Watching small businesses succeed and fail over the years, I'm often reminded of how big a part luck plays. Sometimes it seems as if fate's fickle finger reaches down from the sky and chooses a perfectly ordinary business for huge success; on other occasions the gods seem perversely determined to frustrate the most worthy enterprises.

I have no idea why some businesspeople are luckier than others. Perhaps like a quarter, which when tossed in the air enough times will eventually land on its edge, we are simply observing the laws of statistics applied to small business success and failure. After all, someone is bound to start selling telescopes the day before a huge new comet is discovered, while someone else opens a beachwear business the summer of the hundred-year flood.

But whether we view luck as a statistical, metaphysical, or magical phenomenon, we can probably agree that by its nature it can't be predicted or controlled. Why not, then, just cross our fingers and move on to consider things we can affect? Because, while hoping to be lucky is never a viable business strategy, learning to manage the fallout from both good and bad luck certainly is. And one key aspect of doing this should be the determination to learn the important entrepreneurial lessons that both good and bad fortune so frequently reveal.

The Perils of Good Luck

How you cope with the ups and downs of fortune, as well as what you learn from it, will often have more to say about your ultimate success or failure than whether your luck was good or bad in the first place. To illustrate this point, let me tell you what happened to the five novice publishers I've come to know over my long career in publishing, after they each had the good fortune to publish a highly profitable bestseller—something most publishers never come close to doing.

One recognized that his extraordinary good luck was just that and never published another book, preferring to put his considerable profits into real estate and other good investments outside the publishing business. He retired wealthy from the publishing business at age 38.

Two of the other initially fortunate publishers took a far different approach. Excited by their big success, and convinced it came as a direct result of their brilliance, both immediately plowed all their profits—and, in one case, every dollar she could borrow—into publishing a long list of titles. One of them, Megan, published cookbooks, mysteries, yoga guides, how-to books, and metaphysical tracts. The other, André, was at least sensible enough to stick to how-to sports guides, the area of his initial big score. But like Megan, he, too, made the mistake of publishing so many titles so fast that both editorial quality and marketing focus got lost. Megan's business went belly-up within three years. André's failed in fewer than four.

The last two lucky publishers also published more titles—in one case, regional travel books, and in the other, small business guides. When their subsequent books predictably failed to do nearly as well as their initial bestsellers, each had to face and master the thousands of things it takes to run a successful publishing operation. As they gradually learned to publish books their target audiences really wanted to buy, these two publishers expanded their lists of titles slowly, conserving much of the cash their bestseller had generated. After more than a little struggle, both eventually developed reliably profitable businesses.

It can be convincingly argued that the two publishers who failed did so precisely because they were so blinded by good fortune that they never bothered to learn the basics of running a good small publishing company. And that the two who built solid businesses succeeded, in part, because they understood that good luck doesn't often knock twice at the same door and that they needed to use their initial windfall to help build a solid, long-term publishing company.

Here are a few of the lessons luck has taught me. I share them in the hopes that you won't have to learn as many of them the hard way as I have.

- **Don't mistake luck for genius.** Good luck rarely makes you smarter. In fact, the opposite is far more likely to be the case. A ten-year-old who, by chance, sets up a lemonade stand on the blistering hot Sunday that real estate agents are showing the house across the street is likely to conclude that making money is easy. He'll learn a more accurate, albeit costly, lesson if he tries to repeat his success on a cloudy Tuesday after the house is sold. And like lots of adult entrepreneurs, if he misses the point that his big break has come and gone but, instead, concludes that building a bigger stand and adding grape juice and cookies to the menu will reignite profits, he'll get his knuckles rapped a second time.

- **If you are not blinded by luck, you can often learn from it.** If your first self-published novel goes gold because Oprah's producer discovers it after you inadvertently leave it on an airplane, congratulations—you've been hugely lucky. What you haven't done is to stumble on a reliable business strategy. Even if you write 50 more books and leave them on 500 more airplanes, your big break is highly unlikely to repeat itself. But it is also true that an entrepreneurial insight lurks behind most lucky—and many unlucky—events. For example, if our lemonade kid checks the paper for open houses, and the weather report for hot days, he may be able to move his stand around town, one step in front of a crowd of thirsty house-hunters, turning his lucky strike into a sweet little business. Similarly, the lucky author who now knows that talk show producers play a big part in book promotion may be able to use this information to find more reliable ways to put his subsequent titles in front of them.

- **Bad luck can also teach you how to make a profit.** Whether it's an earthquake, war, or a sudden recession, whenever an unexpected event happens, we all receive a mental jolt. Suddenly our perceptions have been changed. Unfortunately, a big change can quickly flatten a little business; fortunately, creative business opportunities also abound when change is rampant. For example, in the months immediately after the terrible events of September 11, 2001, many New York City tourist-related businesses were hit hard. Among the first to recover were those that realized that while fun-seeking visitors to the Big Apple were at least temporarily a thing of the past, millions of Americans wished to express solidarity and sorrow by visiting the ruins of the World Trade Center and reengineered their business accordingly.

- **Put half your money in your pocket.** Anyone who enjoys the occasional flutter, whether at Las Vegas, Atlantic City, or the little bingo game down the road, knows the heady feeling of hitting a run of luck. Sometimes the slot machine just seems to get stuck producing jackpots. But no one wins forever. To plan for the moment when your luck goes into long-term hibernation, sensible management dictates that you plan to have something in your pockets besides your clenched fists. When my dad, who liked to make a wager once in a while, made a few dollars at the track, the stock market, or cards, he always saved half and continued playing only with the rest. If he lost that portion, he quit, still far ahead. Dad's strategy meant he was a big, long-term winner, unlike some of his friends.

- **When you hit the jackpot, diversify.** In the last years of the 20th century, just as in the 1920s and other periods of investment bubbles, many people came to believe that stock prices would always keep rising. As a result, they put every dollar into the market, sometimes even borrowing money to invest. Each time, for a few years this bet-the-house strategy worked so brilliantly that loads of people became rich, at least on paper. But when the crash inevitably came, it wiped out most of these speculators. The exceptions were people who had the good sense to spread their initial gains over a number of types of different investments, including bonds and cash.

To see how similarly spreading one's risks by diversifying can work brilliantly as a small business strategy, take the example of Anna, a dentist I know. When one of Anna's local competitors died suddenly, and two others unexpectedly retired, Anna's practice turned into a cash machine. Reasoning that new dentists were sure to move into the area soon and siphon off some of her business, Anna used her windfall to buy a small professional building. She then rented office space to the four dentists who opened new practices, allowing her to cut back to three days per week and at the same time enjoy a substantial increase in net income.

Coping With Bad Luck

All businesses, even the biggest, must regularly cope with many events beyond their control. Should an unexpected development shatter your best-laid plans, you can be forgiven for loudly cursing your misfortune. It will seem damned unfair if rapidly rising electricity rates make customers spurn your showroom full of outdoor spas—especially if that's all you sell. And, of course, after September 11, 2001, many travel-related businesses through no fault of their own, lost so much business that they failed.

What should you do if an ill wind threatens to turn your business inside out? Essentially you have three choices. Let's look at each one.

Face It

Nobody likes bad news, and most of us have a tendency to avoid facing it for as long as humanly possible. But no matter where it comes from or how severe it is, putting your head under the pillow and hoping for the best is always a mistake.

Here at Nolo, we have more than once mistakenly persisted with projects Lady Luck seemed determined to spit on. One situation that comes vividly to mind involved commissioning a consumer advocate, who hosted an immensely popular daily radio show, to write a California consumer rights guide. Unfortunately, almost before the author could fire up her PC, the station changed ownership, switched to an all-news format, and killed all nonconforming shows, including hers. Instead of facing up to the fact that without our popular author personally promoting the book on the air, we had little chance of selling enough of what amounted to a laundry list of consumer rights and remedies, Nolo decided to soldier on and hope for a miracle. Not only did we spend months editing and publishing this book, to predictably non-miraculous sales, but we also compounded our costly mistake by keeping it in print for several years.

In hindsight, it's clear that if we had immediately faced up to the fact that events beyond anyone's control had dealt the book a killing blow, we could have redirected our energy to more promising projects. So why, after many years in the publishing business, did we fail to pull the plug on a project we should have known was doomed? The answer, which I think is relevant to many, if not most, businesses, is that it was hard for us to admit to the enormity of the bad news we had been hit with. It was psychologically far easier to deny the worst, hope for the best, and keep marching.

Here are some of the reasons Nolo found to continue with this project:

- We liked the author and wanted to stand by her. We preferred losing money to being thought impolite or disloyal.

- We found it tough to deliver very bad news, even to ourselves.

- Some of our editors had fallen in love with the idea of doing the best-ever California consumer guide, and we chose to ignore the fact that our marketing department repeatedly pointed out that without lots of ongoing publicity it wouldn't sell.

4. We had already done considerable preliminary work on the project and were loath to write it off. Somehow it was tougher to admit that we had already lost some money and quit than it was to spend twice as much more and pray things would somehow work out.

You may have used similar logic to avoid facing difficult situations. If so, you know how easy it is to let a combination of wishful thinking, inertia, and a reluctance to disappoint others blind you to the need to cut losses when faced with unexpected bad fortune. But if you try to ignore unlucky events, a business that could be profitably redirected, or at worst abandoned without devastating loss, may become an expensive albatross. (This is discussed in more detail in Chapter 17, React Quickly to Bad News.)

Outsmart It

It is my experience that no matter how acute your short-term pain, you need to try to come up with creative ways to overcome it—or, when the bad breaks are likely to quickly run their course, to simply outlast them. In fact, I know several very successful small business owners who trace their long-term success to circumventing exactly the kind of ill fortune that caused many others to bolt the doors and run for the storm cellar.

Example:

Craig opened Fish Feathers, a retail fly-fishing equipment business, just weeks before the city discovered a serious soil contamination problem and closed the street in front of his store for three months. After spending an hour kicking a brick around the back yard, Craig accepted the fact that customers would be all but nonexistent until the street reopened.

Deciding to borrow enough money from his sister to pay the rent, Craig set out to use his suddenly free time to create and promote FishFeathers.com, a website offering his merchandise for sale online. Two years later, when his online sales were almost twice those of his shop, he came to see that without the bad luck of the street closing, his business might never have succeeded.

The events that result in both good and bad luck are usually full of information. A spike in electricity prices, a change in climate patterns, or a terrorist act all change the way large numbers of people look at important parts of their lives. And like it or not, when that happens, just as many businesses will find ways to profit as will be economically disadvantaged.

Example:

Emily, an acupuncturist, specialized in helping people coping with depression. Then her area was hit by a devastating earthquake likely to affect peoples' psyches for years. Quickly realizing that during times of war and disaster people's personal feelings of isolation and depression are often relieved by their natural concern for others, Emily decided to reconfigure her practice around the goal of helping people reduce stress. When both her business and her personal satisfaction went up, she knew she had made the right choice.

Sometimes it may be necessary to make fundamental changes to your business to work around the problem.

Example:

Janet, a lawyer who specialized in IRS audits, lost more than 50% of her business when a "kinder, gentler IRS" cut back on punitive collection practices. Instead of exiting the tax business, Janet decided to develop several new tax-related specialties. One was to coach small businesses on how to legally hire independent contractors in a way that would avoid the considerable and expensive risk that the IRS would later classify these people as employees. Another was to counsel divorcing couples on how to understand and cope with the tax aspects of dividing their property. A third was to provide estate tax planning services to upper-income taxpayers. Together, these new initiatives turned out to be more profitable than Janet's old audit-related business.

Cut Your Losses and Move On

A single stroke of bad luck rarely destroys a business. But, although it's unusual, fate can deal your business so severe and lasting a blow that your best approach is to move on to something else. For example, say you open a combination newsstand and used bookstore just down the block from a Starbucks, to take advantage of the heavy foot traffic. If the coffee shop's building burns to the ground the next week, it probably makes sense to rethink the viability of your business—especially if Starbucks announces plans to reopen several blocks away and there are no immediate plans to rebuild the burned-out building.

Unfortunately, it can sometimes be tough to tell the difference between an unlucky event that you can outlast, outsmart, or quickly learn to profit from and one that's a business-killer. Say you specialize in booking tours of the historical treasures of Egypt, and a particularly nasty spate of violence means most travelers decide they don't really need to see the Pyramids after all. How do you know whether it's better to hang on and hope for peace or quit? I'm not smart enough to answer that one. But here are a couple of other (and, I hope, easier) questions I suggest you ask yourself if your business, or a part of it, is buffeted by an ill wind.

- **Does the bad news hit at the core or the periphery of your business?** The harder it hits your core assets, the tougher it will be to outlast it, and the quicker you'll need to face up to its consequences and act. This means you'll need to promptly figure out a plan to circumvent the bad luck, reconfigure your business to profit from it, or cut your losses and run. On the other hand, if only one aspect of your business takes an unexpected hit, leaving others strong, at least you have the option of waiting to see whether or not good luck will soon replace the bad. For example, if you sell both wood stoves and backyard spas, the water rationing that accompanies a prolonged drought may all but kill your spa sales. You may want to emphasize the stove business, but keep stocking spas in the belief that when normal weather eventually returns, you'll be well-positioned to recoup your losses.

- **How long will the effects of the bad fortune last?** Be honest. If a new world-class shopping center is likely to drain much of the foot traffic your candy shop depends on from the slightly tatty older mall you are located in, it will bring you little joy to hang on and hope for a miracle. You need to promptly face up to the need to move, unless you can so fundamentally reinvent your business that the unlucky event will no longer pull you down. For example, if you are able to cook up a new type of candy so delicious and unusual that people will drive out of the way to buy it—or order it by phone, fax, or email—your low-cost location may even be an advantage.

By contrast, if you are located on Main Street and another candy store opens down the block, it may be much easier to come up with a sound strategy, albeit one that may involve short-term pain, to ensure that if there isn't enough business for two shops, yours is the long-term survivor. For example, you could remodel your shop, increase your selection, improve your marketing, and hold frequent sales—things that will be of long-term benefit even if, as you hope, the other shop closes.

■

13

Pay Your Bills Early

"He is rich who owes nothing."

—Hungarian proverb

Business advisors frequently recommend that entrepreneurs wait to pay their bills until the day they are due, or even until they are dunned a few times. They justify this strategy by claiming that businesspeople who pay their bills early or on time don't understand the time value of money. Far better, they claim, to pay as late as possible, putting any money not needed for day-to-day operations into an interest-bearing account, thereby making a profit on the other guy's money.

Sound good? Over three decades of running a successful business have convinced me it's terrible advice. I firmly believe that your best strategy is either to pay up front or to pay your bills early.

The Benefits of Paying Bills Early

Every time I read another article exhorting businesses not to pay until the clock strikes midnight on the last possible day, my first thought is that the commentator has never run a business in the real world where a reputation for keeping one's word is a hugely important asset. Here are five powerful reasons to pay your bills at least a few days early whenever you can afford to—and sometimes even if you must scrimp to do so.

It Builds Trust

Each working day, you (and every other small entrepreneur on Earth) form judgments about the other businesses you come into contact with. For example, even as you read this, business owners are arriving at conclusions like these:

- Business A produces a reliable product.
- Business B employees can be relied on to show up when they say they will and work overtime if that's what it takes to finish a job.
- Business C constantly comes up with new and innovative services that frequently anticipate our needs.
- Business D always seems to be understaffed by surly employees who never return phone calls.
- Some of the younger employees Business E hires are not properly trained.
- Damn Business F to hell. Another day is here, and its check isn't.

When thoughts like these run through your head, you'll doubtless question whether you ever want to deal with business D, E, or F again. And if you had to choose one of these less-than-stellar outfits to head your blacklist, I bet it would be the one that doesn't pay when it's supposed to. And that makes good sense. As tough as it is to cope with late deliveries, unreturned phone calls, inexperienced workers, or even problems with the quality of products or services, it's not as hard as trying to survive without being paid.

The corollary to the rule that a late-paying business gets a high spot on your bozo list is that you'll undoubtedly notice and appreciate customers who always pay you on time. In fact, the only customers you value more are probably those who either hand you a check when your goods or services are delivered or put it in the mail the day they receive your bill. Understanding that it puts them at the front of the popularity parade, shrewd businesspeople make it a policy to pay bills very promptly. And despite the disinformation promulgated in the business press by "pay late, save money" advocates, this insight is far from new. For example, in Abraham Lincoln's time it was a high compliment to say a man "paid cash on the barrelhead," as opposed to asking for credit.

But what about the point that by paying bills early—or even on time—you are giving away money? My answer is that compared to the expense of all the other things you could do to build the same degree of trust and respect in your business's community, the cost of paying a little early is incredibly low.

It Ensures Excellent Future Service

I have long made it a policy to pay small business owners I work with on a personal basis the day I get their invoices. If possible, I put the check in the person's hand the day the job is done; otherwise, I mail it immediately. Paying promptly and in full is the best way to let these people know how much I appreciate their good work. And this simple courtesy almost always pays big dividends should I ever need to ask one of them for expedited service in the future. If, facing a last-minute emergency, I need extra help from Genevieve, the woman I hire to drive my mother to the doctor, or Juan, who occasionally helps care for my yard, I know the fact that I have always paid them very promptly will mean they will do their best to accommodate me.

And, of course, this approach works just as well for small businesses as it does for individuals. Everyone from your freelance bookkeeper and graphic designer to the person who cleans your office will know whether you pay your bills early, on time, or are habitually late. And if you pay promptly without being dunned, they will think more of you and do more for you. It's that simple.

Example:

D&B Concrete Removal made it a policy to pay all the independent contractors it worked with as promptly as possible, often even before the invoices were due. Fred, D&B's president, had never forgotten how important it was, during D&B's early years when money was always tight, to be paid on time, and he wanted to extend the same consideration to the people D&B worked with.

This practice paid huge dividends the day a water main broke, flooding essential equipment in D&B's storage yard at a time when D&B was barely keeping up with a big contract and would face penalties for late performance. Fred was able to pick up the phone and place emergency calls to the shops that maintained D&B's concrete saw and other equipment. Everyone responded immediately and effectively to help D&B clean critical machinery, with the result that D&B was back in business in 48 hours and able to meet its deadline.

It Builds Positive Word of Mouth

Paying your bills promptly is a great way to encourage the people in your entrepreneurial network to recommend your business. It is a far better and cheaper way to build a loyal customer base than is most advertising. (See Chapter 8, Market Your Business Creatively.)

Keep in mind that it's not just your satisfied customers (people who pay you money) who will tell others about your business. All the people who work for and with you are also potentially powerful recommenders. Everyone you cut a check to—from your landlord and insurance broker to the owner of the catering business down the street that occasionally provides food for your meetings—has a stake in your being successful. If they like you and your business—something that is always greatly aided by paying their bills promptly—each can become a powerful marketing ally.

Example:

Doug, an insurance broker, goes to great lengths to help Bluebelle Web Design find an insurance company willing to customize a standard business policy to meet Bluebelle's special needs. Joan, Bluebelle's president, is so impressed with Doug's creative work that after the policy is finally in place and Bluebelle is billed, she ignores the ten-day payment terms and immediately mails the premium check along with a note of thanks. Now it's Doug's turn to be pleased. Later that week, when he attends a local service club meeting at which the subject of small business websites comes up, he favorably mentions Bluebelle to what amounts to a roomful of potential customers. As a result, Joan picks up a couple of excellent new accounts.

Would Doug have still recommended Bluebelle if he hadn't already been paid? Possibly, if he liked Joan and respected her business. But what if the service club meeting took place a month later and, even after Doug had made several phone calls, Joan still hadn't paid? You know the answer.

It Builds a Positive Credit Profile

When your business is tiny, the rest of the commercial world will hardly know you exist. But soon your little operation will begin to leave tracks in the entrepreneurial sand. Your first small financial marks might not be spotted for years—were it not for the existence of businesses whose business it is to find and report them.

Once you incorporate, form an LLC, hire employees, or apply for a bank loan or trade credit, you'll automatically make it onto the radar screen of Dun & Bradstreet or a similar data collection organization. These outfits gather and sell credit information about virtually every American business. Among other things, they note the name of your business, what it does, how many employees it has, who owns it and, probably most important, its credit and bill-paying history. In short, your bill-paying profile is available to anyone who pays a modest fee.

Who is likely to buy such a report? Banks that are considering lending you money, companies considering your application to lease equipment on credit, and suppliers, wholesalers, and other businesses from which you have requested credit. True, an excellent payment record won't guarantee that you'll receive a big bundle of commercial credit or a particular loan; other information is also important. But if Dun & Bradstreet reports that you habitually pay late, your application is very likely to raise a red flag.

It Provides a Safety Net If Things Go Badly

Owners of failed or failing businesses typically tell hard-luck stories. The economy unexpectedly turned down the month after the business committed all its savings to expand, or the most trusted employee opened a competing business and stole the best accounts, or a big customer who owed $50,000 went belly-up—or maybe they all happened at once.

If this sounds like a run of luck so terrible it would be enough to kill any business, I have important news for you: As the bumper sticker says, "shit happens." Instead of making excuses for failure, you need to be prepared to survive when things go wrong, as sooner or later they inevitably will. Sure, your first job is to keep a wary eye out and duck as much dung as you can. But no matter how quick you move, you'll rarely avoid it all. It follows that you need to be ready with a survival and recovery plan. Undoubtedly, the best way to accomplish this is to have a substantial cash reserve. But in the real world, where most businesses need every extra penny to grow or improve their operations, it's no easy job to keep a chunky sum in your bank or money market fund, just in case of emergency.

Fortunately, should the business gods turn perverse, getting into the habit of paying your bills promptly, if not early, can weave a strong safety net. That's because people who run their businesses well enough to pay bills before they are due have considerable leeway, in case of emergency, to postpone paying most bills for at least a month or two. And at least as important, they can also draw on the substantial reservoir of goodwill and respect they have built up by their long-standing scrupulous payment practices.

Suppose Frank's Marine Services, a long-term customer of your engine repair business, faces a difficult business patch as the result of a waterfront fire, and asks for extended credit terms. If FMS has always paid you on time or early, chances are you will be as accommodating as possible—certainly far more generous than you would be if Benji's Boat Repair, your most feckless customer, asked for similar help.

Make Friends by Charging Less

Another excellent technique a service business can use to build a highly positive business reputation is to occasionally charge less than the price quoted for a job. For example, if your service business completes a job in significantly less time than you expected, reduce the customer's bill. Not only is this an honest business practice, like paying a bill before you have to, it's almost sure to result in very positive word of mouth about your business.

Example:

Peter, a stonemason, specializes in the repair of traditional masonry fireplaces, commonplace in houses built before builders found it cheaper to switch to metal fireboxes. Still, in the older residential areas where Peter works, there are plenty of decaying masonry fireplaces to keep him busy. When Peter bids on a major fireplace job (rebuilding the entire unit from the basement up), he estimates his total labor, materials, and permit costs and then marks the total up to allow for a decent profit. Finally, when bidding on bigger jobs in old buildings, he adds on 10% or more to cover unforeseen problems all too likely to crop up. Although real trouble develops only occasionally (and Peter's contract protects him from some potential liabilities), the 10% cushion he charges on every job can be a real lifesaver when he inevitably hits a truly hellish one.

But, occasionally, Peter overestimates how long a job will take. This is just what occurred when he bid $12,000 to rebuild two big and badly degraded fireplaces for Tania, who was

PAY YOUR BILLS EARLY

remodeling her Calvin Coolidge-era house. In fact, the job went surprisingly faster than expected—so well, in fact, that if Peter had been billing after the fact, he would have charged only $10,200, including his 10% cushion. As a result, Peter reduced Tania's final invoice by $1,000. Tania, who already thought Peter had done a magnificent job, was as flabbergasted as she was delighted. Although she had lots of experience with contractors who came up with elaborate sob stories to justify trying to charge more than they bid, this was her first experience with anyone as honest as Peter.

In fact, Tania was so pleased that she told a number of her friends, including Dan, a successful local real estate broker who often sold older houses. Dan, too, was impressed and began to recommend Peter whenever a seller needed to repair a fireplace as part of putting a house on the market. The result was that Peter picked up several additional jobs each year. In fact, over the course of the next five years, Peter could trace $100,000 worth of work back to his $1,000 refund. It was easily the best investment he ever made.

What to Do When You Must Pay Late

Should you find you can't pay all your bills on time, the best strategy can be stated in three words: communicate, communicate, communicate. Don't wait until you receive a third dun letter to talk to the people whose check is not in the mail. As soon as you realize you have a problem paying a bill on time, pick up the phone and call your creditor. Making sure you talk to the person who has real authority to manage accounts receivable, briefly explain what the problem is and when you expect to be able to pay. If you can make an immediate partial payment, even a small one, it's absolutely essential that you do so. As the old saying goes, it always pays to put your money where your mouth is.

Occasionally, people who can't pay a bill on time are tempted to detail all the miserable things that prevent them from doing so. Don't get carried away. Telling too good a story can be counterproductive, since it risks convincing the creditor that your business is in real jeopardy of failing. While it's effective, not to mention polite, to briefly explain a good reason for the holdup, focus instead on knowing when your check will be in the mail, and then do your best to keep your promise.

Be realistic.

If you have had a good payment history, many creditors will let you catch up on past due bills in periodic increments, as long as they believe you'll really do it. It follows that the key to developing a successful plan is usually not in how much you agree to pay on any given date, but that the creditor has faith in your ability to eventually pay the full amount. It follows that it's usually better to negotiate a slow schedule for catching up on overdue debts gradually, and keep your word, than it is to agree to repay them more quickly and have to ask for another extension.

Example:

Mach 7, a motorcycle repair outfit, decided to expand into sales by becoming the franchise for a newly hot line of Italian bikes. Investing a substantial amount in building a showroom and training salespeople, Mach 7 took a big financial hit when its first shipment of bikes was immediately recalled because of a safety-related defect that would take two months to put right.

In the meantime, short of friends, Mach 7 badly needed help from its creditors. To get it, Erin, Mach 7's co-owner, sent a one-page fax to all key accounts, briefly explaining the problem and the fact that it should be taken care of in 60 days. She then requested permission to delay payment of all invoices for three months, promising that if possible she would make a least partial payments sooner. The next day, Erin followed up with a personal phone call to all Mach 7's large creditors, during which she said she could and would pay 10% of what was owed immediately. All were willing to support her, although several wanted weekly updates on Mach 7's condition, something Erin readily agreed to provide.

■

14

Embrace Your Best Competitors

"The trouble with the rat race is that even if you win, you're still a rat."

—Lily Tomlin

Your spouse, best friend, and nosiest brother-in-law, combined, probably don't know your business as well as your closest competitors. Whether you silkscreen t-shirts, import spices, set tile, or run a gymnastics school, the entrepreneurs who vie with you for business will closely track your successes and failures. Given that you often compete for customers, deal with the same suppliers, and promote your businesses in similar ways, they couldn't ignore you if they tried.

Competitors will also play a significant role in defining your business reputation. If you set an extremely high standard (the kids in your gymnastics school love what they do and frequently win regional competitions), you will inevitably earn the respect of others in your field; they may even have to change the way they operate to better compete with your successful example. On the other hand, if you run a slipshod business, your competitors will almost surely enjoy mocking your efforts.

To fully grasp how important earning the respect of your competitors can be, talk to any established local businessperson in a competitive field, such as a doctor, house painter, or copy shop owner. Ask her whether she is able to accurately rank her closest competitors by competence, integrity, cost, timeliness, and other significant factors. My hunch is that she'll have no trouble doing it blindfolded, standing on her head in the middle of a hurricane at 2 a.m. In fact, peer-based evaluation systems tend to be so accurate they are often used as a rating methodology by academics, consumer groups, and others. For example, the editors of the book *America's Top Doctors*, by Castle Connolly Medical Ltd., start their rating process by asking tens of thousands of American doctors a very simple question, "To which doctors would you send a member of your family?" Nominees are then separated by specialty and again rated, this time by teams of doctors in each major geographical area.

Assuming you agree that your competitors are likely to know a lot about your business, you can be forgiven if you still don't see what this has to do with my advice to embrace your best competitors. Traditional small business wisdom, after all, teaches that you should be wary of your competitors; you may even be coached to treat them as outright enemies. Much of the rest of this chapter explains not only why this scorched-earth approach is wrong, but also why a kinder, gentler approach is far more likely to benefit your business and make your personal life more pleasant.

Why It Makes Sense to Cooperate With Your Competitors

In large business, it's at least theoretically possible for one corporation to play hardball so successfully that it largely destroys its competitors. From the Standard Oil Trust of the early 20th century, through mid-20th century category-killers such as IBM, Sears, and General Motors, to 21st-century Microsoft, there are many examples of monopoly-building corporate strategies that have produced huge profits, at least until government antitrust regulators or rapidly changing technologies produced new competitors.

But the rules are different in the small business world. With lots of providers in most fields, it's rarely possible for one company to dominate. Leaving aside the fact that to do so would mean that a small business would have to grow large (something that most small entrepreneurs don't want to do), there are a variety of reasons why a local plumber, Chinese restaurant, t-shirt printer, or law firm can't monopolize its market. One big one is location. Customers often choose these businesses precisely because they are located nearby, so it's hard for a big centralized operator to take over.

Price competition is another big barrier, especially among service businesses, which all have similar labor costs. For example, if ClipMe, a local hair cutting salon, suddenly cuts prices in half, chances are that every other budget hair stylist in town will quickly realize that survival depends on matching or beating ClipMe's prices. The likely result will be that ClipMe's initial increase in volume will dry up and its owner, learning that in most instances no one wins a small service business price war, will put prices back to their former levels. Similarly, if Ready T-Shirt announces it plans to move from a storefront to a large warehouse, install high-speed silk-screening equipment, and embark on an expensive advertising blitz, its local competitors, Graphic Attack, T-Shirt Express, and T-Top are almost sure to spot the danger early and move to counter it. They may lower prices even before Ready T-Shirt makes its move, forcing Ready to similarly slash its prices—and lose the profit margins necessary to justify an expansion loan.

So while being seen by your small business competitors as running an efficient, ambitious, and even highly competitive small business is positive, being regarded as an unfair competitor or business predator is likely to be counterproductive. And it's important to realize that in this context it's often what you say as much as what you do that influences how others regard you. For instance, I'll never forget the self-help law publisher whose president bragged to a prominent journalist, "Nolo is history," or the competing software house whose marketing director loudly proclaimed at an industry trade show, "We'll bury Nolo." Although in both instances these executives may have been as guilty of hyperbole as they were of a real plan to flatten Nolo, we have ever since been extremely wary of both outfits.

Your Competitors Are Your Natural Friends

With some exceptions, most small business owners who stay the course have been drawn to what they do by a real liking for the field. And those who are truly fortunate create a vocation as well as a business. In this context, I think of several of the small business owners I've dealt with recently, including Rick, who gives my softball-mad daughter pitching lessons; Theresa, who owns and runs an excellent Italian deli; my doctor, Alan; and Andy, who owns my favorite bookstore. Without exception, these men and women not only operate profitable businesses, they enjoy and care about what they do. How do I know? Leaving aside the fact that I'm on friendly terms with all of them (another testament to their business acumen), it's easy to see how deeply each is committed to his or her business and the people it serves.

So here's a key question I bet you've never answered: Assuming there are good people like these in your chosen field, who better to be on good terms with? After all, in our big, fast, anonymous world, you are almost sure to have much in common with people who have somehow been drawn to do the same work as you do, in the same place, and at the same time. Except for the fact you see yourself scrapping with these people for your daily bread, at least some might well turn out to be your friends, if not soul mates. Fortunately, in some fields, such as dentistry, landscaping, or real estate sales, where there is plenty of customer demand to support many local providers, it's common for competitors to establish cordial relationships. This is especially likely where a local trade association such as a county dental association offers competitors a regular opportunity to meet and greet each other in a social context, where industry veterans have an opportunity to teach anxious newcomers the long-term value of civil, if not cordial, relations.

But in some occupations—tree trimming, algebra tutoring, or video production, for example—there may be no comparable opportunity for you to mingle with your competitors. Short of starting an organization to provide these occasions (which can be a great idea), your contacts with competitors will necessarily be more informal. Depending on your occupation, your paths may cross at a particular wholesale supply company where your customers gather, at a service club, or just around town. How you act during these encounters will have much to do with defining your relationship. Except when dealing with true charlatans, you'll want to make every effort to establish and maintain at least a polite relationship with all competitors, even those who aren't quite your cup of tea. And to the extent that you can form genuine friendships with your high-quality competitors, you'll not only reap personal rewards, but, as I'll discuss in the rest of this chapter, your business will also likely benefit.

Your Competitors Can Be a Source of Business

By their very size, small businesses are significantly limited in the amount of work they can handle during any given period. A busy dentist, who on average treats 40 people per week and reviews a hygienist's work on another 40, has only a very restricted ability to increase these numbers. If too many patients call in too short a time, some will have to be put off until later or, especially in the case of new patients, referred to another dentist.

And, of course, it's not only a work overload that leads one small business owner to refer customers to a competitor. In an age of increased specialization, the exact specifications of the task often play a huge role in a businessperson's decision to accept work or refer it to someone else. For example, Bill's Pruning may prefer to do high-volume jobs on hedges and small trees up to 30 feet, while sending more complicated and potentially dangerous tall tree jobs to Way-Up Tree Care, which as its name implies specializes in caring for sky huggers. True, the two companies compete to trim medium-sized trees and, in periods where business is in short supply, may further invade each other's vertical space, but most often they find mutual advantage in referring customers back and forth to fit each other's preferred customer profile.

And, of course, it's not only dentists and tree surgeons who frequently refer customers to their competitors. Every busy small business will, at least occasionally, need to do the same, if for no other reason than to be able to meet the needs of their established customers. True, referring an existing or potential customer to a high-quality competitor risks the person's never coming back. But making an excellent referral is not nearly as problematic as is sending a good customer to a marginal business where they are likely to be disappointed, both by the service they receive and the bad steer you provided.

Example:

Jeannie, who is helping plan her daughter's wedding, calls Pour Vous, a local caterer, on the recommendation of her friend Millie, one of Pour Vous' best and most regular business customers. Pour Vous is already fully booked for the date of the wedding, so Jeannie asks Tad, Pour Vous' owner, to recommend another caterer. As a savvy businessperson, Tad immediately understands that he has a lot riding on the success of his recommendation. If Jeannie is satisfied by the caterer Tad suggests, Millie and probably others Jeannie talks to will hear about it. But if the second caterer turns out to be a bust, Jeannie will let Millie know all about it and at least some of the discredit is sure to rub off on Tad. So Tad recommends Good Hands, a business he considers to be thoroughly reliable. And a few days later he calls Deb, Good Hands' owner, to be sure she realizes where the referral came from. Fortunately, Good Hands lives up to its name, and a pleased Jeannie tells Millie all about how successful the reception was. As a result, Millie emails Tad her thanks and asks him to begin planning to cater the big Christmas party.

A year later, when Jeannie needs to plan her 30th anniversary party, she understandably sticks with Good Hands. But two years later, after Deb has closed Good Hands to go back to school,

Jeannie remembers how nice Tad was and hires Pour Vous to handle the catering for her youngest daughter's wedding reception.

Working for Your Competitors

In many fields it is common for independent businesspeople to work at least part-time for one another. This is especially likely when a new business is in the start-up phase. So a freshly minted CPA who opens her own tax preparation service, but as yet has a short roster of clients, may contact several established accounting firms to see if part-time work is available during the tax season rush. Or an independent carpet installer may work two days per week for a floor covering megastore, while devoting the other three to establishing an independent carpet-laying service.

To make these sorts of relationships work typically takes patience, discretion, and good judgment by everyone involved, but particularly on the part of the new entrepreneur who, after all, is in the weaker bargaining position. Until proven otherwise, the established businessperson is likely to worry that the upstart may try to steal customers or clients. This explains why the independent businessperson is often asked to handle only the bits and pieces of jobs that require little or no customer contact.

But if, over time, the freelancer is smart enough to demonstrate that he or she is not a client poacher, the established business's defensive attitude will typically relax. The established business may even begin sending the new business some of the very same accounts it was initially protective of. Although this first paranoid, then generous behavior may strike you as bizarre, in fact it makes sense. That's because by the time the referral actually takes place, the established business owner has had ample time to judge the upstart's work and character. Assuming both prove out—and given the new entrepreneur's clear determination to establish her own business—the established business owner may sensibly conclude that over the long term it will be more beneficial to maintain cordial and cooperative relations than to compete tooth and claw.

Your Competitors Will Help Define Your Reputation

Most small businesses that prosper over the long term do so in significant part by bringing in new business through the positive recommendations of existing customers. (This is discussed in Chapter 8, Market Your Business Creatively.) It follows that establishing and maintaining an excellent community-wide business reputation will be one of your best tools to garner new business.

But your reputation won't be defined only by your customers and others in your day-to-day network, such as your employees, contractors, suppliers, and neighboring businesses. Your competitors will have a great deal of power to define how others regard you. For example, if yours is a field occasionally covered by local media, the reporter who profiles your business will almost always check out your reputation with others in your field. Journalists know from experience that this is one of the simplest and most effective ways to find out both good and bad things about your enterprise. For example, once, several years ago, when a reporter doing a profile on Nolo called a competitor whom I had not been particularly cordial to, the quote he got was "Warner is often an insensitive red-hot, but I have to give him credit for running an excellent company." Realizing that this feedback could have been far worse, I resolved to be a little nicer to my competitors in the future.

And, of course, the prospect of positive media coverage isn't the only way your business can benefit by being well thought of by your competitors.

Before making a decision to patronize a particular business, potential customers often check it out with someone in a closely related field.

Example:

Marcus, realizing it's time to take his two-year-old to the dentist, asks one of the other parents at Playtime Childcare to recommend a children's dentist. He receives a strong recommendation to Dr. Yamaki. But then, realizing that he doesn't know the recommender very well, Marcus decides to check out the recommendation with his wife's "adults only" dentist. When this dentist says, "You couldn't do better," Marcus makes the appointment for his daughter.

If You Can't Say Something Nice ...

If you are new to the small business world, you probably do not fully realize just how frequently you are likely to be asked to express your opinion about your competitors. To see how this might work, assume you own a small interior design business. Here is just a partial list of the questions you might be asked about one of your competitors.

- A potential customer may directly ask, "What do you think of Design Associates' work?"

- Your son's teacher may tell you of a bad experience she just had with Design Associates as part of asking your opinion as to how she should proceed.

- A vendor's representative or someone else in your field may give you the latest gossip about Design Associates, as part of a conversation where you're expected to comment.

- A consumer or industry rating service may contact you to check up on Design Associates.

- You may be interviewed by a reporter from a trade publication or the general media about Design Associates.

- Someone who used to do freelance work for Design Associates may ask you for work and in the process express an opinion about Design Associates.

On these and similar occasions when you are asked to express your opinion about Design Associates, one rule (a version of the Golden Rule, really) should apply: "If you can't say something nice about a competitor, keep your mouth shut." There are many reasons to avoid starting a pissing match with people in your field, the most important being that even a few competitors who are highly motivated to do you harm can hurt your business and try your soul in many ways. Far better to plan to avoid this eventuality, even if it occasionally means being pleasant to people you don't like.

So if you talk about a competitor, be charitable. Secretly, you may think the person sometimes speeds through jobs, charges too aggressively, and often finishes late, but unless he is an out-and-out crook, keep your negative opinions to yourself and accent the positive. Although nice words will never travel as far or as fast as negative ones (especially those imparted to close friends in deepest confidence), eventually your competitor will hear them. And, hopefully, the next time she has a chance to blast or praise your business, she'll be equally well mannered. And even if she isn't, you will still want to continue to avoid mud slinging. In the long run—and possibly even in the near term—your reputation as a fair-minded person will go up, just as that of your mean-spirited competitor will surely decline.

What should you say when asked about a seriously bad or fraudulent competitor? Especially if you're queried by a friend you don't want to mislead, it can be tough to come up with an honest, but nevertheless diplomatic, answer that doesn't risk starting a war. I've found that pausing before changing the subject usually conveys the message loud and clear, without loosing negative words on the local universe to rattle around for years to come. Another approach is to say that as a matter of policy, you don't give opinions on people in your field, but you can explain the criteria you use to judge a good business. This might include a good educational background, on-the-job experience and training, offering a money-back guarantee, or a particular excellent method of doing business. With luck, the information you provide will arm the person you are talking to with enough information to make an independent judgment about a business that probably doesn't meet many of these criteria.

■

15

Don't Buy a Franchise

"The only thing that saves us from bureaucracy is its inefficiency."

—Eugene McCarthy

Somedays it's hard to turn on the TV without seeing ads profiling ecstatic lottery winners. The ads doubtless sell lots of tickets, despite the fact that most viewers surely know that their chances of winning gigabucks lie somewhere between infinitesimal and nonexistent.

The business of selling franchises is eerily similar. Glib salespeople typically profile franchise owners who retired rich just 42 short months after purchasing an Ace Rug Cleaning Service or a Zesty Avocado Burger outlet. Assuming these people really exist, I can confidently tell you that your chances of being like them aren't much better than those of winning $20 million in the SuperLotto.

Almost every franchise presentation emphasizes that nationwide, franchised businesses take in about 50% of the retail sales dollar. What isn't said is that the great majority of these dollars come from just a few categories: automobiles, gasoline, lodging, and fast food. Beyond these megabuck fields, only a small percent of the money retailers take in goes to franchised operations.

Franchises That Are Good Deals

Although I've become convinced that purchasing a franchise is generally a poor way to start a business, let me start with a couple of exceptions to my own rule.

The first involves franchises built around continent-spanning communication networks such as national hotel and motel groups, which maintain 800 phone numbers and websites allowing travelers to easily book reservations. No question, if you plan to be in five cities in five days, booking your bed, car, or perhaps even some of your meals via one or more of these national systems is very attractive. This is not to say, of course, that any particular hotel, motel, or auto rental franchise is a good deal, only that unlike many other franchises, they do sell something of real value.

Second, franchises with brands that really are famous and highly regarded can sometimes be worth the high cost. Franchisees, especially those who bought in years ago at good locations, have made big profits in McDonald's, Pizza Hut, Motel 6, and other world-famous franchises. But it has been decades since an ordinary person could afford to purchase and build out one of the relatively few gilt-edged franchises. Typically, an investor with $50,000 or less ends up with a garage full of low-end vending machines or a couple of panel trucks whose sides are emblazoned with ads for a third-tier rug-cleaning service.

The Problems with Franchises

The biggest problem with many, if not most, franchise operations is depressingly simple: They charge too much for a business that doesn't have enough value to justify the high upfront and ongoing costs. To help understand why this is true, answer these three simple questions:

- How hard is it to make a sandwich?
- How hard is it to clean a house?
- How hard is it to put grout in tile?

If your answer is "not very," then I have another question for you. Why pay a franchise operator a large sum to teach you how to do one of these or other simple tasks when you could learn to do it on your own for far less?

Franchisors say there are at least two good reasons to buy a sandwich-making, housecleaning, or other run-of-the-Yellow-Pages franchise. First, they almost always claim to have developed wonderfully efficient new techniques that have all but revolutionized the business. If you're that gullible, you would probably be investing your money in the nearest slot machine, not reading this book. In truth, although some franchise sandwich shops may serve a decent meal, they have not somehow invented a revolutionary way to put meat, cheese, and veggies between two hunks of bread. And there is no rug-cleaning franchise that really can show you how to clean all types of rugs twice as well in half the time. In both instances, their cleverest techniques are usually in the area that interests them most: separating potential franchisees from their investment dollars. And their amazing new methods are little more than a combination of common sense and heavy sales hype.

Most franchisors' second big sales pitch is designed to convince you that XYZ's 50-state marketing plan is all but guaranteed to make your franchise business the McDonald's of its field. The point here seems to be that if they can convince you, they will hype the hell out of whatever XYZ sells, and you'll want to buy in and rake in the dough when the franchise inevitably becomes famous. But few franchisors ever spend enough marketing money to make a significant impact on the consciousness of the American public. And even if they do, people won't continue to patronize a business unless it's well designed and run. For every franchise operation that has become widely recognized, dozens have struggled and failed, all but unknown except to the people whose investments have similarly disappeared.

Lest you think I exaggerate, consider that few banks—even those that make many small business loans—will lend money to buy a franchise without receiving a security interest in real estate or the personal guarantee of a highly solvent person. They have learned the hard way that lots of these businesses fail, meaning their chances of not being repaid are unacceptably high.

Franchises Cost Too Much for What You Get

A huge part of all franchise sales hype boils down to "we can make it easy for you. Not only can we show you how to wax a floor, clean a rug or make a falafel quicker and better, but we will also explain exactly how to buy all the whizbang equipment and supplies needed to do it (in fact, we'll be happy to sell them to you)." In short, the franchisor promises to provide you with a turnkey business operation that will allow you to skip all the boring start-up details and begin to make money immediately.

Franchisors also emphasize that if you buy in, you'll instantly be part of a well-known and highly respected marketing organization, something you could never achieve on your own. That is, instead of being Joe's Housecleaning Service, you'll be part of the world-famous Scrub n' Shine network. And the right to use the Scrub n' Shine name isn't all you'll receive. You'll benefit from Scrub n' Shine's sophisticated marketing effort that will all but guarantee you'll have a small army of customers knocking down your door to hand you money.

The reality is usually far less exciting. First, you'll pay an up-front franchise fee, which might be $30,000 to $70,000 or more for a little-known housecleaning service. A well-known restaurant or hotel franchise will have a price tag in the millions when you figure the costs to construct the required facility.

Typically, you'll also be required to pay the franchisors 3% to 6% of your monthly gross revenue (big-name fast food operators, such as Wendy's, McDonald's, Burger King, and Subway typically charge between 8% and 11.5%), plus a few cents on the dollar for the franchisor's marketing effort. Put these fees together and it means that in addition to paying the up-front fee for the franchise, you will usually have to pay the franchisor six to ten cents or more of every dollar of revenue. And if the franchisor requires that you buy goods or services either directly from it or from an approved supplier, your costs will probably be higher, because franchisors commonly charge substantially more than do suppliers on the open market. Let's assume that the extra costs would amount to two cents out of every dollar of revenue.

Add it all up, and you'll likely pay the franchisor ten cents of every dollar you take in (more for many fast-food franchises). This is a huge burden to your long-term profitability. But won't a high volume of sales more than compensate for these costs? Consider that the entire profit margin of many small businesses is less than ten cents on the dollar, and few businesses do much better.

And, of course, your franchise fees don't get your business open. If you want to open a business that has a high start-up cost, such as a restaurant, you'll still need to build or remodel a physical space, purchase equipment, and train employees—things that are usually more expensive when you must conform to a franchisor's many specifications. For example, opening a typical upscale bar and restaurant costs between $2 million and $3 million.

But if you don't get a leg up from a franchisor, how will you get the knowledge and skills you need to open a successful business? Chances are you can learn on your own for free. For example, if you are interested in opening a lock shop, nail salon, or copy shop, get a job in one for a few months instead of buying a franchise. Not only will you learn much about how the business works, but you'll be paid to do it.

Example:

Joan, a retired Coast Guard officer, always dreamed of opening a bookstore. Casting around for how to make it happen, Joan discovered that she could buy a turnkey franchise that promised to teach her everything she needed to know to stock and run a bookstore. But before Joan invested, she decided to learn more about the business by getting a job at the local Barnes & Noble chain bookstore. After four months, she moved over to her area's most successful independent store. After six months clerking there, Joan clearly understood two things. First, she had already learned most of the information the bookstore franchise proposed to sell her. And second, because margins were low and inventory requirements high, making a profit selling new books is extremely difficult, something that's only likely to get worse as more and more customers order books online.

Joan decided to take a very decent job running the book and gift shop at a nearby planetarium. Her salary, plus her Coast

Guard pension, would be more than enough to continue expanding her collection of 18th- and 19th-century English literature, books she had already begun buying and selling at a profit on eBay.

But what about all the benefits of the franchisor's marketing efforts? Don't hold your breath. National franchise outfits rarely do a good job of promoting their local franchises, in part because they typically rely on broadcast and print media campaigns, which for small businesses are usually an inefficient way to use precious marketing resources. Even worse, because franchisors are usually headquartered outside a franchisee's area, they are not equipped to implement the many types of low-cost local marketing that can be extremely effective. (See Chapter 8, Market Your Business Creatively.) Add to this the fact that most smaller franchises never have enough money to buy more than a token amount of media exposure and you'll understand that Scrub n' Shine is unlikely to ever become a household name—and even if it does, you probably won't benefit.

You'll Be Bored

To many prospective purchasers, the big appeal of buying a franchise is that someone else has figured out how to run the business. Just pay your money, and the franchisor will explain in great detail exactly how to make a donut, wash a car, or sell sneakers. Often overlooked is the fact that operating a business by following an instruction manual can also be a big negative. Instead of having a chance to exercise your creativity and imagination to improve and change your products and services, you'll be sentenced to endlessly repeating someone else's recipe. Another way of saying this is that the franchise will never really be your business at all—

instead, you'll be little more than a sharecropper working for an absentee owner who retains the authority to make most key decisions. True, recognizing this huge weakness, a few franchisors encourage franchises to experiment with new products and techniques—but if you are going to do that, why not just work for yourself from the start?

Some people think they won't mind running a boring, uncreative business as long as it's solidly profitable. Maybe. But the truth is that you are prevented from actively using your intelligence and creativity to adjust the business to fit local circumstances or take advantage of what you learn, which is almost sure to make the business less likely to succeed. Or put more bluntly: Run a dumb business, get a dumb result.

To help see why a paint-by-the-numbers approach is a poor way to run a business, compare any large franchise operation to other hierarchical bureaucracies where key decisions are made at the center and then communicated to and implemented at the periphery. Whether your model is the IRS, Poland under the Communists, or any one of dozens of once-prosperous multinational corporations such as AT&T, Sears, or Xerox, I think you'll quickly see that inefficiencies inevitably creep into these top-down systems. Especially when it comes to providing local services, sooner or later the best small, nimble operators run circles around centrally planned behemoths. Both the fun and profits in the small business world tend to go to entrepreneurs who learn how to operate lean, innovative businesses able to adjust to changing local conditions. People who buy a business formula and never deviate from it rarely become wealthy or achieve the sense of fulfillment enjoyed by entrepreneurs who work long and hard to succeed at their own enterprises.

The Contract Is Stacked Against You

Franchise contracts, which typically run 50 pages or more, are written and rewritten by skilled lawyers to be sure the franchisor remains firmly in control of the relationship. Like buying a car or an insurance policy, you have no chance to negotiate a change to even one word of these agreements, which by itself should tell you all you need to know about the one-sided nature of your future relationship. Here are just a few of the ways the fine print of these contracts benefits the franchisor:

- **Competition and noncompetition.** Most agreements allow franchisors to sell as many franchises as possible wherever and whenever they wish. So if your business does well, the franchisor can probably brag about your success to sell another franchise to someone in your immediate area. For example, a quick Internet search tells me there are 60 Starbucks locations within ten miles of my Berkeley, California, house. At the same time, should you wish to close the franchise and open a similar independent business, you are typically prohibited from doing so for at least three to five years. Or put another way, even if you want to quit the franchise and go into business for yourself, you can't.

- **Approval of sale.** To sell your franchise sometime in the future, you'll probably have to get the franchisor's approval. Not only can this make the sales process more difficult (the franchisor might reject a purchaser you consider well qualified), but it means the prospective purchaser will have to agree to the terms in the then-current franchise contract. If, as is common, royalty fees and marketing expenses or other costs have been raised significantly since you bought in, your franchise could be all but unsaleable.

- **Resolving disputes.** If you get into a legal dispute with the franchisor, the franchise agreement may require that you file your lawsuit on the opposite side of the country, and be subject to the law of the state whose courts are most favorable to franchisors. The old Mexican curse, "May you have a lawsuit in which you know you are right," is likely to come to mind.

- **Purchasing goods and services.** Many franchisors require that you buy supplies, goods, and even services, such as marketing and advertising services, from the franchisor. Although this sometimes makes sense (all chicken sold at Big Ben's Bird House should look and taste the same), often it's just another way franchisors take money away from franchisees. The obvious problem is that when you agree to buy goods or services from a single provider, you don't get the benefit of the normal competitive marketplace and so almost always pay too much.

Example:

FrostiFruit, a franchisor of frozen fruit concoctions, charges all of its franchises 4% of gross monthly sales as a royalty fee and an additional 3% to participate in a mandatory centralized marketing plan controlled by FrostiFruit. Candy, FrostiFruit's president and principal stockholder, sets up an ad agency, Candy & Associates, to handle systemwide advertising, paying herself a generous salary as agency president. FrostiFruit hires Candy & Associates to do all its advertising. As long as the agency does a reasonably competent job placing ads, the courts of many, if not most, states would find nothing wrong with Candy's feathering of her own nest. And this would be true even if a local franchisee could prove that it could pay half as much for a far more effective local ad campaign.

Evaluating a Franchise

Even after reading my anti-franchise arguments, you may remain convinced that a particular franchise really does have such a valuable name and reputation that buying in may be a good deal. Despite initial fee and ongoing royalties and marketing costs, you are sure that if you can run the local Subway sandwich shop, 7/11 convenience store, or Sir Speedy printing center, you'll do extremely well.

If that's so, I recommend you go through this step-by-step process to investigate the business and its prospects before you write your check.

Get the Franchise's Circular

Your first step should be to ask the franchisor for a copy of its Uniform Franchise Offering Circular (UFOC). This is a federally mandated document that contains loads of information about the franchise company's history, operations, franchise network, rules, and costs. Read it extremely carefully. And if you have limited business experience, ask a friend with a successful business to review and discuss it with you.

Further information on franchises.

The Legal Guide for Starting & Running a Small Business, by Fred Steingold (Nolo), contains a useful chapter analyzing the UFOC, as well as other legal issues having to do with purchasing and running a franchise.

Talk to Franchisees

If you talk to a number of people who already own a franchise in the outfit you are attracted to, I can virtually guarantee you'll learn many very interesting things the salespeople somehow never told you. The UFOC lists (see Item 20) existing franchisees and will tell you whether the system has grown or shrunk over the last three years. Obviously, if you learn that the franchise operation is shrinking—or if it's too new to have a history— you'll just want to say "no." There is little reason to pay for a system that hasn't proved itself.

If the franchisor suggests that you talk to particular franchisees, don't bother. One way or another, these people are part of the franchisor's sales team and are unlikely to give you fully objective information.

Ask whether there is an association of franchisees. If so, contact this group and ask for an objective assessment of the franchise. Also check out the list of franchisees who have left the system in the last year, and call some of these people.

Look at All the Costs

Carefully study Sections five and six of the UFOC for answers to these questions:

- How much is the upfront franchise fee?

- How much money do you have to pay the franchisor by way of a monthly fee, often called a royalty? As noted, this will often be 3% to 6% of your sales—not your profits—but can be much higher. (Subway charges as much as 11.5% of sales, according to the December 24, 2001, issue of *Forbes*.) With most franchises, even if you are operating in the red, you must pay this fee.

- Is there an additional marketing or advertising fee? If so, how much is it?

- Are there other fees for such things as travel, training, audits, and attorneys?

- Do you have to buy equipment or supplies from the franchisor? If so, how much cheaper could you buy them from an industry wholesaler or even at the local warehouse club?

- How much will it cost you to actually get into business? If you'll have to construct a building and buy equipment, it could be several hundred thousand dollars or, in the case of a fancy restaurant or hotel, many millions. You'll find the franchisor's estimate in Item 7 of the UFOC, but of course this won't include all your time, effort, and worry (that without the franchise, could likely be turned to other profit-making pursuits). And also remember this number doesn't include your operating costs during the start-up period, when business may be so slow it doesn't cover your costs.

Find Out About Recent Lawsuits Against the Franchisor

You want to know whether or not any unhappy franchisees have sued the company recently. Any such lawsuits should be listed near the beginning of the UFOC. If you find a history of litigation, contact the people involved to get their side of the story. Or, if the case was decided by an appeals court where a formal court opinion was written and published, find out what the judge had to say. (You can find court opinions in a law library or, in many instances, on the Internet. For help with online legal research, see Nolo's Legal Research Center at www.nolo.com.) For example, a few years ago, a federal appeals court ruled that it was legal for

Meineke Mufflers to set up its own in-house advertising agency and hire it to handle franchise system advertising, in effect ensuring itself millions of dollars in fees to handle franchise advertising. (*Broussard v. Meineke Discount Muffler Shops*, 155 F.3d 331 (4th Cir. 1998).)

Check Out the Competition

Open the local phone book and count the competitors in the particular market niche. In any popular field, chances are there will be a number of other competing franchise operations, as well as many independents. Personally visit or patronize a number of these businesses. Do the franchise operators really have an advantage over the well-run independents? How hard would it be to set up on your own?

Analyze Your Options

Finally, compare the cost of a franchise to the cost of opening and operating a similar independent business for a year. I suspect that you'll conclude that it's much cheaper to go it alone. If, for example, you would save $50,000 by operating independently, pretend you invest this money in United States bonds and leave it there until you retire. Depending on your age, it will double, triple, or, if you are young and leave it alone for many years, do even better. Obviously, it makes sense to invest in the franchise only if you are pretty sure you would earn more than you would take in running an independent business plus your annual investment income.

■

16

Sell Services, Not Goods

"Business without profit is not business any more than a pickle is a candy."

—Charles F. Abbott

In a Wal-Mart world, it's usually tough to succeed—or even survive —by retailing most kinds of goods. Whether it's clothing, hardware, sporting goods, pet food, or almost any other physical object, unless you operate in a niche so tiny the big players can't be bothered with it, competition from hypermarkets and other mass retailers will typically force you to set prices too low to make a decent profit. As thousands of struggling retailers have noticed, the big box stores, because of their huge market clout, often can sell stuff cheaper than the small guys can buy it.

By contrast, in an age where time is the most precious commodity, it's relatively easy to prosper by selling any one of a huge variety of helping services to individuals or businesses. Depending on the level of local competition, you can normally earn a very good living unclogging toilets, strengthening teeth, doctoring feet, laying tile, teaching kids advanced sports techniques, or providing any of a thousand other types of help. As long as there is a real demand for the type of assistance you provide, and it can't realistically be delivered long distance from a low-wage county, you normally have a great opportunity to establish and defend a robust profit margin.

To illustrate why it's far easier to succeed selling locally provided services than selling physical items, here is a short list of people I know whose businesses are solidly profitable:

- Wendy, whose four-person business designs and maintains up-scale gardens

- Ted, whose eight-person company installs, replaces, and fixes electric garage-door openers

- David, who is working with his partner, Wilbur, tutors high schoolers preparing for SAT exams

- Roy, whose three-person business repairs and replaces masonry fireplaces

- Cecily, whose small law firm (three partners, two staff) helps small businesses cope with employee-related problems

- Ling, whose family runs a photography business that specializes in children's school, church, and sports-team portraits

- Kyle, whose one-person business teaches batting skills to young women who play fast-pitch softball, and

- Andrew and Sid, who own an antique shop specializing in 18th- and 19th-century furniture.

Now here is a second list of business owners I know who are doing markedly less well:

- Faith, who runs a boutique dress shop with the help of four part-time employees

- Paul, whose independent bookstore employs two full-time and two part-time employees

- Ali, who retails TV and consumer electronics and repairs big-screen TVs (90% of his profits come from the repair business)

- Helga, who operates a three-person ice-skating equipment store (fortunately, Helga's second business, teaching people to skate, is profitable), and

- José, whose futon shop barely survives despite the poorly paid help of several long-suffering family members.

Interestingly, the only successful business that exclusively sells tangible items is the antique shop. It does well because it focuses on one-of-a-kind items not sold by major retailers. Even more telling, all the less successful businesses are retailers. Of course, not every service business prospers, and not every retail shop struggles. Loads of factors, including consumer demand, marketing savvy, location and, often most important, the proximity of low-price competition have a lot to do with whether a particular enterprise thrives or withers. Nevertheless, the trend away from being able to make a decent living selling goods is both strong and inexorable. It began way back in the mid-19th century with the advent of mass-produced consumer goods, and has accelerated ever since the large discount chains opened after World War II. Today the marriage of super-efficient, computer-driven, just-in-time inventory systems to low-cost but highly reliable foreign production has produced goods that are actually becoming both cheaper (in inflation-adjusted terms) and better quality.

Certainly there can be little doubt that many, if not most, Americans prefer to shop at the huge low-cost megastores that have all but taken over the retail environment. If you doubt it, walk along the main street of any American town or small city a year or two after Wal-Mart, Home Depot, Staples, or other big box retailers move into the area. Despite the best efforts of many established retailers to defend their traditional markets, you are almost sure to find many empty storefronts. As discussed later in this chapter, unless yours is a niche business specializing in products not available from the big players, such as antiques, luxury goods, or crafts, you are not looking at a future you want to be a part of.

By contrast, most service businesses have great potential to do well. Overbusy Americans are increasingly likely to buy help with all sorts of tasks. And most service businesses, which have the great virtue of being cheap and easy to start, are all but immune from the scorched-earth price competition so common in retail business. The exception, of course, is services such as telephone order taking and software development, which are easily amenable to being transferred to low-wage countries.

You Can Keep Start-Up Costs Low

It's often possible to get a highly profitable service business up and running with little up-front investment. The millions of people who have started one of these businesses from their homes, or in low-cost offices or warehouses, prove the point. For example, one highway engineer I know has run a one-person consulting business from his home for over 20 years; he has never netted less than $100,000 per year and often considerably more. And a freelance paralegal who very profitably handles the legal research needs of half a dozen small law firms from the corner of her bedroom often makes as much as they do.

A quick comparison between two animal-related businesses, one that offers services and one that sells products, illustrates this point. To open a pet supply store, Penny must rent a physical space, buy or lease equipment, purchase a wide variety of insurance, buy inventory, and hire employees, to mention just a few of her larger expenditures. By contrast, Philip, who catches and relocates raccoons, skunks, and other small animals that have become a nuisance to suburban homeowners, can start his business with a couple of dozen live traps, a Yellow Pages listing, some cat kibble, and an answering machine.

In many instances, retailers pay so much for a prime location that it's difficult to make a decent profit even when sales are strong. By contrast, your electrician, plumber, garage-door repairperson, and dozens of other service providers are probably headquartered in low-cost digs so far off the beaten path that you've never visited them. And, of course, the millions of consultants, tutors, Internet-centered resellers, and others who work from home pay little or no rent. Even many dentists, doctors, accountants, lawyers, and other professionals whose clients expect them to operate from appropriately "professional" locations find that their rent consumes only a smallish fraction of their gross income. In part this is because the ones with the best business smarts have learned that customers prefer to visit functional, rather than fancy, offices, and value practical things like free or affordable parking far above a faux-marble lobby or Persian carpet. After all, if you hire a business lawyer for your small business, do you really want to be billed an extra $50 per hour to cover the cost of the firm's penthouse suite?

Example:

Josephina decided to locate her law firm in a small but tasteful office complex on the edge of a light industrial area, rather than paying twice as much for space in the new professional building downtown. Before inking the lease, Josephina and her partners even got the landlord to trade a small but significant portion of the rent in exchange for legal services. The result was a yearly rent bill of only $50,000, not bad for a small firm that expected to bill about $700,000. By contrast, if Josephina's firm had located in the new professional building and negotiated no discount in exchange for services, the rent would have been close to $150,000.

Even service businesses such as car repair shops or dry cleaners, which do need to rent easily accessible space, still usually spend far less on overhead than do most retailers.

Example:

Don, an experienced car mechanic, dreamed of running his own business to repair luxury cars. Recognizing that the local Lexus dealer charged high prices for average service and that there were plenty of older, out-of-warranty Lexus cars in the area, Don sensed an opportunity for an independent garage charging less. Having very modest savings, he looked around for a relatively low-cost location from which to operate his new business. His hope was to rent a corner of an existing garage and pay an additional monthly fee to use its sophisticated diagnostic equipment. (Like most mechanics, Don already owned his own hand tools.) Unfortunately, every one of the 15 or so local garages that had good facilities and equipment turned him down. Then, just as he was planning to look further afield, Don got a call from Vincent, the owner of one of the first repair shops he had visited. It turned out Vincent's partner had just been diagnosed with cancer, and Vincent suddenly faced the prospect of buying him out and running the business alone. Renting part of the garage to Don was now attractive, and the two men quickly struck a bargain.

Now Don needed customers, and he needed them pronto. Instead of following more conventional marketing techniques, Don wrote a personal letter to Lexus owners announcing his new repair service and explaining why he believed he could do a great job for them. His next problem was how to deliver his messages effectively. An early morning jogger, Don tucked his letter under the wipers of literally hundreds of cars as he made his morning rounds. In addition, he hired school kids to distribute his flyer at several upscale shopping areas on weekends. Almost immediately Don got his first customers. With every repair job for a new customer, he included an elegant stainless steel, lidded beverage cup with a note thanking the customer and mentioning that as a new entrepreneur he would appreciate referrals. Before long, Don's small operation was making a profit.

Not every service business, of course, can be started or operated cheaply. If you want to open a car wash or instant printing operation, obviously you won't be able to do it from a spare bedroom. But even if you'll have to purchase or lease machinery and your rent approaches that of a similarly sized retail operation, you'll still have one big cost advantage: no need to pay to stock an inventory of expensive merchandise. You can tie up a lot of money in inventory—and if your stock is less popular than you had hoped, it will be a long time (if ever) before you get that money back.

You Can Keep Marketing Costs Low

When my younger daughter was facing the dreaded college board examinations (SATs), I looked around to find her some help in preparing. I had heard negative reports from older kids who had worked with a couple of national test preparation chains, so I hunted for a smart, experienced person to coach my daughter, one-on-one. I started and, as it turned out, quickly ended, my search by calling several friends whose bright children were a year or two older than my daughter. When all three highly recommended David, a local SAT tutor, I immediately called and booked a series of sessions. A few months later, after my daughter aced the exams, I passed David's name along to other parents. When, the next fall, word spread that she had been accepted at an excellent college, I received several more calls from parents of high school sophomores and juniors asking for tips. Again, I highly recommended David.

The point of this little story is obvious. David, like so many other service providers, gets most of his new customers from the recommendations of existing ones with no need to advertise. Combine this with the fact that like many other service providers, David's overhead costs are low, and the happy result is that almost all of his $60 hourly fee plummets straight to his bottom line. The result is that if David works 40 hours per week, he both grosses and nets substantially more than $100,000 annually. Not bad for a business whose principal physical asset is an eight-year-old answering machine.

If you are selling a skill that's in demand, positive word of mouth about your business can be all or most of the cheap and powerful marketing fuel you need to power your small service enterprise. But how do you get your business talked about in the first place? When you first open your doors, obviously you won't yet have any satisfied customers beating the drum for you. To get your marketing tom-tom started, you'll want to do many of the things discussed in Chapter 8, Market Your Business Creatively. But a crucial point bears emphasis here: As long as the service you provide is needed and you do an excellent job, there will be many cost-effective ways to attract customers. And since marketing a service is almost always a contact sport, you'll surely have many opportunities to use your own efforts and energy to spread the word about your business.

Example:

Tomiko opens a legal document preparation service specializing in helping people prepare the paperwork for uncontested divorces, bankruptcies, guardianships, and other routine legal matters. As part of developing her marketing plan, Tomiko follows the advice in Chapter 7, Target Your Customers, and asks: "Who are the people most likely to purchase my services?"

For divorces and bankruptcies, Tomiko decides her prime targets are "younger adults of limited financial means." By contrast, for guardianships, Tomiko sensibly concludes that her target market is largely made up of grandparents who suddenly find themselves raising their kids' kids when the parents can't.

To best serve the people in these target audiences, Tomiko opens a small office in an older, but still respectable, office building easily accessible to lower-middle-class and working-class neighborhoods. She then creates several flyers describing her legal document preparation services and has them translated into Spanish and Vietnamese—after English, the most common languages spoken in her area. Drawing a 20-mile circle around her office, Tomiko's next step is to hand-carry her materials to the social services and other helping and counseling organizations from which her target customers might seek help. At each place she tries to talk to the frontline people most likely to come in contact with people who have divorce, bankruptcy, guardianship, or other legal problems. Here is a partial list of the groups and organizations Tomiko contacts:

- public library reference librarians
- legal services (legal aid) offices
- battered women's shelters
- immigrants' help organizations
- law librarians at courthouses and law school libraries
- community services referral agencies and directories
- marriage counselors and family therapists
- court clerks
- Gray Panthers and other senior advocacy organizations
- Parents Without Partners and other singles groups
- women's organizations, and
- the local military base, (especially the Judge Advocate General law office).

In addition, Tomiko prepares a press release describing her new service and why it represents such a powerful and effective way for people who can't afford to hire a lawyer to gain affordable access to the legal system. She sends it to a long list of local print, broadcast, and Internet media, including those that reach Spanish and Vietnamese speakers. With the help of an experienced freelance publicist, she follows up a few days later and arranges for several interviews about her much-needed service.

You Can Set Prices at Profitable Levels

Unlike most retail and small manufacturing businesses, service businesses enjoy the huge advantage of being able to establish and maintain prices at a profitable level. As mentioned, instead of having to compete with the 21st-century retail juggernaut, which typically links highly efficient, low-wage foreign manufacturing with computer-driven, football-field-sized stores, most service businesses are by their nature locally based and labor-intensive. Because people in Thailand or Guatemala are obviously not available to unplug sinks or toilets in Scarsdale, Sacramento, or Santa Fe, this means that a typical service business's competitors are almost always other local enterprises that must pay wages on an American scale. True, in a few low-skill fields, such as lawn maintenance and house cleaning, recent or even illegal immigrants willing to work cheap may drive down prices, and in a few others, work can effectively be done from overseas, but for the most part, skilled service businesses are remarkably free of low-wage competitors. Even when you're competing against big companies and franchise operators, the fact that they must pay their workers locally competitive wages typically means they can't operate much more cheaply than you can. When it comes to providing essential services, corporate America can't use the same "build it big, sell it cheap" formula it so successfully employed to dominate the shopping mall.

To illustrate, consider that even in the service niches where large corporations are significant players, including tax preparation (H&R Block), unplugging drains (RotoRooter), rug cleaning (The Rug Doctor), and mail service (Mail Boxes Etc.), none of them has been able to eliminate the tens of thousands of independently operated small businesses that also populate these fields. To check this out, simply open your Yellow Pages and count the number of independent tax preparers, plumbers, and rug cleaners listed right next to the nationally advertised franchise outfits. You'll not only find plenty, but if you are able to talk to a few, you'll learn that on balance the big outfits do not try to undercut the prices of the independents.

Local service providers—whether or not they are affiliated with national franchises all have roughly similar labor costs, meaning few see anything to be gained by competing primarily on price. This helps explain why if you check the prices of several local dentists, chiropractors, or electricians, most are likely to quote roughly similar rates. With no need to engage in illegal price-fixing to maintain solid margins, these businesses have all learned that everyone does better if no one engages in predatory pricing. True, in some service fields, consumers who comparison shop can find someone who will charge a little less. But the cheaper players tend to be tiny outfits that typically offer limited or spotty customer service, underscoring the rule that most top-drawer service providers charge roughly the same fees.

When national service operations do try to compete on price, results are at best mixed. For example, in the legal field, both Jacoby & Myers and Hyatt Legal Services failed to make a profit running lower-cost, clinic-style law practices, even though the local lawyers they competed against often charged upwards of $200 per hour. One reason why these name-brand legal operations failed in their efforts to run full-service law offices was that, as in other fields, it proved hard to hire and retain workers (in this case, lawyers) at affordable salaries. After all, these people could opt to work for other law firms that paid better or even open a competing business across the street.

SuperCuts, a low-cost hair cutter, offers a more successful example of a price-competitive national service business. But because SuperCuts must pay its hairstylists decently or risk losing them, any price advantage it enjoys vis-à-vis nonfranchise independents is very small. In fact, every SuperCuts shop I've checked is surrounded by other independent hair-cutters, many of whom loudly trumpet that they charge a dollar or two less. And, of course, SuperCuts has had virtually no impact on the large number of more expensive hair salons, whose customers seem happy to pay a premium for a little extra pampering.

Retail and Other Nonservice Businesses That Work

A few types of retail businesses have been able to buck the long-term negative trends that have made it difficult for independent operators to prosper in most nonservice fields. Most of them are businesses whose products are handmade or one-of-a-kind, or which occupy niches so small or specialized as to be beneath the notice of the big operators. True, some stores that sell high-priced goods to upper-income consumers can also do well, especially when economic times are rosy, but for the most part these are not businesses that continue to do well in recessionary times.

Let's look briefly at why these types of businesses are the exception to my stay-away-from-retail rule.

Publishing

Businesses like Nolo and other small book, newsletter, and software publishers have a huge advantage over most businesses. Their output is protected by copyright, meaning that competitors can't directly copy it. Thus, as long as Nolo invests the time and energy to create and constantly improve its books and software, competitors must continually play catch-up. True, since ideas and facts can't be copyrighted (only their expression), all successful nonfiction publications—be they restaurant guides, genealogy software, or a popular series of investment advice titles are sure to attract imitators. But as many niche publishers like Nolo have shown, small outfits that adopt a strategy of continual improvement can both thrive and prosper.

Arts and Crafts

Although the starving artist is an enduring part of American mythology, in fact, many artists, artisans, gallery owners, and others who work in arts and crafts enterprises make a good living. In part, this is because the very ubiquity of mass-produced items has to some extent boomeranged, making significant numbers of consumers search for something different. With virtually everything at the shopping mall made by a machine, many people are willing to pay extra for handmade or unusual products.

The result is that in all sorts of fields, including furniture, clothing, garden sculpture, weaving, and the fine arts, many small arts- and crafts-based businesses are thriving. Often these businesses start when a creative person finds that his or her works are actually saleable and begins to dream of turning passion into profit. To judge if an arts- or crafts-based enterprise might work, many aspiring businesspeople often make a crude calculation along these lines: "If I can create five whatchamacallits a week and sell each for $250, I can make $65,000 in a year, which is more than enough to support myself." Sadly, this sort of naïve approach to small business economics has doomed many arts- and crafts-based businesses to failure. That's because, of course, by the time materials, sales costs, transportation, and a dozen other expenses are figured in, $65,000 will melt down to a starvation wage.

Although Achilles himself had but one vulnerable heel, the owners of small arts and crafts businesses tend to have two. The first, as just mentioned, is their lack of entrepreneurial experience and business sense. Second, even those artists and artisans who master business basics must confront the fact that it's no easy task to both create and market products. This helps explain why these functions are often separated, with galleries, crafts shops, catalog companies, or Internet sites doing the selling. But whether a creative person does the marketing or hires someone else to do it, marketing is time-consuming and costly. In fact, recognizing just how expensive it will be to sell your creations and designing a business model that will allow for an adequate profit after subtracting marketing costs is usually the key to designing a successful arts or crafts business.

Example:

John and Elaine create garden art—lifelike bugs, birds, lizards, and other creatures cut out of steel with a blowtorch and designed to be displayed on poles or wall-mounted. To make their business, called Critters, work, they carefully divide their time between production days and selling days, sometimes working together and sometimes going different ways. Like most artists, John and Elaine find that creating their sculptures is both a lot easier and more fun than selling them. But by personally marketing their sculptures at a number of quality craft and street fairs, they are nevertheless able to sell lots of product with low out-of-pocket marketing costs. Unfortunately, operating booths at fairs, craft shows, and other sales venues, in addition to designing and making sculptures, requires so many long days that John and Elaine have too little time left to have a decent life. Clearly, to make their business a long-term success, they need to find additional sales channels.

Deciding to avoid galleries and stores because they don't want to pay chunky commissions or get bogged down in keeping track of and trying to collect accounts or manage consignment deals, they focus instead on the Internet. First, they display their wares on several sites that aggregate the work of a number of craftspeople and charge reasonable commissions. Then Elaine takes a website design course and creates their own basic Critters website.

Now, she and John give everyone they meet at a fair a small brochure promoting their site. And because they know many of these will be tossed, they also point out that their Internet address is etched unobtrusively on the back of each sculpture. Their hope is that should someone admire one of their creations, its owner will remember how to point them to Critters.com. Over the next year, Critters' Internet business grows surprisingly robustly. Even allowing for the higher than anticipated costs of running a website, it provides a nice stream of profitable retail sales, enough to allow John and Elaine to scratch five of the least profitable weekend fairs and hire someone to go in their place to several others.

Niche Businesses

A successful "niche" retail business is typically one that's popular enough to make you a decent living, but not big enough to be flattened by the price-cutting, profit-eliminating competition from mass retailers. Although finding just the right niche can be tough, when accomplished successfully, it is a path that can lead to a profitable and lasting business.

Example:

Tod opened The Lizard House, a shop that sold snakes, reptiles, and amphibians and the often pricey equipment needed to keep them healthy. By stocking a far greater variety of cold-blooded creatures than any of the large pet retailers within at least 500 miles, and providing a superior level of education about how to care for reptiles, Tod was able to create a store that drew committed customers from a huge area. He made a very solid profit.

The Internet, with its worldwide reach, is often an excellent way for a niche business to reach enough customers to be profitable. So if you sell unicycles, unusual hats, fencing equipment, or custom-sewn sweatshirts with embroidered names and pictures of horses and dogs, you will almost surely want to establish an online site. Although most websites that attempted to sell goods in direct competition with major retailers have lost gobs of money, lots of highly specialized online retailers are solidly profitable. For example, a Missoula, Montana, store that sells a wide variety of animal bones is almost sure to increase its business by going online to reach the bone collectors of the world, not just those willing to stop by its shop in central Montana. Similarly, Nolo's self-help law site, which offers more plain-English legal materials than are available anyplace else, is another good example of how combining a specialized product with the long reach of the Internet can succeed. Every day Nolo sells hundreds of self-help law products, many of which are too specialized to be stocked in local bookshops, to people all over the U.S. and, increasingly, in other countries.

Paradoxically, one of the biggest enemies of long-term online profitability is too much success. A good niche business, such as one that sells French cookware or Peruvian sweaters, can easily choke on its own success if its products become sufficiently mainstream that they attract lots of price-cutting competitors. Similarly, a unicycle sales site may work as long as there is no mass market in one-wheeled cycles, but will almost inevitably face trouble the day K-Mart decides it can sell lots of them at a low price. It follows that if your niche threatens to grow too big, you'll want to look for a way to reorient your efforts to a specialized slice of it. Unicycles built for two, perhaps....

Antiques and Collectibles

Antique shops, used book stores, and high-end used clothing shops are also retail businesses that can do well. Although eBay and other Internet auction sites offer ways for collectors to find antiques, rare coins, old books, and other unique items without going to a physical store, so far there seems to be plenty of business to go around. (A quick count of the antique shops in your area should verify this.) In fact, many businesses that specialize in collectible items very profitably combine a physical location with the use of online auction sites such as eBay. Frequently, the idea is to use the physical location primarily as the place where goods are bought at reasonable prices, and the Internet as the place they are marked up significantly and offered for sale to a potentially huge audience. For example, a sports card dealer I know sifts through tens of thousands of cards hopeful collectors bring in each year. Purchasing less than 5% of them last year, he resold 1,500 on eBay, usually at a very nice profit.

Many one-of-a-kind businesses do well for the two reasons discussed at the beginning of this section: Lots of people are attracted to unique or rare goods, and the big box retailers have not found a way to efficiently serve, let alone dominate, this market. But the opportunity to succeed and the ability to actually do it are very different things. For example, despite bright prospects, a high-end, previously owned clothing business that doesn't buy the right items at the right price and resell them quickly can die a quick death.

But when a solid market and a smart buyer come together, profits usually follow, in large part because the markup on used items is usually much fatter than for new ones. For example, a used book store that pays about 25% of the cover price for certain categories of used books can resell many of them for 60% of the original list price, providing a markup of 150%. By contrast, a small, new book store will be lucky to buy inventory at 45% off the cover price and, at least with bestsellers, be forced to give customers at least a 20% discount, ending up with a dismal profit margin.

Buying, not selling, is often key.

This point bears emphasis. An antique, collectibles, or used merchandise store will prosper if it buys enough of the right items at the right price. That's why experienced owners usually concentrate on finding the right merchandise. Once they do, the sales side of the business often all but takes care of itself.

Luxury Goods

Mass retailers make money by selling lots of products to lots of people. When it comes to items where a few sizes fit most, such as appliances, tires, and many types of clothing, they are all but impossible to compete against. But for clothing, furniture, and a number of other types of goods, people crave novelty. As discussed, one way to get it is to purchase handmade items. Another, obviously, is to buy luxury goods not available at the mall.

Flight from the mass market makes it possible for shops selling some types of upmarket goods to prosper. But even though loads of people will pay $300 for a sweater, $600 for a pair of shoes, and many thousands for just the right chair, particularly when economic times are good, succeeding long-term in a luxury goods business requires plenty of entre-preneurial savvy. For one thing, you'll need an expensive address; people willing to splash out big bucks for items they don't really need are not likely to do it at the downscale strip mall out on the old state highway. Add to this the fact that the wealthy are famously fickle. One year every-one seems to need a $10,000 watch; the next, only a $50 Swatch will do. And finally, while the very rich are always with us and continue to spend during tough economic times, the merely well-off often cut back on non-essential purchases at first whiff of a recession.

But despite these negatives, lots of retailers do well selling to the Jaguar trade. The trick is to pick a product enough people are willing to pay extra for. Fancy lighting is one good example. Big box stores carry lots of serviceable lamps and light fixtures. But no matter how many styles they stock, it barely scratches the surface of what's available from small lighting manufacturers and custom designers. For example, one specialty shop I occasionally patronize stocks lamps from 144 manufacturers, only two of which are carried by the nearby Home Depot. Affluent customers willing to pay hundreds of dollars for specialty lamps and lights make this little lighting business solidly profitable. What's to stop mass retailers from trying to capture this business? Nothing—and by constantly expanding their lighting sections and keeping prices low, several are formidable competitors of the smaller store. But as long as many tiny manufacturers produce small quantities of expensive designer lamps, well-run indepen-dents can succeed marketing to upmarket customers who want their houses to look a little different.

17

React Quickly to Bad News

"When the horse dies, get off."

—Kinky Friedman

Small enterprises are incredibly sensitive to both good and bad fortune. A run of good news can result in quick growth and outsized profits. Unfortunately, the opposite is also true; when things go wrong—often for reasons beyond anyone's control—profits can turn into losses faster than the neighbor's nuisance of a cat disappears when you reach for the garden hose.

It's usually exciting and fun to expand a successful business by hiring additional employees, buying more equipment, renting space, and doing all the other things necessary to grow. But there is precious little joy in downsizing a business that has become overextended or otherwise hits a rough patch—so little, in fact, that many entrepreneurs whose businesses are caught in stormy seas refuse even to recognize that they are in trouble. Often the result is that owners of a sinking, but nevertheless savable, business delay necessary cutbacks and changes until their enterprise is so waterlogged it can't be kept afloat.

Act Quickly on Bad News

Huge, once highly successful companies, such as Kodak, Xerox, or AT&T, can deteriorate for years or even decades without closing. But small entrepreneurs rarely have the luxury of being able to ride their declining businesses slowly into the sunset. In the small business world, if revenues drop significantly for more than a few months, you must both prune expenses and address the causes of the decline. If you don't, you risk quick and brutal failure.

How do you know when it's time to cut back? Anyone who runs a small business will immediately know about—and may well have anticipated—negative events such as a precipitous sales drop, the loss of a big contract, or the emergence of a tough new competitor. The real problem is not spotting a disturbing event or trend, but admitting that it is serious enough to require quick and decisive action. Thus, the owner of the small Reader's Corner bookstore who learns that Barnes & Noble is planning to open a megastore on the next corner is all too likely to carry on business pretty much as usual, even as the walls of the huge new competitor rise. Similarly, the operator of a motel on the main street of a town bisected by a good-sized highway may do nothing when it is announced that the construction of a nearby freeway will shunt tourists several miles away from its front door.

Whistling in the face of entrepreneurial adversity will rarely work. Once you see—or better yet, anticipate—that your current business faces a boulder-strewn path, your most important job is to immediately come up with a workable plan to either clear the boulders, choose another path, or sensibly deal with the problem in some other way. Depending on your business and the new problem it suddenly faces, this may involve moving, introducing a new product or service, developing a better way to reach customers, cutting expenses, or selling the business. But since survival depends on quickly reversing business-killing losses, it's usually less important what you do than it is that you act before insolvency turns the boulders in your path into gravestones.

Fix the Problem, Change Direction, or Quit

What exactly should you do when your enterprise is suddenly surrounded by hostile forces? Obviously, I can't give you a survival plan for your unique business, but I can remind you that the owner of a troubled business who gets beyond the denial stage commonly has three choices: fix the problem, take the business in a new direction, or close down. Let's look at each.

Fix the Problem

When times are good, it's easy to expand too fast or into too many unproven areas. As has happened in countless wars, when a victorious army advances so quickly it outraces its own supply lines, a rapidly growing business can easily become a victim of its own euphoria, in effect snatching defeat from the jaws of victory. In an effort to open a second café, hire more workers for your carpentry business, or expand your nutritional supplements website, your business can similarly become financially, personally, and logistically overextended. And when this occurs, new or newly invigorated competitors are almost sure to attack your core profit centers.

As you might expect, both in war and business, often the best anti-
dote for advancing too far too fast is to quickly pull back and consolidate
your initial success. Executing a strategic retreat isn't the only way to fix a
broken business, but absent a clear culprit, such as an embezzling bookkeeper, incompetent manager, or radically new competitive environment
that puts your whole business plan in question, it's usually the first one
you'll want to consider.

You'll probably want to focus energy on your profitable core competencies while shucking off other money- and energy-draining activities.
To develop a back-to-basics plan, start by looking at the profit margins in
all parts of your little empire. Often you'll find that the areas that made
you successful in the first place are still your cash cows. For example, a
coffee shop that has begun to serve dinner, only to be hit by a business-
dampening economic downturn, may find that most of its profits are still
made before 10:30 a.m. and that the new supper business, no matter how
excellent its long-term prospects, is causing unsustainable losses. Fine—
cut dinner, take a hard look at whether lunch is also a money loser, and
reemphasize coffee and breakfast. When the operation is profitable again,
and sunnier economic times return, take another look at expanding into
pork chops and pasta.

Opening a second or third location is a particularly tough transition
for many small businesses, especially when the enterprise is simultaneously
hit by a profit-flattening event such as a recession, tough new competitor,
or natural disaster. Leaving aside the issue of whether it's usually wise for
a successful small business to open additional locations or find other ways
to create new customers, one thing is sure: If your expanded operation
isn't quickly profitable, close it. If you don't, you are at high risk of transferring precious time and energy from the successful part of your business
to the bit that is failing, almost always a terrible strategy.

At Nolo, we have several times had to resize our operations in light of less-than-hoped-for revenues. For example, in the late 1990s, we were suddenly faced with competition from a number of consumer-oriented legal websites funded with free-flowing venture capital. Looking at them, we concluded that we either had to invest far more in Nolo's website or risk becoming an also-ran in this critical new self-help law market. Eager to answer the online challenge, we hired Web programmers, reassigned legal editors from our book and software operations to Web development, bought equipment, and took a number of other expensive steps to quickly expand and improve Nolo.com. Nolo planning documents of those years confidently looked forward to a day, not far off, when Nolo customers would be able to handle most of their legal tasks, including filing court documents online using Nolo.com's interactive legal wizards. Unfortunately, the cost of jump-starting Nolo's digital future outstripped our online revenues to such an extent that for two years running, Nolo operated far in the red.

Clearly, a reassessment was in order. In reaching eagerly for the future, Nolo was obviously in danger of compromising its core book and software operations. To fix the problem before it finished us, we decided to severely downsize our online efforts by laying off programmers and Web designers, cutting our website budget for such things as new equipment, and renting less space. We slowed down development of many new interactive features and decided to treat the website primarily as a vehicle to sell our existing books and software. With expenses cut drastically, Nolo quickly returned to the black.

Fortunately for us, at the same time a number of our online competitors who had emphasized growth and ignored profits, exhausted their venture funding and went bust. So, even as Nolo reduced online expenditures, our Internet market share actually increased. Today, Nolo.com not only brings in millions of dollars, it's solidly profitable and steadily growing.

Don't blame the economy.

When a local or national recession hits, it's easy for struggling business owners to excuse their inability to make a profit by blaming their red ink on economic factors beyond their control. Like the right fielder who claims he would have caught the ball if he hadn't slipped on the over-watered grass, this is a cop-out. Although, admittedly, it can be tough to make money in a recession, you need to focus on your business's fundamentals and on how you can overcome the adversity you face. Just as lots of outfielders catch balls despite wet turf, many nimble small businesses survive even severe economic downturns.

Go in a New Direction

Closing a poorly performing satellite location, shedding side businesses and concentrating on your strengths, or fixing another problem such as poor management won't always put a staggering business solidly back on its feet. If suddenly no one wants to buy your most important product or service, or a huge competitor has siphoned off a large chunk of your business, cutbacks or leadership changes obviously won't help. Unfortunately, it's fairly common for yesterday's highly profitable business model to become today's big bust. For example, if you own Stoveland, a business that sells wood stoves, in a semirural area where new air pollution regulations have begun to drastically restrict their use, there may be little you can do to save your core business. Similarly, if your venture-funded

Internet e-commerce business suddenly loses its one profitable business niche, cutting back won't help.

Quickly moving to find a new product or service, or otherwise diversifying your business, is often your best chance to survive if your core business begins to fail. If you have built a culture of continuous innovation into your operations, you may know just how to do this. (See Chapter 6, Innovate Now and Forever.) For example, in the last decade, Amy, a travel agent who specialized in booking business travel, faced serious problems as a result of the airlines' gradual but relentless move to cut commissions on domestic air travel. But if Amy had been farsighted enough to early on spot this trend, as well as the related one of customers increasingly booking air travel online, and as a result began developing a sideline planning reasonably priced trips for baby boomer retirees, she would now be well-positioned to turn the side business into her main business. Similarly, the owners of a rural bed and breakfast, hit by the double whammy of too much local competition and an areawide economic downturn, may be able to reenergize their operation by using a website to market to urban families looking for an affordable and friendly place to hold reunions.

If your business loses key markets or otherwise faces a severe drop in revenue, I suggest a two-step approach to analyze your situation. First, inventory and list your enterprise's core skills or competencies. Then assess whether or not you can market them in new ways. If you do see new marketing possibilities, exploring them is probably your best strategy, because there is far less risk in finding new customers for an existing business than there is in trying to create an entirely new enterprise. Only if you're sure there's no way to target and reach new customers should you consider trying to save your business by fundamentally reinventing it.

Example:

In 1999, Sandrine, Mavis, and Paul formed SMP & Associates to design websites for e-commerce companies. For two years, business was so good SMP's headcount ballooned to 60, and it was about to sign a lease for thousands of square feet of office space in a pricey area called Web Alley. Then, in 2001, the bottom fell out of e-commerce and new business dried up. Still, for months the partners thought they could survive until business picked up by completing SMP's many existing contracts. But when in early 2002 three of their best remaining customers suddenly declared bankruptcy and two others simply packed up in the middle of the night and slunk out of Silicon Gulch without paying their bills, it looked like SMP was toast.

That's when Mavis mentioned that River People, a nonprofit environmental group whose board she chaired, needed help with its website. With nothing else on the horizon, SMP made River People a proposal and landed a fair-sized job, albeit at an hourly rate far lower than they were used to charging profit-making enterprises. The partners decided that redeploying their skills to design Internet sites for nonprofits was their best strategy to stay in business at least until higher-margin commercial business again became available.

To get started, they made a list of the 100 largest area health, environmental, and education groups. Next, Sandrine, Mavis and Paul systemically studied each organization's website. Identifying a number that obviously needed improvement, they began pitching SMP's design services. Although more than a few of these potential customers claimed to have no funds to improve their sites, a number of others were open to SMP's reasonably priced bids, especially when Mavis explained how River People had quickly raised the needed money through a focused membership appeal.

Over the two years, SMP worked with a number of nonprofits but was still officially committed to eventually returning to the profitable world of e-commerce. But, at an owners' meeting in early 2004, a funny thing happened. In the middle of outlining his planned proposal to a potential client in the child health field, Paul said, "You guys—I'm having so much fun working with people who really stand for something, I don't want to do anything else." When Mavis and Sandrine agreed, the owners realized that they hadn't just temporarily adjusted their business plan in reaction to a financial emergency, they had fundamentally and happily changed it.

Example:

Jorge and Guillermo thought they would be tremendously successful opening Los Padres Grill, a mid-priced Mexican restaurant across from a university's large complex of married-student housing. With the exception of a McDonald's, there was no real competition nearby. Still, no matter how tasty its food, Los Padres Grill never drew the number of lunch and dinner customers Jorge and Guillermo needed to prosper. After two years, mostly in the red, they finally had to either quit or try a different approach.

With the help of a loan from their uncle, they converted their sit-down restaurant to a takeout place with just a few self-serve tables. Because customers now lined up at a counter to order food, there was no need for table service, meaning prices could be reduced. More students were able to afford the food, and Los Padres' dinner business improved.

But still, because business was decent only at supper time, it was obvious Los Padres Grill needed to develop additional markets. Jorge and Guillermo decided to try to find one in the light industrial area that surrounded the student housing. Taking a few days to talk to workers at an auto body shop, metal fabricating company, wholesale plumbing supply outfit, and a number of similar businesses, the partners learned that workers didn't patronize Los Padres at lunch primarily because they were so busy they didn't take a formal lunch hour. Instead, they grabbed a sandwich off a roving lunch truck or brought one in a bag. To improve access to their food, Jorge and Guillermo decided to create what they called "the Taco Wagon." Converting Guillermo's pickup truck with several warming ovens, coolers, and food display units, the partners began taking their food to the workers, something that immediately proved popular and profitable.

With their business finally doing better, Jorge and Guillermo next decided to use their core skill of making tasty Mexican food to diversify into catering. Realizing that virtually all small businesses sometimes entertain or order food for meetings, celebrations, and other events, and that even the financially challenged students occasionally have parties, Los Padres created a menu of reasonably priced catered meals. When flyers were distributed at all businesses on the Taco Wagon's route and to customers in the student housing, orders quickly began to come in.

Taking an under-performing business in a completely new direction, instead of finding a way to take advantage of its core skills, is a more difficult task, especially if the business is already in trouble. So the owners of Stoveland, the wood stove business mentioned earlier in this chapter, would have at least a decent chance to develop new endeavors if they began a well-planned diversification into septic tanks at the first hint that air quality rules would be tightened. But, like a hotel guest who, when awoken by a fire alarm, decides that it's a false alarm and rolls over and goes back to sleep instead of heading for the exit, their chances of survival decrease if they wait and hope for the best. And even if a desperate, last-minute switch into septic tanks keeps Stoveland out of bankruptcy, it may still not assure it long-term success. That's because in their haste to find a new business that will pay the bills, Stoveland's owners may end up working in a field they don't enjoy and won't stay committed to over the long term.

Close Down

For a variety of reasons, including new competition, a changing market-place, bad luck, and, of course, owner mismanagement, many small businesses don't succeed. Unfortunately, some enterprises fail despite the fact that their owners work hard and do lots of things right, often because their imagined market simply never existed. But it isn't just marginal businesses that are vulnerable to trouble. Even initially successful ones can sail into heavy weather.

Especially when a small business is hit by very bad news, as was the case in New York City after 9/11 for many travel-related businesses, there can often be little recourse, absent a government bailout, but to close down and move on. Or put another way, if there are no tourists to ride your excursion bus, no amount of entrepreneurial CPR will resuscitate your business, at least in the short run. And because your business is losing both money and hope, no one is likely to want to buy it. In Chapter 12, Learn to Live With Luck, I discuss several indicators that help you decide when you would do better to close up and move on, as opposed to hold-ing on and hoping for better days. The most important factors are the scope or severity of the bad news and how long it is likely to last. Thus if a new digital technology makes your signature mechanical product completely obsolete, there is probably little you can do to recover. Like a manufacturer of carbon paper for typewriters who can't wait until people tire of computers, you need to move on. But, as was predictable in New York after the horrors of September 11, 2001, the business-dampening effects of many types of catastrophic events are likely to pass relatively quickly. This explains why many of New York's tourist-related businesses that hung in there—sometimes with the help of government financial assistance—through a very bad couple of years eventually returned to profitability.

How to Cut Expenses

If your suddenly troubled business still has a heartbeat and you sensibly decide to quickly reduce expenses, you'll have the time you need to either outlast the problem, market your goods or services more effectively or diversify. Moving quickly to cut expenses without killing an already troubled business is no easy task. Here is an ordered approach that I think makes sense.

Decide How Much to Cut

Your first step is to decide how much you need to cut. Lay off the Prozac and start by creating a "worst case" budget for the rest of your current fiscal year. List only revenue you are absolutely sure will materialize. If, because of widespread state government budget cuts, sales of your public library-centered consulting business have dropped 25% in the last three months and there is no economic rebound in sight, your budget for the immediate future should obviously reflect this. It follows that to balance your budget you'll need to cut expenses at least 25% and probably significantly more, since reduced volume is likely to further savage profits.

Sharpen your knife.

Just as it's human nature to delay pruning your business while continuing to hope for the best, when you finally do reach for the knife, you may be tempted to cut too little too slowly. If you do, your business, already weakened by losses, will continue to droop, making additional and often deeper cuts necessary soon.

Cut Discretionary Spending

If you planned to paint the building, buy new equipment, or hire additional employees, don't. Only if a particular expense is crucial to an essential diversification plan should you go ahead. In virtually every other instance, it makes sense to put new expenditures on hold. And you should try to do this even where contractual commitments have already been made. If you are willing to pay a reasonable buy-out fee, you can legally and honorably negotiate your way out of most agreements. After all, once clued in to your financial problems, the other party may be happy to avoid working with you.

In addition, you'll want to examine every part of your operations to make sure pennies aren't being wasted. For example, depending on your business, a surprising amount can often be cut by reducing perks such as expense account lunches or nonessential travel expenses. And often by focusing attention on paring even basic expenditures to the bone, such as phone service, copying, janitorial services, and payments to a variety of independent contractors, you can probably achieve significant additional savings. Even in areas where cuts are more symbolic than significant, working hard to chop every possible expense sends a message to everyone associated with your business that you are determined to do what it takes to survive.

Cut Your Pay and That of Any Managers

The biggest expense for many small businesses is the payroll. If this is true for your enterprise, cutting other expenditures is unlikely to realize the savings your troubled business needs. Sooner or later—and the sooner the better—you'll need to reduce the size of your payroll.

The first place to look should be employee perks. For example, if you match your employees' contributions to a 401(k) plan or have other generous benefits, consider cutting them back. Although often painful, it's usually better to cut benefits before you reduce pay or lay off people.

The first person to take a pay cut should be you. Even if your compensation is already modest and cutting it won't save much, trimming your own salary is sure to get employees' attention—and their respect—in ways a dozen dire pronouncements never will. Next, you should sit down with any well-paid employees to help them confront the need to voluntarily accept similar reductions. Depending on pay levels and other circumstances, a cut of 10% to 20% is usually reasonable.

This cut-from-the-top approach usually makes sense for several reasons. First, if you explain it correctly, you'll save money without losing essential employees. Second, and perhaps more important, it sends a message to everyone connected to your company that you and other managers take personal responsibility for coping with tough times.

Example:

John and Adelle own HillTop, a 60-room country hotel near a ski resort. Although the hotel does decent business year-round, in most years the lion's share of profits are made from the winter ski crowd, who cheerfully pay high-season rates and eat and drink everything in sight. After a decade of hard work during which they invested most profits back in the business, John and Adelle were finally able to pay themselves and several key employees, including the reservations manager and head cook, comfortable salaries. Then came the year when the snow failed to arrive in their corner of the woods, and the skiers went elsewhere. It didn't take many weeks of brown slopes and terrible business before John and Adelle realized that HillTop was in serious trouble.

Calling a meeting of their five highest-paid employees, they suggested freezing all nonessential expenditures, such as replacing older but still serviceable equipment, repainting several hallways and rooms, as well as cutting nonessential items such as subscriptions to periodicals and memberships in trade organizations. They even decided to ask several employees to turn in their cell phones. In addition, they resolved to severely cut the budget for outside services, transferring work to employees who now had time on their hands. Next they announced they were cutting their own pay by 20% and were asking all managers to accept a 15% reduction. A couple of people grumbled, but all they had to do was look out the window to understand the problem. Respecting John's and Adelle's determination to take the biggest hit, they accepted their lower paychecks.

Cut Jobs, Not People

Unfortunately, in many small businesses, reducing your pay and that of top managers won't save all that much, since the business probably hasn't matured enough to afford to pay generously in the first place. In short, while salary cutbacks, combined with other reductions in spending, are usually a big step in the right direction, they probably won't save nearly enough to balance your new bare-bones budget. For most small enterprises, where people are the biggest expense, it follows that layoffs will be required. Again, don't act like the hotel guest who assumes it's a false alarm when she hears the fire siren. Delay, and you risk having to face a business-destroying conflagration—which, of course, will throw everyone, including you, out of work.

Unfortunately, unlike the big business world, where the CEO can order 10,000 job cuts without ever meeting anyone who has been laid off, reducing your small workplace entails the excruciating task of firing people you know well and are on friendly terms with. It's so hard that some businesspeople watch their business fail rather than wield the axe. But to survive the economic ups and downs that affect any business, you absolutely must accept the proposition that your duty to your employees is limited by economic reality. You agreed to hire employees in an effort to make a profit, not to pay them in all circumstances forever.

Recognizing that laying off people is always an unhappy proposition, there are nevertheless some good and bad ways to approach it. First, the bad. Things are likely to further go further and faster downhill if you base your cuts on the needs of the people who work for you. No question, it's tough to lay off Jeff, who just made a down payment on a new house, or cut back Morisette's hours when you know she is already financially stretched helping support her cancer-stricken mother. But, as I learned the hard way many years ago, if you spare the people who have the most sympathetic personal problems, or have worked for you longest, or are related to you, you'll almost always end up laying off other, better workers. The result will be a business that is less efficient and competitive, and therefore more likely to fail.

Far better to base your cutback decisions strictly on the needs of your business. Look at the task that needs doing, not just the person filling it. If your brother-in-law is in charge of an activity that is losing money, his position should be cut. And so should every other position that isn't truly needed. If it makes good business sense, transfer a beloved employee whose task is no longer essential to a still-needed job he can perform well. But if the longtime employee isn't well-qualified to do the work, don't let sentiment cloud your vision.

In a very small enterprise, it will fall to you to decide which jobs must go. But if you depend on others to help with management decisions, it's extremely important to solicit their help in deciding who you should lay off, unless of course you have decided that managerial cuts will be necessary. It's key to involve others because it is often your managers, not you, who have the best frontline knowledge of which tasks are essential and which expendable. And because they are the ones who will be responsible for accomplishing the essential work with a smaller staff, they are likely to be highly motivated to hold onto the most talented workers, while shedding the less efficient.

Example:

Returning to our example of the HillTop hotel, it became clear to John and Adelle that to survive, it wouldn't be enough to cut discretionary expenses and managerial pay. To plan deeper cuts, Adelle, the financial officer, prepared a revised budget that matched expenditures to their newly drafted worst-case scenario. This rebudgeting process revealed that to achieve balance, an additional $200,000 needed to be cut, pronto.

Some cuts were obvious, such as laying off several maids and restaurant workers who, given the lack of guests, were already underemployed. To help plan other staff cuts, John and Adelle convened an off-site meeting of their top people. Fortunately, when the managers shared their opinions about how best to reduce staff, a consensus emerged. For example, Constantine, the head cook and restaurant manager, suggested that while things remained slow, the jobs of bartender and restaurant host be combined. He pointed out that most customers ordered easy-to-serve beer or wine, and that the person who handled both jobs just needed to know how to mix a few basic drinks.

Then Phyllis, the reservations manager, suggested that while business was in the dumps she could handle reservations herself, without an assistant. She pointed out that occasionally, this change would mean that customers would get a message machine with the promise of a prompt call back, but given the low volume of calls, this didn't seem like a serious problem. Finally, John himself proposed taking over many maintenance tasks. This would allow HillTop to eliminate the position of in-house maintenance manager, one of whose main tasks, removing snow from the parking lot, obviously did not need doing.

The result of these and several other job restructurings was that $200,000 in salaries could be cut without significantly reducing essential guest services or eliminating key employees who would be immediately needed when business eventually picked up. All told, ten people—including John and Adelle's niece, who worked as a part-time desk clerk—lost their jobs, and contracts with several outside businesses were cancelled.

Act Slowly to Reverse Cutbacks

After you've had to make painful cuts in jobs and salaries, you would only be human if you were tempted to quickly reverse them the minute business improved. Although eminently understandable, especially when you are dealing with loyal employees whose personal budgets you know are already stretched, there are at least two reasons why this approach is almost always a mistake. First, if significant cutbacks were needed in the first place, it will almost certainly take time for your business to bounce back to health, even if the factors that triggered the need to downsize begin to dissipate. Before you should even think about increasing expenditures, this typically means your business not only needs to return to profitability, but to dig itself out of its financial hole. In many instances, you'll want to repay borrowed money, catch up on deferred maintenance, and buy long-needed equipment before you give a thought to restoring paychecks. For example, if you have borrowed $100,000, deferred the purchase of $50,000 worth of new equipment, and failed to repaint your tatty-looking building, you've got lots to spend money on before adding to your payroll expense.

A second reason why you don't want to restore jobs and raise pay to precut levels too quickly is to avoid the possibility of a double dip. If after a couple of months your business again underperforms, it will be emotionally devastating to you and your staff to have to reimpose the cuts. To say your credibility as a leader will be shot will surely be an understatement.

It's also important to recognize that all employee costs are not alike. Rehiring laid-off workers is often a lower priority than is restoring at least some of the pay of the employees who have stuck with you during the hard times and worked extra hard to achieve the recovery. In fact, if you really did adopt a good process to cut your least important functions and your most inefficient people, it may not make sense to reverse these decisions, no matter how much business prospects have improved. You will often be smarter to hire fewer, more efficient workers at the same time you lift the pay of those who have experienced cutbacks. A highly motivated employee can be at least several times more efficient than a weak one, meaning you may even be able to get more done than you did before the cutbacks, when you had more employees. (See Chapter 9, Hire and Keep Good People.)

Example:

Finally, in the last week of February, HillTop and the surrounding mountains experienced a deep snowfall. Even though business immediately improved, John and Adelle decided to keep a lid on costs until they could reduce the bank line of credit they had all but maxed out. So except for rehiring a couple of essential room cleaners and restaurant staffers, and in the process replacing the two who had been least diligent, John, Adelle, and the other HillTop managers continued to fill in behind the front desk and grab the now happily jingling phones. Adelle, subbing behind the bar, even learned to make a killer martini (use cold gin and just one drop of vermouth).

Only when a long and busy spring ski season gave way to an equally good summer, allowing HillTop to reduce its line of credit to a comfortable level, did John and Adelle finally restore half of the salary reductions. A month later, when business stayed good, they hired back the assistant reservations manager. But the old bartender, who was not missed, was replaced with a new hire willing, when necessary, to pinch-hit as a waiter. They also kept a number of the efficiencies imposed during the downturn, including contracting out maintenance and snow removal instead of paying a full-time employee. Only when bookings for the fall "color season" came in strong was the decision made to restore all salary cuts to their predrought levels and to rehire the final couple of needed workers. That next Christmas, with business still strong, everyone who had survived the tough year received a small bonus along with a personal note from John and Adelle thanking them for their loyalty.

■

Index

targeting customers, examples,
146–147, 148, 153, 154
Southwest Airlines, 210–211
Specialization, 91, 96–97, 112, 123
Sponsorships, 175, 179
Starting on a shoestring, 71–86
dangers of overcapitalization,
72–73
examples, 73–79, 83
service vs. nonservice businesses,
300–303
spending money wisely, 79–86
Success. *See* Business success;
Profitability
Suggestions forms/boxes, 136–137,
222. *See also* Ideas
Superior service. *See* Customer
service; Excellence
Suppliers
benefits of early payment,
259–265
if you must pay late, 267–269
Sustainability, 18–19

T

Targeting customers, 141–156
ad targeting, 163–165
current customers, 152–156, 160
customer outreach, 147–148,
178–179

examples, 146–147, 148,
150–152, 153, 154–156
identifying potential customers,
141–146, 177–178
novice vs. experienced
customers, 149–152
Testing job applicants, 196
Texas UPLC, legal battle with Nolo,
7–9, 11–16
Thanking people, 227
Toyota, 26–27
Trade associations, 275
Training employees, 192–194
mentoring, 205–206

U

UFOC (Uniform Franchise Offering
Circular), 293, 294
Unauthorized Practice of Law
Committee of Texas. *See* Texas
UPLC
Uniform Franchise Offering Circular
(UFOC), 293, 294

V

Vacations, 47

W

Website design businesses,
examples, 43–44, 324–325

CATALOG

...more from nolo

ESTATE PLANNING & PROBATE

	PRICE	CODE
8 Ways to Avoid Probate	$19.99	PRO8
9 Ways to Avoid Estate Taxes	$29.95	ESTX
Estate Planning Basics	$21.99	ESPN
How to Probate an Estate in California	$49.99	PAE
Make Your Own Living Trust (Book w/CD-ROM)	$39.99	LITR
Nolo's Simple Will Book (Book w/CD-ROM)	$36.99	SWIL
Plan Your Estate	$44.99	NEST
Quick & Legal Will Book	$16.99	QUIC

FAMILY MATTERS

	PRICE	CODE
Child Custody: Building Parenting Agreements That Work	$29.99	CUST
The Complete IEP Guide	$24.99	IEP
Divorce & Money: How to Make the Best Financial Decisions During Divorce	$34.99	DIMO
Do Your Own California Adoption: Nolo's Guide for Stepparents and Domestic Partners (Book w/CD-ROM)	$34.99	ADOP
Get a Life: You Don't Need a Million to Retire Well	$24.99	LIFE
The Guardianship Book for California	$39.99	GB
A Legal Guide for Lesbian and Gay Couples	$29.99	LG
Living Together: A Legal Guide (Book w/CD-ROM)	$34.99	LTK
Medical Directives and Powers of Attorney in California	$19.99	CPOA
Using Divorce Mediation: Save Your Money & Your Sanity	$29.95	UDMD

GOING TO COURT

	PRICE	CODE
Beat Your Ticket: Go To Court and Win! (National Edition)	$19.99	BEYT
The Criminal Law Handbook: Know Your Rights, Survive the System	$34.99	KYR
Everybody's Guide to Small Claims Court (National Edition)	$26.99	NSCC
Everybody's Guide to Small Claims Court in California	$26.99	CSCC
Fight Your Ticket ... and Win! (California Edition)	$29.99	FYT
How to Change Your Name in California	$34.95	NAME
How to Collect When You Win a Lawsuit (California Edition)	$29.99	JUDG
How to Seal Your Juvenile & Criminal Records (California Edition)	$34.95	CRIM
The Lawsuit Survival Guide	$29.99	UNCL
Nolo's Deposition Handbook	$29.99	DEP
Represent Yourself in Court: How to Prepare & Try a Winning Case	$34.99	RYC
Sue in California Without a Lawyer	$34.99	SLWY

HOMEOWNERS, LANDLORDS & TENANTS

	PRICE	CODE
California Tenants' Rights	$27.99	CTEN
Deeds for California Real Estate	$24.99	DEED
Dog Law	$21.95	DOG
Every Landlord's Legal Guide (National Edition, Book w/CD-ROM)	$44.99	ELLI
Every Tenant's Legal Guide	$29.99	EVTEN
For Sale by Owner in California	$29.99	FSBO
How to Buy a House in California	$34.99	BHCA
The California Landlord's Law Book: Rights & Responsibilities (Book w/CD-ROM)	$44.99	LBRT
The California Landlord's Law Book: Evictions (Book w/CD-ROM)	$44.99	LBEV
Leases & Rental Agreements	$29.99	LEAR
Neighbor Law: Fences, Trees, Boundaries & Noise	$26.99	NEI
The New York Landlord's Law Book (Book w/CD-ROM)	$39.99	NYLL
New York Tenants' Rights	$29.99	YRW
Renters' Rights (National Edition)	$27.99	NYTEN
Stop Foreclosure Now in California	$29.95	CLOS

IMMIGRATION

	PRICE	CODE
Becoming a U.S. Citizen: A Guide to the Law, Exam and Interview	$24.99	USCIT
Fiancé & Marriage Visas	$44.95	IMAR
How to Get a Green Card	$29.99	GRN

	PRICE	CODE
Student & Tourist Visas	$29.99	ISTU
U.S. Immigration Made Easy	$44.99	IMEZ

MONEY MATTERS

	PRICE	CODE
101 Law Forms for Personal Use (Book w/CD-ROM)	$29.99	SPOT
Bankruptcy: Is It the Right Solution to Your Debt Problems?	$19.99	BRS
Chapter 13 Bankruptcy: Repay Your Debts	$34.99	CH13
Creating Your Own Retirement Plan	$29.99	YROP
Credit Repair (Book w/CD-ROM)	$24.99	CREP
Getting Paid: How to Collect from Bankrupt Debtors	$24.99	CRBNK
How to File for Chapter 7 Bankruptcy	$34.99	HFB
IRAs, 401(k)s & Other Retirement Plans: Taking Your Money Out	$34.99	RET
Money Troubles: Legal Strategies to Cope With Your Debts	$29.99	MT
Stand Up to the IRS	$24.99	SIRS
Surviving an IRS Tax Audit	$24.95	SAUD
Take Control of Your Student Loan Debt	$26.95	SLOAN

PATENTS AND COPYRIGHTS

	PRICE	CODE
The Copyright Handbook: How to Protect and Use Written Works (Book w/CD-ROM)	$39.99	COHA
Copyright Your Software	$34.95	CYS
Domain Names	$26.95	DOM
Getting Permission: How to License and Clear Copyrighted Materials Online and Off (Book w/CD-ROM)	$34.99	RIPER
How to Make Patent Drawings Yourself	$29.99	DRAW
Inventor's Guide to Law, Business and Taxes	$34.99	ILAX
The Inventor's Notebook	$24.99	INOT
Nolo's Patents for Beginners	$29.99	QPAT
License Your Invention (Book w/CD-ROM)	$39.99	LICE
Patent, Copyright & Trademark	$39.99	PCTM
Patent It Yourself	$49.99	PAT
Patent Pending in 24 Hours	$29.99	PEND
Patent Searching Made Easy	$29.95	PATSE
The Public Domain	$34.95	PUBL
Trademark: Legal Care for Your Business and Product Name	$39.99	TRD
Web and Software Development: A Legal Guide (Book w/ CD-ROM)	$44.95	SFT

RESEARCH & REFERENCE

	PRICE	CODE
Legal Research: How to Find & Understand the Law	$39.99	LRES

SENIORS

	PRICE	CODE
Choose the right long-Term Care: Home Care, Assisted Living & Nursing Homes	$21.99	ELD
The Conservatorship Book for California	$44.99	CNSV
Social Security, Medicare & Goverment Pensions	$29.99	SOA

SOFTWARE

Call or check our website at www.nolo.com for special discounts on Software!

	PRICE	CODE
LLC Maker—Windows	$89.95	LLP1
PatentPro Plus—Windows	$399.99	PAPL
Personal RecordKeeper 5.0 CD—Windows	$59.95	RKD5
Quicken Legal Business Pro 2005—Windows	$109.99	SBQB5
Quicken WillMaker Plus 2005—Windows	$79.99	WQP5

Order Form

Name

Address

City

State, Zip

Daytime Phone

E-mail

Our "No-Hassle" Guarantee

Return anything you buy directly from Nolo for any reason and we'll cheerfully refund your purchase price. No ifs, ands or buts.

☐ Check here if you do not wish to receive mailings from other companies

Item Code	Quantity	Item	Unit Price	Total Price

Method of payment

☐ Check   ☐ VISA   ☐ MasterCard
☐ Discover Card   ☐ American Express

Subtotal	
Add your local sales tax (California only)	
Shipping: RUSH $9, Basic $5 (See below)	
"I bought 3, ship it to me FREE!"(Ground shipping only)	
TOTAL	

Account Number

Expiration Date

Signature

Shipping and Handling

Rush Delivery—Only $9

We'll ship any order to any street address in the U.S. by UPS 2nd Day Air* for only $9!

* Order by noon Pacific Time and get your order in 2 business days. Orders placed after noon Pacific Time will arrive in 3 business days. P.O. boxes and S.F. Bay Area use basic shipping. Alaska and Hawaii use 2nd Day Air or Priority Mail.

Basic Shipping—$5

Use for P.O. Boxes, Northern California and Ground Service.

Allow 1-2 weeks for delivery. U.S. addresses only.

For faster service, use your credit card and our toll-free numbers

**Call our customer service group
Monday thru Friday 7am to 7pm PST**

Phone   1-800-728-3555
Fax   1-800-645-0895
Mail   Nolo
                950 Parker St.
                Berkeley, CA 94710

Order 24 hours a day @
www.nolo.com

Remember:

Little publishers have big ears.
We really listen to you.

Take 2 Minutes & Give Us Your 2 cents

Your comments make a big difference in the development and revision of Nolo books and software. Please take a few minutes and register your Nolo product—and your comments—with us. Not only will your input make a difference, you'll receive special offers available only to registered owners of Nolo products on our newest books and software. Register now by:

PHONE
1-800-728-3555

FAX
1-800-645-0895

EMAIL
cs@nolo.com

or **MAIL** us
this registration card

fold here

- -

Registration Card

NAME _____ DATE _____

ADDRESS _____

_____

CITY _____ STATE _____ ZIP _____

PHONE _____ EMAIL _____

WHERE DID YOU HEAR ABOUT THIS PRODUCT? _____

WHERE DID YOU PURCHASE THIS PRODUCT? _____

DID YOU CONSULT A LAWYER? (PLEASE CIRCLE ONE)   YES   NO   NOT APPLICABLE

DID YOU FIND THIS BOOK HELPFUL?   (VERY)   5   4   3   2   1   (NOT AT ALL)

COMMENTS _____

_____

_____

WAS IT EASY TO USE?   (VERY EASY)   5   4   3   2   1   (VERY DIFFICULT)

We occasionally make our mailing list available to carefully selected companies whose products may be of interest to you.

☐ If you do not wish to receive mailings from these companies, please check this box.

☐ You can quote me in future Nolo promotional materials.
   Daytime phone number _____ .

THRV 1.0

Nolo in the NEWS

"Nolo helps lay people perform legal tasks without the aid—or fees—of lawyers."
—USA TODAY

Nolo books are ..."written in plain language, free of legal mumbo jumbo, and spiced with witty personal observations."
—ASSOCIATED PRESS

"...Nolo publications...guide people simply through the how, when, where and why of law."
—WASHINGTON POST

"Increasingly, people who are not lawyers are performing tasks usually regarded as legal work... And consumers, using books like Nolo's, do routine legal work themselves."
—NEW YORK TIMES

"...All of [Nolo's] books are easy-to-understand, are updated regularly, provide pull-out forms...and are often quite moving in their sense of compassion for the struggles of the lay reader."
—SAN FRANCISCO CHRONICLE

fold here

- -

Place
stamp here

Nolo
950 Parker Street
Berkeley, CA 94710-9867

Attn: THRV 1.0